LIGHT MY FIRE

Arabella Melville has a doctorate in psychology, has been a relationship counsellor, and is an experienced lecturer and broadcaster. She writes frequently for magazines and newspapers. Her several books include *Cured to Death: The Effect of Prescription Drugs*, *Natural Hormone Health* and *Eat Yourself Thin*. She lives in Wales.

By the same author

EAT YOURSELF THIN
NATURAL HORMONE HEALTH

With Colin Jackson

CURED TO DEATH
PERSISTENT FAT AND HOW TO LOSE IT

ARABELLA MELVILLE

Light My Fire

Rekindle Your Relationship and Revitalize Your Sex Life

HarperCollins*Publishers*

HarperCollins*Publishers*
77–85 Fulham Palace Road,
Hammersmith, London W6 8JB

This paperback edition 1995
1 3 5 7 9 8 6 4 2

First published in Great Britain by
Michael Joseph 1994

Copyright © Arabella Melville 1994

The Author asserts the moral right to
be identified as the author of this work

ISBN 0 00 638366 1

Set in Ehrhardt

Printed in Great Britain by
HarperCollinsManufacturing Glasgow

All rights reserved. No part of this publication may be reproduced, stored in a retrieval system, or transmitted, in any form or by any means, electronic, mechanical, photocopying, recording or otherwise, without the prior permission of the publishers.

This book is sold subject to the condition that it shall not, by way of trade or otherwise, be lent, re-sold, hired out or otherwise circulated without the publisher's prior consent in any form of binding or cover other than that in which it is published and without a similar condition including this condition being imposed on the subsequent purchaser.

Contents

ACKNOWLEDGEMENTS

I should like to thank all those who supported and encouraged me through the struggle of writing this book. I am particularly grateful to Rachel Holtom, Charleen Agostini and my agent, David Grossman, for helping me to keep going; and to my partner Colin Johnson for permitting intimate details of our life together to be made public.

Foreword

Loss of desire has been called 'a disease of the nineties'. It's a deeply distressing, though rarely discussed, problem for many thousands of couples, the most common reason for consulting a sex therapist, and the most consistent forerunner of separation and divorce. Surveys of the prevalence of sexual problems over the past twenty years reveal that loss of desire is becoming increasingly common, affecting 35 per cent of American women and 16 per cent of men.[1]

This book, written from personal experience, is about overcoming that problem. It describes how I lost interest in sex with my long-term partner, and how I was able to rediscover desire and rekindle passion. We reached the verge of separation and then, through a process of consciously directed change, rebuilt closeness at a deeper, more intimate level. I reveal the sometimes painful but ultimately tremendously rewarding process of learning about myself, about my partner, and about the way we interact to create our relationship.

I have tried to write in the most candid way I can, using my experience to illuminate the truths I've discovered. Although I touch on theory, this book focuses on everyday reality, the sort of reality many people live with. I believe that those who read about my experience will be able to learn from it and, I hope, find effective solutions to similar problems of their own.

I realise that we are all unique and that my life is not the same as anyone else's. Yet at the same time, through talking to many other people and through extensive reading, I have found that the sort of difficulties I've confronted are very common, and the solutions I've discovered can be applied to many problems. At an emotional level, we share a great deal; details may differ, but broad reactions tend to be very much the same.

Colin and I have been living and often working together for more than nineteen years. Ours has been a difficult relationship. We both tend to be stubborn, opinionated, demanding in our different ways. At first the attraction between us was overpoweringly intense, concealing our differences, distracting us from conflict; but gradually the passion faded, as it eventually does for everyone. By our twelfth year, I had lost interest in sex with him; two years later, I felt sure I should leave him, so destructive had the relationship become.

But I didn't leave him, nor did he leave me, though we both considered the option very seriously. Instead, we decided to try to make our relationship work. When we looked at our situation, we realised that the deterioration of our sex-life reflected a decline in the overall quality of our relationship – a decline that had gone much further than either of us had been willing to admit. There were recurring destructive patterns in the way we behaved in relation to one another. Where we had been affectionate, we had become antagonistic; instead of resolving conflicts, we tended to turn away from each other. Over the years, bad habits and inappropriate assumptions had multiplied as problems deepened in every facet of our intertwined lives.

I knew, from the time when I had worked as a relationship counsellor, that couples who aren't happy together rarely enjoy sex together. What I didn't anticipate was how difficult it would be to reawaken my sex-drive when our relationship began to improve. Even when we had progressed to the point where I could honestly say once more that I loved and cherished Colin, I just didn't have any sexual feelings at all. That made him feel frustrated, rejected, and eventually very angry. It seemed that all the work and goodwill we had put into caring for each other would be wrecked on the bleak rock of my loss of desire.

For a whole host of reasons, I had come to believe that Colin should be my only lover. We should have a monogamous relationship. But now I was confronting the painful possibility that staying with him could mean giving up sexual pleasure for the rest of my life, and that just wasn't an acceptable option for me. I desperately wanted to experience again the delight that I used to get from sex. Anyway, I knew our relationship wouldn't last unless we could restore the sexual part of it. Colin is a highly sexual man who would never be content to live with a woman who rejected him sexually, whatever the nature of the relationship outside the bedroom.

I realised that unless I could unlock my responsiveness, our relationship was doomed. I had to discover the nature of the blocks in my mind, to learn how they could be overcome. So I embarked on what was to be a protracted exploration of myself as I searched for the wellsprings of desire.

My journey took me through scenes of childhood, relived and reassessed with the vision of maturity; through the development of my sexual nature, with all the learning experiences of young adulthood, the fears and anxieties, the joys and revelations. I re-examined my patterns of interaction with men, the ways of being and of reacting that I had learnt from parents, teachers, and all the people who had touched my life at each stage of my development.

As I discovered myself, I began to understand my sexuality anew. I learnt to recognise, identify, and understand my feelings so that I could speak clearly about them. I became more responsible for myself, more fully my own person than ever before. This process forced me to challenge some of my most cherished beliefs about myself. I had seen myself as a liberated woman, I had thought I knew a great deal about sex. But I found, time and again, that I had been following unquestioned assumptions, responding to unrecognised fears, reacting to unacknowledged pressures. Knowing the theory of sexuality wasn't enough: the mechanics of making love are just a superficial part of the whole experience. I was finding out about the deep emotional levels of my sexual nature, the levels where the fires of passion are kindled and nourished. It was here that my problems lay; this was where I had to create change in order to function as a whole person once again.

I discovered how the ways I reacted to Colin could sometimes damage me – and him; how misunderstandings developed and persisted between us; how frequently we both acted on beliefs that were simply not valid. I began to learn new ways of behaving that were beneficial to our relationship and that allowed me to flourish in every way. As a result of this journey into myself, questioning my motivations and my emotional nature, I have been able to identify and share with Colin my problem areas, my personal demons. We have come to recognise his, too. We can't pretend we've conquered them all, but we have largely succeeded in drawing their teeth. And at least they don't come on us unawares, undermining our relationship without our knowledge.

Loss of desire on the part of one member of a couple is a problem for both. It causes a great deal of sadness, especially when it seems to make no sense, when love remains but passion has flown. Solving the problem is a challenge for both partners, but only one needs to start the sequence of changes that have to be made, for when one partner begins to behave in a new way, the relationship inevitably changes.

Because I am a woman, I write from a female perspective; I am not capable of doing anything else. Inevitably, women will identify with my experience more than men, for the two sexes differ in the way they see the world and in their emotional experience of life. But men are just as likely as women to experience loss of desire,[2] and I believe that my insights will be helpful to them too, because the root causes are generally similar for both sexes. Just as importantly, those who want to understand why their partner's sexual interest seems to have died will find much in this book that could help them to deal with the problem.

The sorts of changes I describe are challenging. They challenge your self-concept, your beliefs about your partner and yourself. They may seem threatening or dangerous. But ultimately, such a process of discovery is always beneficial. Even if a particular relationship is not strong enough to survive the changes that new understanding can create, the knowledge you will gain by going through this process will help you to make your next partnership more rewarding. Unless we understand how to make relationships work in the long term, we repeat our mistakes with one partner after another.

Relationships that remain rewarding over long periods of time adapt as both partners grow and mature. We have to learn to cope with the developing reality of our own and our partner's natures. When we rise to such challenges, the whole relationship becomes deeper, stronger, more capable of nurturing our innermost selves.

Surveys reveal that the most satisfying relationships are those that have lasted for many decades. Such relationships don't just survive through happy chance; they reflect the willingness of both partners to adapt, to understand each other and strive to meet each other's needs. Almost every couple, when they commit themselves to sharing their lives, whether in formal marriage or private, individual ways, have a shared dream of living happily ever after. A minority succeed in making the dream into reality. This book explains how to achieve such success.

Throughout, I tend to use everyday language, rather than Latinate medical or biological terms. I know that some readers will dislike my choice of words, for our native Anglo-Saxon sexual vocabulary has been hideously misused and thus, for some, rendered ugly and unacceptable. I hope such reservations will not distract those who don't share my feelings about language from the messages of the book. As Erica Jong wrote in *Parachutes and Kisses*, 'At least these words represent the language of *feeling*, the language of poweful emotion, while the Latinate words smell of disinfectant . . . If these words were good enough for Chaucer and Shakespeare and Joyce, then they're *certainly* good enough for Isadora.' And that goes for me, too.

Although sexual passion is at the heart of this book, I don't devote much space to sexual technique. Most of the forces that determine sexual feeling operate outside the strictly sexual context; the emotions we take into the bedroom – the feelings that make sex ecstatic or depressing – are generated by the way we relate to each other as we go about our everyday lives. The attitudes that determine our behaviour in bed are present in our minds long before we get there. So this isn't a sex manual; it goes much further than that. Frankly, I had no interest in sex manuals when I didn't want sex; refining love-making technique is irrelevant when you don't have any desire to make love.

But when you do want to make love, you want the experience – sometimes, at least – to be wonderful, memorable, mind-blowing, all-consuming. It doesn't matter if you've been with your partner for four, fourteen or forty years: ecstatic sex *is* still achievable. I believe that this book will make the greatest human delights available to some who had lost hope of such pleasure. Rediscovering sexual pleasure rejuvenates relationships, bringing joy in place of boredom, love where there was antagonism, caring instead of coldness.

Building a rewarding partnership that has the resilience to stand the test of time includes creating a mutually delightful sex-life. Sex is the glue that holds male and female together when gender differences could blow us apart, the element that makes relationships between men and women special. Sex is a uniquely powerful force – one that we have to understand and value, and for which we can create a context that makes it into a positive force. It can so easily become negative, destructive, dangerous. Good sex, as June Reinisch of the Kinsey Institute points out, is not 'always easy fun'. 'If we continue to perpetuate the false message that . . . all one has to do is let go, many people will simply stop having sex (or passively endure sex without enjoyment) and continue to view themselves as failures.'[3]

To harness the power of sex to strengthen our relationship, I had to recognise the way my sexual feelings are tied in with all my other feelings, how our sexual interaction mirrors other facets of our interactions. I had to learn how to nurture the fire of my sexual drive by working on my sexual self as well as on every other aspect of myself.

I discovered the synergy between sex and love – love both for Colin and for myself. And through this voyage of discovery, I found the path to ecstasy. This is the knowledge that I share in this book.

Part I

Learning From Experience

1

Sex in the Nineties

The nineties give me a sense of *déjà vu*. So many themes that were being developed when I was growing up in the sixties and seventies have re-emerged in new forms, reshaped by today's concerns. There have been profound changes in the last few decades, changes that touch every level of our lives, but the seeds of those changes began to germinate in the flower-filled wild years of three decades ago.

In the nineties, we are experiencing the reality of ideas which small groups of people began to discuss way back then. The fight against environmental pollution, which used to be regarded as cranky, is now recognised as crucial to future survival. Issues like women's rights are no longer minority concerns; they have practical force enshrined in law and reflected in changes both in the workplace and in personal relationships. Today the majority see their environment and themselves in a different way: we are more realistic, but that realism comes mixed with higher expectations, tempered by apprehension about the future and a desire for stability in the face of painful change. Rewarding relationships have become perhaps more important than ever to buffer us against the difficulties we now face.

We have recognised that attempts to escape reality are futile. Turning on and dropping out was no answer, mother's little helpers harmed us, every silver lining seems veiled in cloud. We haven't forgotten the dream of ecstatic sex that obsessed rock groups like The Doors and fired the sexual revolution, but in the Age of Aids we have to find it at home: casual sexual sharing is *out*. Young people, in particular, are not likely to have more than one sexual partner at a time, although they may change partners frequently.[1] Nobody suggests any longer that open marriage, 'swinging' or group partnerships are desirable options; the risk of transmitting incurable infections is too prominent in our cultural consciousness.

Nothing seems so straightforward any more. We used to feel that fun was there to make or to take; today we know there's a cost. Many imagined that technology would solve the world's problems; now we know the techno-fix has inherent hazards. The easy, optimistic sixties, the laid-back seventies, the greedy eighties are over. This decade has been dubbed 'the Caring Nineties'. At last we are looking beyond the superficial, searching for depth and satisfaction beyond tinsel-town trivia. We want relationships that fulfil us, that bring us joy and last a lifetime. But what's actually happening? The reality we are creating fails to match our expectations.

Paradoxically, disappointment and despair are all around in the Caring Nineties. Climbing divorce statistics reflect the rate at which people are giving up on their marriages. With 160,000 divorces in 1991, England has the highest rate of marriage breakdown in Europe, but divorce is rising throughout the world.[2] In England and Wales, annual divorce rates increased more than six-fold between 1961 and 1991, from 2.1 to 13.8 per thousand population. Changes in legislation made divorce easier and cheaper but the figures began to climb before the law was liberalised; new legislation reflected changing attitudes. The same pattern can be seen in all Western countries.[3]

Although the popularity of marriage has declined slightly over the past twenty years, committed one-to-one partnerships remain the preferred option for the majority of people. Fewer couples marry but cohabitation is becoming increasingly common. In 1989, about 10 per cent of people between the ages of sixteen and sixty were cohabiting, an arrangement that was particularly popular among women in their late twenties.[4] While many of these couples eventually marry, a large minority choose – like Colin and I – never to do so. But those who choose not to marry are not necessarily less committed, or less emotionally involved in their relationships.

However committed couples may feel in the first years together, a great many partnerships fall apart within a decade. The peak time for divorce comes between the fifth and the ninth year – that seven-year itch is real!

According to popular mythology, it's the husband who is likely to get itchy feet and leave his wife for another woman. In fact, although about two out of three husbands are unfaithful, this does not often lead to divorce. The overwhelming majority of separations are instigated by women who are no longer willing to settle for the sort of relationships that their mothers might have tolerated in the fifties. The most common reason for divorce, according to Zelda West-Meads of Relate, is a breakdown in communication. Usually, the woman feels her partner doesn't listen, that he criticises her excessively and fails to give her the emotional support she needs. Increasing numbers of women refuse to tolerate this demoralising situation, withdrawing first emotionally and sexually, and eventually giving up on the relationship.[5]

Now that divorce and single womanhood carry little, if any, social stigma, women have more options; few are willing to endure loveless, empty marriages, or violent and miserable ones. As more women began to see possibilities beyond the roles of child-bearer and kitchen skivvy, they recognised that they could earn their own livings and fend for themselves.

Changes in sexual attitudes, especially the recognition

that sex can be just as important and exciting for women as for men, have meant that more women now regard sexual satisfaction as something to which they are entitled. Expectations have risen since the sixties. For most women today, wonderful sex matters far more than a well-equipped kitchen.

Nancy Friday's collections of women's sexual fantasies, *My Secret Garden* and *Women on Top*,[6] reflect the way that women's sexual horizons have shifted. The contrast between these two books, the first published in 1973 and the second in 1991, is illuminating. 'Those first voices,' Nancy Friday wrote in 1990, 'were tentative and filled with guilt, not for having done anything, but simply for daring to admit the inadmissible: that they had erotic thoughts that sexually aroused them.'[7]

In the sixties and early seventies, most women still saw themselves in passive roles. In their fantasies, they protected themselves from guilt, shielding themselves from acknowledging responsibility for sexual desire by imagining scenes of rape and lovers who always took the initiative, sweeping them off their feet and into bed. Fifteen years later, the pattern had changed; women were fantasising about overpowering the men for whom they lusted, enjoying sex with a succession of people, giving and getting all the sexual pleasure they wanted, in the way they wanted.

Women have discovered their power. They are no longer willing to live as victims, submitting to someone else's desires and priorities. The nineties woman is not only physically stronger than her sixties counterpart, proudly displaying muscles that would have been thought utterly unfeminine; her will is stronger too.

In the fifties and early sixties, in the aftermath of the post-war utility years, expectations were material: we wanted goods, shiny things to decorate and extend our personal environment. Most of all, we wanted money. Men, the providers, offered these things; women traded their bodies for the fruits of their husbands' wage-packets. They didn't necessarily expect to enjoy sex: that was for men, who paid for sexual relief. Men bought, possessed and owned women.

None of this was overtly acknowledged. The realities of sex and marriage were hidden behind a romantic veil. After the roses and the courtship, his lips would brush hers and she would be transported to heaven ... The bruising, strangely, would be on her mouth, not her cunt; the intimacy of nakedness, the shocking thrusting of his cock, the strains of living together ever after for rich and poor, good and ill, were never mentioned. Our heroine just had to make the best of it. As Sheila Kitzinger explains, 'The thrill of sex, the snatched romantic moments, are supposed to compensate for all the other feelings of being trapped and, for the woman, of having surrendered her autonomy and her very identity as an individual ... Sex cannot be enjoyed simply because it brings pleasure ... The price of sex is seen as nothing less than a lifetime spent together in undying devotion.'[8]

The contrast between fantasy and reality was the starting-point for the growth of the women's movement. Betty Friedan's *The Feminine Mystique*[9] and Germaine Greer's *The Female Eunuch*[10] heralded a new vision of woman – a vision of an independent person who didn't need to hide behind men or romance, who could appreciate the reality of her being. Freed from enfeebling self-denial, millions of women discovered the pleasure of sex in the seventies. I was one of those millions. I realised then, for the first time, that guilt-free sex, separate from marriage, possession, or obligation, could be tremendous fun. Reacting against all this frothy romance, freed from fear of unwanted pregnancy by the Pill, the attitudes of a generation swung to the opposite extreme, expecting sexual pleasure as a right and condemning repression as a twisted distortion of a miserable culture.

Feminists proclaimed the power of sisterhood and nurtured a new, positive attitude to female sexuality. And while few women counted themselves among that band of idealists at the forefront of the movement for radical social change, their voices were heard and their message made an impact that none could deny. *Cosmopolitan* and other women's magazines encouraged wives to expect orgasms. Women throughout the Western world recognised their sexuality; promiscuity became more acceptable and we learnt how to enjoy ourselves sexually. Women began to expect men to be sexually competent: bang, bang, thank you ma'am, was no longer acceptable.

With each action comes an equal and opposite reaction. The men who rose to women's new levels of expectation began to demand that women should know how to please them too, and that put a strain on women. Learning to lie back and enjoy sex instead of merely tolerating it, was the first change; the second, and often more difficult, change was learning to be an active participant. Women had to find out what men liked, just as men had to discover the mysteries of female sexuality. A mutual escalation of pleasure-demand ensued, with accusations of ball-breaking from the men's side countered by resentment at being used as sex-objects on the women's. Both sexes felt the strain.

While some were able to leap the hurdles and have a ball, the carnival didn't last. The discovery of antibiotics gave us a few decades when we could change partners without worrying about disease, but the infections that threaten us also changed. First herpes, then Aids and a variety of other sexually transmitted diseases which cannot be cured by modern medicine, emerged and began to spread with a speed that few anticipated. Now, we know that casual multi-partner sex is not safe and it is unlikely that it will ever seem safe again.

Sex remains important; we aren't returning to soft-focus non-genital romance. Role-models like Madonna, flaunting female sexuality in all its variety, ensure that everyone recognises that women do enjoy sex, want sex, and refuse any longer to act as passive objects for the delectation of men. After centuries of denial, female orgasm reached the top of the priority-list. But orgasm alone is not enough. We can masturbate for our personal pleasure; we want to share love. Women rapidly found that they did not wish to separate sex and emotion, as many men seemed able to do: we realised that we would not be truly satisfied unless we could experience the whole gamut of feelings, physical, emotional and spiritual.

Before the sexual revolution, when few women seriously expected to get much pleasure from sex, husbands provided security, not ecstasy. Women were less critical, less demanding. Male sex-objects used to be romantic, dominating figures like Clark Gable in *Gone with the Wind*; while this remains true for some women, a new dimension has emerged. Today's male sex-objects are more flamboyantly sexual; women watch the muscular bodies of men like The Chippendales flaunting their bodies in a display of naked sexuality. Both women and men have high expectations and many are disappointed most of the time. Knowing our capacity for delight, we want to feel the excitement that makes us take leave of our senses, to experience the build-up, the orgasms, the heights of passion and sensation in the context of caring relationships.

When we didn't know about the joy of sex, it didn't seem to matter. Now that it does matter, most of us don't know how to achieve it – or, at least, not within long-term committed relationships; not after years together, when we have become set in our ways and the magic has gone, taking with it the automatic boost of pure lust. It can be no surprise that loss of desire is now such a common problem, and so difficult to overcome.

We want sex to remain exciting. But how? We can't return to our honeymoon days, when the least touch thrilled; few people actually *want* to live like Elizabeth Taylor, continually having new honeymoons in a desperate search for eternal love through serial monogamy. There are those who believe that this is the emerging pattern of the nineties, arguing that it is a lot more honest than swearing eternal fidelity, only to break those vows when boredom sets in and problems mount. But I believe that this pattern of repeated short-term relationships is ultimately less rewarding than an enduring partnership within which both individuals can grow and develop.

Although many people try to overcome the problems of marital dissatisfaction and boredom through serial monogamy, it isn't an ideal solution. The honeymoons are too brief, the partings too painful and disruptive, the repeated search for new partners too depressing, especially when change can bring exposure to terrifying risk. And few do better in second and subsequent marriages: these fail twice as often as the first.[11]

In the nineties, we have become aware of the power of our sexuality and shed much of the burden of guilt that used to hold us back, but the risk of fatal disease has killed the old notion of free love. Despite the heady excitement of fresh lust-objects, deep down we feel the need for total trust and fulfilment with partners who ultimately become so close, so intimate, that they are, in a very real sense, part of our selves.

The dilemma can be resolved through learning how to build partnerships that retain their excitement; through nurturing relationships which allow both partners to flower and flourish sexually and in every other way, where commitment is rewarded with growing understanding and deepening love. In the sixties and seventies, I imagined that this was a fifties romantic dream that could only be achieved by some form of mental self-mutilation. Now, I am convinced that we can make it a reality without compromising our individuality – if we want it badly enough.

2

Young Beginners

Early experiences can be very important for later sexual happiness. I am not referring to the sexual desires of small children; I find Freud's theories as unconvincing as Hitler's and I don't believe that toddlers think about raping their mothers, or worry about castration. But it is undoubtedly true that our adult sexual responses are founded on a broad base of feelings and attitudes that begin to form when we're very young indeed.

Early learning has a special, intense quality. It shapes our reactions throughout our lives at a level so fundamental that we may imagine we are behaving naturally, instinctively. This sort of learning is not conscious or deliberate; it is automatic and its effects are long-lasting. The great ethologist Konrad Lorenz observed that ducklings who saw coloured wellingtons rather than Mother Duck in the hours after hatching would follow those wellies as though they were their mother, and attempt to mate with them when they reached adulthood. Lorenz called this irreversible form of learning that happened rapidly at a critical period, 'imprinting'. Imprinting in humans is more complex than that, but for us, too, the learning that takes place in the early period of life is extremely important for our social development.

We learn about ourselves in relation to the world from

the day we are born. Through holding our mothers, being held, fed, cuddled, kissed, stroked and tickled, and through playing, we learn about love. We bask in the knowledge that we are loved – or wither in the belief that we aren't. We learn to trust, or distrust. Even things that most people imagine to be innate, built-in, like the way we experience pain, are actually learnt very early in life.

We cannot change what happened to us as babies. But trying to recreate the events of the first few months of my life has helped me to understand some of the feelings I still have, especially the recurring sense that I am not loved or wanted, which tends to make me alternate between clinging, over-dependent behaviour and voluntary isolation; I retreat from conflict into a world of my own. While I can see clearly now that these are the feelings of the baby who lives on in my mind, they are not appropriate to my adult situation, when I have control over my life. I can now let those feelings pass, feel them surge up but not take too much notice of them. Gradually, they are losing their power to damage my relationships.

For me, childhood was not a particularly happy time. I remember my parents' obvious affection for one another, but I don't recall anyone showing much warmth for me. My mother and father, born in the second decade of this century, were brought up by servants in families which behaved with Victorian stiffness. Middle-class British families of that period didn't believe in having fun or showing love. Duty and honour were the dominant values.

My problems began the day I was born, in 1948. My mother told me about my birth and its aftermath quite recently, when I specifically asked her about it. She had kept quiet for over forty years, believing that such things are better forgotten. But the truth has helped; it has helped me to make sense of the way I am now.

I was an enormous baby. Weeks overdue, I was altogether too much for my unfortunate mother, who was badly damaged internally by my passage into the world. She was admitted to hospital, where my father took me to be fed every day. My mother insisted on breast-feeding me, but this caused her so much pain that she would faint. Was I sensitive enough, as a new baby, to perceive the pain I caused as I clung to my suffering mother? I must have felt desperately rejected, left alone in my cot, separated from her except for a few distressing minutes each day. When my mother returned home, she found me a difficult, demanding baby. By that time, I'm sure I was already convinced that I was unlovable.

My two-year-old sister Joanna's rage and jealousy didn't help. For most of my infancy, she often seemed to hope I would be eaten by monsters or otherwise removed from her world. And then there was the fact that my parents had wanted a boy. William, the son for whom they had been longing, was born a year later.

All in all, the circumstances of my early life conspired to make me feel pretty rotten about myself. Even now, this deep-rooted feeling re-emerges at intervals, despite a life filled with affection. I remember, when I was a little girl, often regretting that I had ever been born; I felt certain that nobody loved me. I used to have screaming fits – hysteria, they called it – when I felt so desperate, so alone, so unwanted, that I just wished I had never existed. They tried to shut me up by pouring cold water over my head.

My mother always had problems in showing her love for her children. Paradoxically, she was obsessed by love; she wanted to be loved so much that she could never get enough for herself, let alone give love. She taught us a version of Christianity that was entirely about love, denying hell, hatred, and anything at all unpleasant. We came to see it all as make-believe.

In 1920, when my mother was four, she had been sent to a boarding school for missionaries' daughters while her parents went preaching Christianity to the people of India. Poor little Joan! She had no visitors, no friends, no toys, no letters, and no love. Her two sisters and her brother were in India; she, alone, was left behind. The school was a place straight out of Dickens, with man-traps in the garden, cold baths and weevils in the porridge. She used to say she could eat anything: when you have to make do with weevils or starve, you learn to accept anything.

How could my mother show love, when she had never experienced it herself?

I don't remember kisses and cuddles and closeness as a child. I did learn to love and trust Dinah, the family cat, who purred and rubbed her soft body against me. But humans? They were as likely to be cruel as kind. Usually they ignored me. Not that my mother was cruel. She was a passive, gentle person who spent a lot of time on the sofa being ill. While my sister and I looked after the house, Mother retreated from the demands of her growing family into the irresponsibility of the invalid role. She didn't value herself. She always assumed that other people were more likely than she to be right about almost anything, apart from colour and design, for she was a talented artist.

I learnt from her and from my father, a Scots engineer whose sense of duty was very strong, that I should not make demands, I should always put others first. Like my mother, I find it difficult to be assertive in love relationships, difficult to communicate clearly what I want, difficult even to know what I want. I found her determination always to follow, never to lead, infuriating; yet I see the same passivity, the same lack of confidence that leads to a fading and diminution of self, in myself. Learning to feel for myself, ask for myself and live for myself is still difficult. It goes against what I learnt as a little girl.

Learning to suppress anger was part of this pattern of feminine passivity. Mummy was never angry and she didn't like quarrels or cross children. She wanted everybody to be loving all the time. So I learnt to deny my anger even to myself, and had difficulty dealing with conflict. As with my mother, submissive tears came much more easily than rage.

Of course, every one of us has a different upbringing, and this contributes to our differences as adults. Usually the patterns of behaviour we develop help us to fit into our social background. But when our parents' experience is at odds with our wider social background, we may grow up with a variety of social and relationship problems.

If I had grown up with parents who fought constantly, I would have brought a different set of problems to adulthood. Most likely, I would react to conflict with rage instead of depression, and if the household in which I grew up had been violent, mine would probably be violent too. We tend to repeat the patterns that we experience when we are very young. But just as understanding where my passivity comes from helps me to deal with it, so seeing the roots of other recurring problems that we experience in our relationships can help us to work on handling them more effectively.

Sharing my memories of growing up with Colin and discussing the ways my early experiences continue to colour my reactions, has been helpful for both of us. When he understood better why I felt the way I did, he was able to be more patient and gentle with me. This is a common reaction. From her work at the Marriage Counselling Centre in Montreal, Dorothy Freeman observed that 'sharing a growing-up problem often brings out an empathic response from the spouse'.[1]

We all have different struggles, different problems to understand and work through. Perhaps the most difficult are those that result from sexual abuse in childhood, which leads to terrible confusion and anxiety about sex in later life. In almost every case, specialised professional counselling is necessary to help the victims to recover from such severe early damage.

More common than such extremes are the problems caused in families where children grow up, as I did, with too little close physical and emotional contact with parents and peers. When play is not an integral part of family life, children don't learn about having fun. I still have difficulty with play, jokes and fun: my parents didn't play with me and I became rather a serious little girl. Even now, my sense of awkwardness with physical games, with rough and tumble, can make me a bit wooden in bed. But understanding why I am the way I am, Colin is aware that there's no personal rejection involved and he's able to encourage me to relax and have fun.

You can look at the way your problems developed, just as I did. One way to start is to write down, quickly, without thinking, your earliest memories. What do they tell you about your childhood? What can you learn from them? Were you happy or hurting? Where was your mother? What part did your father play?

I had help in looking back into my childhood from a counsellor, Charleen, a wise and beautiful woman who practises psychosynthesis, a therapeutic technique that aims to free people from past conditioning, to assist resolution of inner conflicts and develop the creative potential of the individual.[2] Charleen encouraged me to identify the voices of my parents and teachers which had become internalised and fossilised in my mind. Sometimes they said things which I don't accept and don't wish to hold on to; sometimes I couldn't recall what had been said, but I discovered strong feelings associated with faded memories from long ago. Finding those voices and remembering those feelings, seeing their separateness from my chosen direction, I have been able to start to let them go, just as I can dismiss views that I don't share. Once they emerge into consciousness, I am able to deal with them more easily.

We learn specific sexual attitudes, and attitudes to our own bodies, through interaction with the people closest to us as we grow up. These issues may never be openly discussed. Children learn by watching, by imitating other people, and attitudes are absorbed, without awareness or thought, from those who surround them. Young children are especially receptive to this type of learning; this is how they learn to speak their local language and fit into their social environment.

I learnt to feel ashamed of my body, to cover myself up.

I remember my mother's insistence that I keep my knickers on when I played in the garden as a nine-year-old: for some reason, I always preferred to have a bare bottom. But I had to be covered up 'down there'. Why, I didn't ask: children don't. Mummy says so, and that's enough.

Sex was something my parents didn't talk about in front of the children, and my earliest attempts to raise the issue were dismissed. It was unfortunate that I chose to ask Mummy whether Daddy jumped on her like male frogs do, when she was giving a dinner party! Whenever anything remotely to do with sex was mentioned, it was clouded in a romantic haze. I had problems speaking even mildly sexual words. I recall a word-association game with schoolfriends when I was thirteen; when one said 'robin' and the next said 'red', I said 'breast' – and blushed beetroot, wishing the ground would swallow me!

Another clear memory is of my mother stopping me touching myself between my legs. 'Have you got an itch?' she asked. 'Perhaps you've got worms.' It was not a pleasant idea. Obviously, this experience – brief though it was – made a strong impression on me. I believe it may have spelt the end of my childhood exploration of my sexual organs, for I never did learn to masturbate as a child. After that I didn't consider touching myself, let alone discover the capacity for delight that resided there, for many years.

And even now, as a middle-aged woman who – consciously at least – celebrates her sexuality, masturbation sometimes causes me problems. The disapproval that I heard as a little girl from my mother is still there in my mind. At least now I recognise that voice, I can tell it to get stuffed!

Shame about my body, and especially my sexual organs, has had lasting effects, but I have fought back. Realising that shame could only diminish my pleasure in life, I made conscious efforts to overcome my fear of being seen naked. I told myself firmly that such fears were groundless and forced myself to take deep breaths and go ahead and do what I believed to be appropriate to whatever situation I was in. I didn't want anyone to see my sexual organs, but joining a women's group where we looked at each other helped me through that. Early learning made it particularly difficult for me to relax and enjoy cunnilingus, partly because I couldn't imagine that my cunt could be desirable, and partly because I felt it was selfish; but with the help of some delightful men, I learnt to love it.

Changing deep-seated attitudes is never a quick or easy process. I am still aware of remnants of those early blocks against experiencing my own sexuality. Even though I reject them intellectually, and I continue to work at overcoming them, I still feel their effects. By deliberately choosing to ignore the anxiety, calming myself mentally and then actually doing the things that brought up that sense of shame, I have reduced it to the point where it rarely affects the way I behave or feel. I talk to myself, encourage myself, insist on my right to follow through my own choices. That way, I become my own person.

Childhood taboos re-emerge most strongly when I feel anxious or stressed. Predictably, when I'm having problems relating to Colin or I feel rejected, the old inhibitions surface – precisely when they are most dangerous. But Colin, knowing all this, usually tries to be sympathetic, supporting my struggle to become free of taboos that we both reject.

Thankfully, the strong sexual taboos in Western culture need not damage us irreparably; we can recover from old wounds. In my bathroom, there's a rubber plant that was thrown out because it was broken almost in half. We rescued it, repotted it and splinted its damaged stem; eventually, it recovered. Whenever I look at that scarred but healthy plant, it reminds me that living creatures can survive even the most adverse pressures with a little help from their friends. Unlike women in some Muslim cultures, Western women are not subjected to physical mutilation; and problems in the mind can be solved by the mind.

Whenever I have the sense of being unable to do something that part of my mind wants to do, I ask myself where the block comes from. Is it baggage that I'm carrying from childhood, that I would be better off without? If so, I try to look at it, defuse its power, let it go. Who needs it?

Deciding whether particular attitudes are important parts of our personal moral code, or unwanted baggage dumped on us by people with a different set of beliefs, can be difficult. I grew up with the remnants of Victorian morality, which the sixties winds of change blew almost away. My own morality is different from that which I was taught, although my parents and I agree on many fundamental values. I don't believe, for example, that society has any right to condemn victimless 'crimes', whether they are unusual sexual acts enjoyed by consenting adults, buying and watching sexually explicit videos, or using drugs in one's own body. I do believe that my freedom ends where another person's begins; I take responsibility for my own actions, but not for those freely chosen by other people. Working through some of these issues can be complicated and I do not accept answers that are given to me without considering them very carefully.

I have learnt to respect and listen to some of my inner voices; others, I tune out and ignore. Moral issues are tremendously important to me, as they were to my parents. Their voices formed the foundation of my conscience, and I am grateful for its strength, even if it sometimes gives me a hard time!

Adolescence was the time when issues of this sort became important to me. I was a late beginner in my relationships with boys. I was shy, quiet, and self-conscious, while unflattering glasses and a penchant for comfort-eating meant that I was no beauty. I longed to step into the shoes of the vivacious party girls, but I didn't know how to do it. Boyfriends? You had to be joking.

I did try making babies with Ben, the boy next door. I was ten, he a couple of years older. He'd heard that a boy could make babies by putting his thing into a girl; we tried it out in the air-raid shelter at the bottom of the garden. It was clearly impossible. We ended up giggling at the absurdity of the idea. I didn't even know I had a vagina until my first period. That air-raid shelter had been dark and we didn't investigate very thoroughly. My mother, embarrassed, had been putting off the day when I had to be told the horrendous secrets of my sex; she never imagined that my periods would start so early. The blood came as a horrible shock to me. I hated it, hated the smell, the pain, the shame of it all.

My body generally was a source more of embarrassment than pleasure. A shy, chubby schoolgirl, I was out of touch with my physical self, hopeless at sports, consistently last in races. Teased and bullied by working-class children whose culture I didn't understand, I took refuge in reading and drawing. Other children played kiss-chase; I avoided loneliness by becoming expert at marbles, a game that I was able to analyse intellectually in order to win. It was easier for me to do that than to learn social skills.

With physical maturity comes a rapid acceleration of the mental and emotional maturing process. Although I wish I had been warned about periods, perhaps my mother had been right in waiting before talking to me about sex; such information makes little sense to most girls before they reach their early teens. I remember trying to explain to my nine-year-old stepdaughter what people photographed in sex magazines were doing; like me when I tried making babies with Ben, she found it difficult to believe that anyone would want to do such things.

By thirteen, I felt differently. I'd fallen in love with my doctor when I was ill with bronchitis. With his big square head and strong hands, his gentle manner overlying hidden power, I found him tremendously attractive. I wanted him to touch me; when he did, I tingled all over. Deliberately, I sought to make my illness last so that he would come and see me in my nightie. Desire had stolen upon me; I wanted him to touch my firm young breasts, to stroke my nipples, to put his arms around me. At that age, I didn't think my desires through. I burned with wanting, not knowing what I wanted. I tried to appear sophisticated, didn't admit my ignorance. Had I been less inhibited or moved in a different social group, I might have sought sexual experience in defiance of parental rules and society's blind insistence that I was too young for sex. Physically, I wasn't too young. Psychologically, I was very vulnerable.

Rebellious, physically strong and emotionally unstable, I felt unable to relate to my parents' values and the assumptions they tried to impress on me. It was important to my mother that her daughters should not 'marry below themselves'; I reacted by rejecting the whole idea of marriage.

Fear of pregnancy added to my anxiety about sexual matters. My mother had become pregnant by accident at seventeen; her family insisted that she marry the father for the sake of the child, my half-sister Judith. At the time, my mother wanted neither husband nor baby. Determined that none of her daughters should find herself in a similar situation, she warned us repeatedly about the risks. When I did start going out with boys, in 1964, contraception was for married couples and abortion illegal. I realised that boys could buy condoms if they were bold enough to face the chemist, but I also knew that contraceptives were not totally reliable. I wouldn't risk going all the way and I didn't know how far we could go before a boy might lose control.

Despite my fears, I trusted my boyfriends enough to learn that there were amazing pleasure centres in my body. I still remember the rush of excitement mixed with apprehension the first time a boy put his hand in my knickers. I loved it, I longed for more – and I ran away. As time went by, I found that boys could produce incredible effects by stroking my sexual organs, but I didn't know how. At eighteen, I still didn't realise I had a clitoris.

Sex education at my school was called 'hygiene'. We

were taught about the vagina and the uterus, about eggs and sperm and how babies come into being, but never, never about pleasure. The clitoris wasn't on the genital maps in our textbooks. We didn't hear about arousal or female orgasm. There was no hint that people might touch each other, much less lick or kiss each other. Eroticism didn't exist. We learnt only about the most basic mechanics of procreation.

Teenage informants tell me that sex education hasn't changed greatly since my day. It is still about physiology and internal organs, not about emotion or pleasure or excitement. But many adolescents today have the opportunity of learning from explicit videos, and they show far less fear and ignorance of sexual matters than my generation did. Even though the social and emotional content of such videos is usually very limited, at least they suggest some variations on basic missionary-position fucking!

Today's adolescents become sexually active at an earlier stage than we did. Twenty per cent lose their virginity before the age of fifteen; very few see any reason for 'saving themselves' for marriage.[3] They are far more sophisticated than we were, twenty-five years ago, and they have thrown off much of the guilt that held us back. What scares me is that so many children, thinking they've done it all by the age of fourteen, decide that the next thing to do is to have babies. Babies are fashionable. To me, that's a horrifying idea in a world facing the social and ecological pressures that are so obvious in the nineties.

When I was a teenager, virginity was still deemed important. The Pill, and the sexual revolution that followed its availability, changed all that. We laughed at boring old farts who said that sex was only for marriage and that nobody would marry a girl who wasn't a virgin. Nowadays, few people even consider such ideas.

Whatever our upbringing, whatever the cultural context in which we learn about sex and relationships, growing up is about becoming fully ourselves, independent of our parents. We may not be able to completely erase disapproving parental voices from our minds – I will never entirely forget the disgust in my father's voice when he called me a whore because, at seventeen, I had put on make-up for a date – but those voices need not control us to the same extent.

I believe our task, as the parent generation, is to inform our children as fully as we can, to give them as complete a picture as possible of adult life, pleasures and responsibilities; not to teach them shame, but to give them confidence and pride in themselves. We have to be honest with them, because if we are not honest they pick up confused messages; and that means we must first try to understand ourselves and come to terms with our own feelings and behaviour. Being a good parent is not an easy task but it's one we have to take very seriously, because so much of adult emotional life depends on how we were treated by our parents. Of course, nobody gets it all right. I know my parents tried hard, and they always did genuinely love me; but they passed their difficulties on to me.

As I became an independent adult, I learnt to relate to my parents as two very special people. Our relationship grew closer and more genuine with every decade. My father learnt that he did not need to protect me; in time, he came to respect my viewpoint, even if we did not always agree. Now he's almost eighty and I love his company; our attitudes and interests are very similar and we talk for hours together.

My love for my mother grew stronger as we grew older. Once I felt I really didn't *need* her, I lost the sense that she had failed me. In the last decade of her life, she was the one person with whom I could share my deepest feelings without anxiety or doubt; she alone had the depth of insight that I came to rely on in my darkest moments. When I was young, I had felt she didn't listen to me; by the time I passed forty, I knew she did. She listened and she understood. Her death was a terrible loss to me.

3

Flying Blind

My first lover was to become my husband. I barely remember our first act of intercourse. There was no pain, no blood, no delight, certainly no ecstasy. It was only one step removed from the sensation produced by the speculum wielded by the doctor who prescribed my first pack of contraceptive pills. It was not an act inspired by irresistible passion; having decided that I would do it, I had already dealt with the risk of pregnancy by going on the Pill and waiting the requisite three weeks until I knew I was safe.

Well, I thought, this is it. Sex. Why do people make such a fuss about it? I put it very low on my personal priority list. Yet it was a significant occasion, more significant than I was willing to acknowledge at the time. It marked the move from casual relationships with boys to my first committed partnership.

Spring came early in 1967. I was in my first year at university when Bob and I were matched by a computer dating company that had flooded the campus with detailed questionnaires. What a marvellously rational way to find partners, I had thought – how much more efficient than hoping the next boy who asked me to dance would turn out to be a soul mate! And we did feel well-matched. Our attitudes were similar, especially our emphatic rejection of romance and determination to embrace rationality at every level. We both saw ourselves as intellectuals, scientists (he was studying biology, I psychology) and rebels; Bob braved catcalls, wearing his hair long and his jeans frayed; my style, with skirts just below the bum or skimming my ankles, matched his in daring. Within a couple of months, we were lovers: alike in our naïvety yet interested in serious experiment, consciously seeking a new way of living.

Before long, I had moved into his flat. This was my means of escape from the family home that I found oppressive. He represented a new security. I imagined we could be self-sufficient, free from our parents and their assumptions.

We didn't talk about sex. Although we discussed pregnancy and I took obsessive care to avoid it, we didn't share the personal meaning of our sexual interaction at all. The possibility that we had only tasted a tiny part of the whole experience didn't occur to us. I dismissed the idea of overwhelming passion as a fantasy, the sort of dream my mother indulged in. If people like her wanted to believe such things, that was up to them. I was interested in reality.

New and exciting ideas were in the air in the sixties: different attitudes to life, a sense of freedom from the restrictions of convention. Girls were throwing away their panty girdles and crippling stilettos, adopting tights and micro-minis, going on the Pill. We experimented with drugs, smoking joints in each other's candlelit flats. We painted the ceilings black or maroon, hung Indian tapestries on the walls, played Hendrix as loud as we could. Everybody tried to be super-cool while young men competed for the biggest speaker systems, the most powerful amplifiers. Music was the focus of much sexual symbolism.

Sex was omnipresent – in our provocative style of dress, the burgeoning alternative press, the heavy rock bands with their colourful album covers and posters. There was a heady sense that we were the first generation to be free – free to live as we wished, to grow our hair, to live with our lovers, to have sex without fear.

It was the Swinging Sixties: sex, drugs, rock'n'roll; we talked of fucking in the streets, and never mind the horses. But for me, as for so many in reality, the party was always somewhere else. We believed we welcomed radical change yet we barricaded ourselves behind mental walls, keeping our inner selves uninvolved by staying cool, or – as in my case – by adopting a pose of scientific rationalism that ignored emotion.

Girls, acquiescing unwittingly with the expectations of a male-dominated society, tried to be Barbie dolls: pretty, painted, leggy and compliant. Some of us couldn't quite create the image; my short, stocky build didn't fit. I hated my heavy legs, my rounded body. Bob agreed, and encouraged me to carry on dieting. Unhappy and out of touch with my body, I had been dieting since I was fifteen; my babyhood experience of deprivation had made me an expert at self-deprivation. I didn't know how to enjoy anything physical. Deep inside, I was still the dutiful girl who denied her own desires, substituting 'oughts' for 'wants'.

Not surprisingly, I didn't enjoy my early experience of sex particularly, though it seemed pleasant enough at first. But within a couple of years, the underlying reality of unconscious conflict began to make itself felt. The effects of suppressed distress were exaggerated by the unrecognised side-effects of oral contraceptives. I became deeply depressed and developed vaginismus, an uncontrollable tightening of the vaginal muscles that made penetration impossible. Vaginismus was a relief to me, although I never admitted it. The truth was, I didn't want sex. I didn't want Bob to come close enough to feel the rolls of fat on my body.

The student health service treated me with antidepressant drugs and tranquillisers. Nobody – neither the psychiatrists, nor Bob, nor I – looked at the reasons for my condition. I just thought I had gone mad, as many women in my family had before me. I felt desperately ugly, like a rhinoceros struggling in heavy mud. My capacity for rational thought was overwhelmed by the sense of deep misery that shrouded my mind. Day after day, week after week, I sat and cried.

It didn't occur to me that the roots of my depression might also lie in the distortions in my mind. I didn't realise the extent to which I had boxed in my emotional self, repressed my unpredictable, irrational and passionate nature; or that my apparently harmonious relationship with Bob depended on an elaborate construction of defences. I wasn't aware of the way my feelings were subjugated to these defences, nor that I would rather deny my self than challenge Bob. I just felt I had failed, but at what, I had no idea. Finally the drugs had their desired effect. Even though the underlying problems had not been recognised, let alone resolved, the incessant misery had gone and I could cope with everyday life. But I still felt half-dead inside.

Bob and I married that summer. He wanted to marry so that he could cease to worry about his parents' disapproval of our cohabitation. I wore black. I didn't want to marry, but I thought I understood Bob's reasons so I went along with it. There was no party, we invited nobody except our parents who acted as witnesses.

'But do you love him?' my mother asked anxiously as we walked to the registry office. 'You don't have to go through with this.'

'No,' I said, honestly. 'I don't love him. We get on well together.' I didn't believe in romantic love. I thought sex was overrated. Marriage, I imagined, would change nothing as far as I was concerned.

Despite my attitudes to the institution of marriage, I tried to be a good wife. I looked after Bob, cooked his favourite dishes, darned his socks, made clothes for both of us. The dutiful girl who had done her best to look after the family home while Mummy lay in bed being ill had become a dutiful wife, denying her own needs. It is, according to Dorothy Freeman, a common pattern.[1]

I admired Bob. He seemed so efficient, so competent when I felt I was not. He could solve practical problems. At that time, we were living on a canal boat which he converted into a home; his designs were elegant and effective, his systems worked. He seemed quick and clever, able to argue very convincingly for his point of view and against any vague doubts that I might have. I spoke little, held no independent opinions; our friends were his friends and my part in our mutual life seemed insignificant. He maintained his dominant role in our relationship, it seems to me, looking back, by putting me down, dismissing and belittling me. I had too little self-respect even to recognise what was going on most of the time, let alone to fight against it.

He didn't ill-treat me physically: he would not have dreamt of doing that. He never shouted at me, he was always logical and reasonable, and his careful, rational approach to life fitted in neatly with the defences that I had constructed around myself. We reinforced each other's protective illusions, but at great cost: the other facets of my nature – aspects of myself that should have been developing and maturing at this stage of my life – were ignored.

My sexuality was one of these unexpressed facets. Dressed in the short tight skirts that were fashionable at the time, my feet crushed into shoes with heels as high as I could bear, I worked on being desirable. I bought black stockings, a frilly suspender belt, a half-bra. It didn't help. We were both too inhibited to let ourselves go sexually and we collaborated in denying our feelings. Bob was rarely interested in sex, and when he was, it didn't turn me on.

But I wanted sex with him, despite the fact that it wasn't exciting, because I wanted to feel loved and desired. I still felt awful about myself, saw myself as fat and boring, trailing around behind Bob like a hopeless puppy. Bob seemed to reinforce my poor self-image, criticising my body and continually pressuring me to lose weight.

Whatever I did, I felt he was never satisfied. Eventually, I became anorexic; the very thought of food filled me with such horror at one stage that I totally stopped eating for three weeks. Starvation proved astonishingly easy. It gave me a sense of power over the body I hated. Secretly, I was proud of my refusal to eat and delighted with my twenty-two-inch waist although I hated my still-plump legs.

Even then, Bob told me I was too fat. I remember one day in the psychology department animal laboratory when one of the lecturers complimented me on my slender figure, Bob immediately retorted that he should look at my fat tummy. The lecturer smiled, commenting that my belly merely had a lovely feminine curve to it. Bob didn't agree.

Fortunately, I realised that my obsession with dieting was getting so far out of control that my academic career could be threatened by it, and I began to make myself eat again. Just as I had turned to reading as a lonely schoolgirl, I lost myself in my work as a student. I became the brightest star in my year, fascinated by the intellectual challenge of behaviourist psychology. This sort of psychology fitted me perfectly: it dismissed the unconscious and anything that might be going on in the mind and concerned itself only with objectively observable behaviour. It relied on the study of rats and pigeons, effectively ignoring the unpredictable complexities of humans. Introspection was taboo.

Although I denied it, my subconscious mind was in turmoil. Eventually, all the anger that I had turned in on myself, all those repressed desires, would bubble up and wreck my apparently solid marriage . . . but I anticipated that only to the degree that I couldn't honestly believe in monogamous marriage as a lasting commitment. I couldn't imagine that I would stay with Bob – or any man – for the rest of my life.

Bob and I lived together for five years. When I finally left him, I looked back with astonishment at having endured such a depressing relationship for so long. But I was immature, insecure, lacking in confidence. Deep down, I didn't feel I deserved anything better. I had been thinking and behaving like a victim.

My second committed relationship began nearly three years after I left Bob. I had grown up considerably. I now found my body acceptable, I had learnt to enjoy my sexuality, and I had much more self-respect when I met Colin in 1974. At first, our relationship seemed totally different from my marriage to Bob. It was years before I began to recognise the same patterns repeating themselves.

By the time I met Colin, I had been single for long enough to have had a wide variety of lovers, refusing to commit myself to any of them, to settle down to the role of wife or even exclusive mistress. I saw marriage as a trap where I risked losing my individuality and my freedom of choice. Freedom had become very important to me.

Freedom was important to Colin, too. After a year's separation from his second wife, he was as cynical about marriage as I; and his anarchistic philosophy, which I recognised as very similar to my own, held that no one should be treated as another's property. We fell passionately in love. I sang in the streets, danced round my flat brimful of fierce joy at discovering a soul mate.

Having recently come to the conclusion that I was much happier alone than living with a man, it was ironic that Colin and I missed each other so much every moment we were apart that I quickly moved in with him. My second honeymoon began the day we met; that night we shared a bed. Sex was simple and delightful, remarkable more for the frequent repetition of the basic act of fucking than any sophistication.

Our lust was intense. We would have sex anywhere, everywhere we could, even up a tree with Sunday strollers walking the path beneath us. As he drove his car, I would unzip his jeans and suck his cock; when we reached his flat, we would fall through the door in a close embrace, pulling our clothes off in our haste to get at each other's body.

The honeymoon continued for two years, two years when the nights when we didn't make love were remarkable for their rarity. We didn't need elaborate foreplay: the very idea of sex was enough to turn us on. I was always available for him. Orgasm came quickly, easily, repeatedly. We never doubted our compatibility. I saw Colin as clever, funny, honest, sexy, generous and playful. We shared the same beliefs, loved each other's bodies, respected each other's intelligence, encouraged each other to develop and grow.

During this period, our work, like our leisure, overlapped. I had given up my academic career after confronting the realisation that experiments on animals were morally unacceptable. The fact that the science of behaviourism, based on the suffering of animals, could not be morally justified had been a shattering revelation, one that destroyed my carefully nurtured progress up the academic ladder in a single stroke.

Shedding the blinkers of scientific rationalism was a painful experience. Some of the experiments that I watched were just too revolting even for my hardened perception. In these experiments, rabbits were subjected to operation after operation to produce terrified creatures with half their brains removed, yet sufficiently conscious to react to pain and, through their reactions, to generate the data that the scientists wanted. They proved that a rabbit does not need a cerebral cortex to learn discrimination; to me, they proved that the pursuit of academic success and knowledge for its own sake could be used to justify any excess of cruelty. The scientists called these rabbits 'good preparations'; I knew they were living, feeling animals. They called me a sentimental woman. I resigned from my research post.

Unemployed, over-qualified – for by this time I had my doctorate – and inexperienced in everything apart from the animal-based research work that I now refused to contemplate, I was in limbo. My carefully nurtured dreams of a career as a scientist had turned to nightmare, my certainties were shattered. Psychologically, I was devastated.

Penniless, I earned money as a nude model, posing for seedy photographers in gloomy London basements. I could scarcely have taken myself further away from the academic world. It was at this point that I decided I would be a writer. It seemed like the only option open to me. I borrowed a typewriter and worked through typing exercises between modelling jobs.

One of the men who took photographs of me was publisher Gerry Kingsland, who was later to become famous as G in Lucy Irvine's story, *Castaway*. He encouraged me in my writing ambitions, commissioning my first article for his magazine, *Curious*. It had been through Gerry that I met Colin, whose company distributed Gerry's publications.

Gerry's publishing company didn't survive long enough for me to get paid for that first article, but money no longer mattered to me. Colin and I took over one of Gerry's magazines, and that gave me the opportunity I wanted to learn to write. Together, we created *Libertine*.

The spirit of the times encouraged both our personal philosophy of freedom and our totally positive, lighthearted attitude to sex. In *Libertine*, we promoted our belief in sexual freedom, and our personal lives were inseparable from our work. We had sex with many partners, both gay and straight, in groups or alone; the sole requirement was informed consent. Naively, we saw sex as harmless fun, a form of pleasure for which our capacity was almost unlimited, as well as an easy way of relating to people. We wrote and talked openly about our lovers without fear or jealousy: we didn't believe in possessiveness or secrecy. Believing that denying and concealing reality led to sexual unhappiness and the breakdown of relationships, we, and those who worked with us, aimed to explore and expose our sexuality as we experienced it. We hoped that the fresh breeze of openness would blow away the mists of guilt and shame that diminish sexual enjoyment for so many people.

We knew that breaking down the barriers of sexual inhibition and celebrating a view of sexuality that accepted the full breadth of human variability, and acknowledging that sexual pleasure must be based on equality and mutual respect between the sexes, would have profound implications for society. Intuitively we recognised, as Naomi Wolf was to write fifteen years later, that 'the result would be more radical than the establishment's worst nightmares. A mass heterosexual deviation into tenderness and mutual respect would mean real trouble for the status quo . . . The power structure would face a massive shift of allegiances . . . Such love would be a political upheaval more radical than the Russian Revolution and more destabilising to the balance of world power than the end of the nuclear age. It would be the downfall of civilisation as we know it – that is, of male dominance; and for heterosexual love, the beginning of the beginning.'[2]

We were not alone in this knowledge. The establishment feared the openness we promoted for precisely the same reasons. A senior officer of Scotland Yard's Obscene Publications Squad commented, 'Don't you realise that if people were to believe what you write, that they could enjoy sex and not feel guilty about it, you would change the whole way of life in this country.'[3]

We did not believe in sexual censorship. This, we knew, maintained the status quo. So we deliberately flouted convention and openly challenged the laws that censor publishing in Britain. We were courting trouble but we didn't care.

I was alone in our publishing offices when the police raided us, one sultry day in August 1975. I was afraid, my knees trembled, I felt nauseated. But to Colin it was an exciting challenge, and before long I came to share his view. That's what kept us going for the next eighteen months, before we eventually came to trial.

Colin and I were charged under the Obscene Publications Act. We faced the possibility of imprisonment and unlimited fines. But we were willing to stand up for our principles. We were fighting for freedom of publication and against censorship and sexual repression, and we discovered that we had many supporters. Hundreds of *Libertine* readers – a cross-section of the British adult population, somewhat skewed towards the intelligentsia – volunteered to take the witness box at our trial and declare that the magazine did not deprave or corrupt, but merely informed and entertained its readers.

We were finally acquitted in the High Court at Leicester in February 1977, after a trial where our defence counsel, John Mortimer and Geoffrey Robertson, had the court howling with laughter time and again about the sheer absurdity of the prosecution case. We would have found the whole thing great fun if we had been sitting in any other place but the dock. At the end, we had, we imagined, won a great victory for freedom, and gained a measure of immunity from police raids.

But the heady *Libertine* years did not last. For one thing, I found myself suffering from a condition I christened 'the sex-mag blues' – a sense of erotic overload, a surfeit of sex. I was haunted by visions of serried ranks of voyeurs, watching my every move as they masturbated. I felt pressured by the massed lust of uncounted faceless men. I was getting turned off.

There were other pressures, too. Although I knew, intellectually, that sexual freedom means freedom to say no as well as yes, I found refusal very difficult. I feared that my inability to enjoy swinging parties, sex with women, or masturbation without penetration, revealed that I was still riddled with inhibitions. I started to feel inadequate again, that I was failing to live up to the expectations of my role as editor of a radical sex magazine.

Meanwhile, Colin's business was in trouble. Having won our case, we were now perceived as a real threat to the girlie-magazine trade. This business depends on censorship to maintain an enormous and perpetually unsatisfied market. The trade feared what they called 'a Danish Situation', for the sex-magazine market in Denmark had crashed within a year of the country's decision to abandon censorship. When the Copenhagen evening papers could publish explicit stills from sex films, very few people bothered to buy tawdry magazines. So the British girlie-mag distributors instituted self-censorship: any magazine that was to reach the shops had to be passed as acceptable by the trade. We were not at all surprised to find that nothing we produced, however innocuous, was acceptable.

Then Colin's business was suddenly bankrupted. His competitors, who distributed millions of copies of girlie magazines, ordered hundreds of thousands of magazines from Colin's small group of publishers, only to return them unsold three months later. Over the course of a single week, truck after truck arrived at Colin's warehouse, unloading pallets piled with what was now unsaleable paper. And with each truckload came a massive invoice. Thus Britain avoided a Danish Situation. We left London penniless, unemployed, with very few possessions and no prospects.

We settled in Wales, our relationship strained by the pressures of poverty. Gradually the conventional roles of husband and wife began to assert themselves: once again, I became subordinate, an inefficient and frequently morose domestic servant. Colin was irritable, resentful, prone to depression. His pride had taken a severe dent with the change in his fortunes; I tried to prop him up, not wanting him to feel inferior or deprived because it seemed that the outside world had rejected him, but he was often moody and aggressive. Our sex-life lost its colour, its spontaneity, its delight. We didn't think about it, much less discuss it.

I found a research job at Swansea University – studying doctors, not rats or rabbits – and became the wage-earner for our small family. By this time, one – if not more – of Colin's children was living with us and I took on the role of stepmother as well as housekeeper and cook. I often felt incapable of holding it all together. Alone in my office, I wept. The patterns that had marked my years with Bob were beginning to repeat themselves.

When the research centre closed down, neither of us had a job. Everyday survival became a challenge. Fortunately, we had hope: my research had been the starting-point for our first book, a controversial study of the damaging effects of prescription drugs. *Cured to Death* was to be published in 1982.

During this phase of our lives together, we concentrated on practical matters. Here, too, the patterns of my relationship with Bob were being repeated; Colin knew how to build, how to create a vegetable garden, how to keep the home fires alight. I had the knowledge we needed for the book, but outside my specialised area of academic expertise I felt incompetent. And Colin reinforced that view by finding fault with almost everything I did.

Although we discussed our emotional problems with a counsellor, Colin was not willing to get involved in the therapeutic process and it didn't seem to help me. He was unable or unwilling to curb his temper. I remained a victim.

Life was not entirely bleak, however. There were good times too: long walks in the Brecon Beacons when we'd talk for hours; eating delicious fruit and vegetables that we'd grown in our kitchen garden; watching our small flock of tame chickens whose greatest desire seemed to be to move back into the kitchen where they has been reared. The house was primitive but we could do just about anything we wanted with it – so long as it cost nothing. Colin became creative in wood and stone, and I learnt valuable skills like plumbing.

Living in this tumbledown cottage by a gurgling river, we were close to nature. I shall never forget the night we lay side by side on our home-made garden table, my head cushioned on a hollowed boulder as we watched shooting stars in the clear dark sky. I loved the trees, the wild creatures, the flowers in the meadow; I loved the hills and the rocks and the waterfalls. In many ways, though we were poor, our life was rich with delight.

I learnt a great deal during those years. Colin encouraged me to use my body, teaching me to run, ride a bicycle – which was less easy – dig the garden and saw logs. For the first time in my life, I began to feel proud of my body and enjoy physical fitness. It was a whole delightful dimension of life that I had never explored before.

We shared our intellectual lives too. Working on books together, we would edit each other's drafts, discussing the text in detail. We had animated editorial arguments which sometimes got very heated; suddenly I found a fluent certainty in myself when I defended points that I considered important. I had discovered a new form of excitement – but I could only argue in this way about books. It was the one significant area of life in which I felt I was Colin's equal.

Our problems lay in our emotional and sexual lives, which we didn't tend to discuss. Both of us looked to others to fill the gaps. I had close friends and family who offered support when I needed it; Colin had a long-standing love-affair with a buxom coffee-coloured woman in London. I liked her; we're still friends. She helped to balance our relationship so that Colin didn't get so bad-tempered with me.

For the next ten years, we stumbled from crisis to crisis. Our interactions developed predictable patterns, from the way I made porridge in the morning to the way we made love at night – or on a minority of nights, anyway. Colin was often fed up, while I was subdued. We quarrelled but I was rarely angry: that was the part he played. He raged while I cried. Then I would try to behave better, to avoid angering him again. I never succeeded for long.

At frequent intervals I would ask myself why I stayed with Colin and whether it was time I left him. But the mood would pass, he would turn sunny again and I would hang on, persuading myself that, on balance, life was better with him than without. Deep down, I was convinced we had an abiding love that was different in quality from anything I had ever experienced before.

Inevitably, perhaps, bad habits accumulated over the years. Like my inability to raise issues that I feared might bring forth his rage; like our readiness to assume that we each knew what the other wanted, without checking; like Colin's assumption that he always knew better than me, and my unwillingness to speak up for myself.

Sexual bad habits became fixed too. In bed, as elsewhere, I was passive, often disinterested but unwilling to admit this even to myself; Colin, bewildered, attributed my lack of passion to my age. We both fantasised about other people, exciting people, people who would make us feel marvellous. At intervals I had brief affairs, never deceiving Colin, but not really sharing either. As with Bob, the pattern of my sex-life with Colin was one of dominance and submission. He decided how much foreplay there should be, and when to penetrate me; if I wasn't ready, I didn't tell him. I was almost always underneath him, controlled by his weight. I wanted sex, because without it I felt rejected, neglected, undesirable, unloved; but I contributed little to its success.

Always I took low-risk options. I rarely confronted him, suppressing my distress when I felt put down; often, I thought I deserved the treatment I got. I tried to please Colin, as I had tried to please Bob years before, making fitful efforts to stay attractive and look after my body. But slowly, steadily, our sex-life deteriorated.

Our relationship dwindled. More and more topics of conversation became taboo: he wasn't interested in my twaddle. He became predictable; I knew all his stories, his opinions. When he started to talk about philosophy or physics, my eyes glazed over. When I talked about my family or our animals he turned away, his attention on the TV.

For too long, we coexisted in sullen silence punctuated by sharp comments. We both felt chronically frustrated, sexually and in every other way. At intervals his irritation flared into fury and he shouted at me, attacking my failure to keep tidy, to finish jobs, to organise my life. I reacted with brief anger, extended despair. More and more, we separated our lives.

We lived in a featureless landscape of boredom and unsatisfied needs. Our relationship had gone stale and we knew it.

4

From Freedom to Fidelity

Sexual boredom and disinterest usually reflect unhappiness in other aspects of relationships. That was certainly true for me, both in my first marriage and in my partnership with Colin. By the time most couples decide to divorce, they can look back on an extended period when sex had turned sour. While sex is good, it keeps you close, reminds you of your love, maintains the warmth between you. It defuses anger, soothes resentment, lifts the spirits, brings shared laughter. But when the pressures and challenges of partnership smother your sexual fires, problems build one on top of another. The crucial bond, the bond that ties man to woman and woman to man across the abyss of sexual and individual differences, is weakened.

Bob's constant put-downs had shattered my fragile confidence. When another man told me, 'Your husband doesn't appreciate you', it made a tremendous impact. Bob didn't appreciate me, it was true, I knew it. This man was demonstrating what appreciation meant: paying total attention to me, treating me like something precious, taking me to heights of passion that I hadn't believed possible. The contrast with my marriage was immediate, shocking, undeniable.

It happened when I was a graduate student, the first time I had spent more than a day away from Bob after four years of living together, when I went with my tutor to an international psychology conference. I was just one of a handful of women mixing with over a hundred men: grown men, handsome men, intelligent, sophisticated men. And they all seemed to want to meet me. I could scarcely believe it – at twenty-two, I had no experience of being treated like a desirable woman.

I was dazzled. At the introductory party on the first evening, I chatted with one charming man after another. But I was naïve: when Jim, a Jewish American working at Oxford, asked me up to his room, I suspected nothing. My tutor had warned me before introducing me that Jim was a womaniser; I had never met one of those and the concept intrigued me. I was impressed by his obvious intelligence, but he was a short, slight man who didn't fit the stereotype of my imagination. I certainly never anticipated that I would end up having sex that night with both Jim and his friend Tony.

When I understood what they wanted, I went along with it in my usual passive way. I hardly thought about what I was doing. I was more drunk than I realised – I wasn't used to alcohol – and I could think of no reason why I should refuse. Bob and I had agreed that fidelity was unnecessary to our relationship – we believed that the fashionable concept of free love was totally rational – though neither of us had actually had any other lovers. I had gone to the conference to learn, and I regarded this as part of my education.

Jim fucked me first while Tony sat on the bed watching. In my mind, I was a spectator too, waiting to see what they would do next and whether I would feel anything. I don't remember whether I enjoyed it, though I'm sure I didn't object. I cannot actually recall much about that night at all, except that Tony and Jim took turns fucking me.

I woke late the next morning in my own room with a crashing headache and half my clothes missing. I felt awful. What had I done? Memories of Jim and Tony filtered back . . . What would they think of me? How could I face them?

But I had to face them. The conference had only just begun. And my clothes were in Jim's room.

My face was running with uncontrollable tears when I knocked nervously on his door. I wished the ground would swallow me. I felt sick. Jim was still in bed when I entered. Shocked at the state I was in, he persuaded me to stay a while so that we could talk it over. He was gentle, kind, comforting. He hadn't realised how innocent I was, how naïve, how completely inexperienced. But he was a believer in sexual freedom and I was receptive to his message.

I began to question the fears that had welled up inside me. What was this anxiety I felt about my reputation? What reputation? That I was a virtuous married woman? To hell with that! How boring can you get? I wanted to develop a reputation as a serious scientist: the stereotyped role of good wife was not for me. It seemed like no fun at all. So maybe now it was time I learnt to enjoy life, discover sex and adult forms of play. Jim was more than willing to help.

My transformation from sexual innocent to lustful woman was completed on the last day of the conference. Jeff, a famous professor, singled me out. I was overwhelmed. This great man, a leader in his field, wanted to be with me! I trembled with excitement. We talked and walked outdoors and held hands. He seemed curiously gentle for such a giant of a man. Although I knew he must be at least twice my age, he seemed at once mature and boyish. I was very drawn to him; he wanted to know all about me. I confessed all that had been happening to me over the past few momentous days, told him about Jim and Tony and my utterly miserable marriage, and left with him for his London hotel.

Lust – lust as I had never felt it in my life before – overwhelmed me. Everything seemed incredibly intense: colours so bright, sensations so acute that the slightest brush against him made me shiver. I longed to feel his body naked against my own; my cunt was hot, aching to be filled. I wanted him so much, I could think of nothing else.

It seemed to take forever to reach his hotel room. Time was stretched tight, my impatience intolerable. The journey from Brighton seemed interminable; I wanted to make love on the train but he resisted, counselling me to be patient, to wait just a little longer. Then at last we were alone, the door shut, Jeff and me together.

We undressed in poignant silence. Strangely, I did not feel awkward. Aware of his eyes on my body, I felt no shame, no embarrassment. Perhaps it was the relaxed half-smile on his face; perhaps it was the warm tingling of my skin, the tension of flesh longing for his touch, overwhelming any uncertainty. Or perhaps, after all that had happened to me during the past few days, I had exhausted my capacity for embarrassment.

Spring sunshine poured through the window as we gazed at each other, our hands starting to explore, kisses becoming more and more passionate. His fingertips brushed my belly and I trembled. His erection grew, insistent. My cunt answered, hot and wet, aching with longing.

The first thrust was like fire entering and stretching my whole being. I didn't know I was capable of feeling so much. I was transported, just him and me separate from the rest of the world, with the unbelievably wonderful sensation of his cock inside me.

Nothing had ever felt like this. The way the velvet of my tissues clung to the satin of his; the way he watched me, his blue eyes penetrating my emotions as his cock penetrated my body; his hands caressing my super-sensitive skin – it was heaven!

Orgasm exploded through me. I was consumed by glowing red sensation, expanding from deep inside, wave upon wave, forcing sobbing cries from my throat. He paused, holding the pressure within, watching my face intently. The tension in my body dissolved, leaving me limp, helpless, totally at his mercy. He began to thrust again.

We lay scissor-fashion, his hand on my hip, his eyes fixed on mine. Slowly, irresistibly, he moved, pulling and pushing the engorged tissues of my cunt as they clung to his cock. Suddenly, convulsively, we grabbed each other close, fucking desperately, all control lost.

Spent, we dozed a while. Lazily, I looked at him, admiring his muscular torso, the grey hairs on his broad tanned chest. He was so much bigger than me! So powerful. So virile. Desire was mounting again. How could this be? After all that, I wanted him again? Yes, I did – more and more!

The affair could not last. I had to deal with the unresolved issues of my personal life; he had a wife and family in America. I cried bitter tears of loss as I caught the train home. I had discovered ecstatic sex and I wanted more.

A decade after I had felt the first stirrings of desire for a man, I was no longer a virgin. I know that technically I had not been a virgin since my first fuck with Bob, but emotionally I was: my sexual nature had remained hidden, untouched. Jeff had unlocked – shattered – that secret door.

As soon as my husband saw me, he knew I had changed. I told him little about what had happened, I just said I needed to go away for a while to think things over. I packed my bags and left. Over the course of the next week, a tide of rage flowed through me. Suddenly I realised how angry I was with Bob, how much I resented his seemingly constant put-downs, the way he devalued me. I covered scraps of paper, old envelopes, anything I could find in the friend's house where I had found sanctuary, with uncharacteristically tiny handwriting, cramming years of accumulated resentment into bitter words. How I hated him!

He came to see me. Fury clogged my throat. He was quietly reasonable, as always. I felt sick. I screamed at him till he left.

I found solace in music. Among my friend's records was Beethoven's F Minor string quartet. The rage, the pain, the distress and finally the freedom that flowed through the music soothed my seething mind. I played that quartet again and again. Eventually, I started to dance.

Alone in the house, the picture window reflecting my

moving image, I danced through the pain, anger and repression to touch the joyful fire at my core. Leaping and stretching, running and twisting, I found myself.

In the weeks that followed, I felt like a butterfly newly emerged from the chrysalis, stretching damp and delicate wings, learning to flutter and fly. Years later, I met Jeff again when he travelled five hundred miles out of his way to spend a night with me. It was a pleasant, friendly reunion but the magic had gone. We reminisced about the day we'd met; he told me I had seemed like a flower, just on the point of opening to greet the sun. He had felt privileged, he said, to be there at that time.

For me, the events of that conference had opened floodgates of emotions I had never experienced before. Other men showed me that Bob offered less than I needed. Poor Bob, his background seemed to have made him even more repressed than I; young for my years, passive, lacking in confidence, I had followed his faltering lead. In retrospect, I believe that Bob was afraid of my potential emotional, sexual and intellectual power: afraid that he could not match it, could not keep up with me. He had succeeded in controlling me by playing on my fears – until I escaped. I was growing. I had left Bob behind.

During the period of self-discovery that followed, when I became promiscuous, seeking affection, sexual knowledge and pleasure in a succession of relationships, I was trying to work out my own moral code, questioning everything as I searched for valid reasons to underpin my choice of lovers.

After a while, my personal life ceased to make any sort of sense. The loneliness was getting to me. All my relationships seemed superficial; when I felt tired or weak, there was nobody to comfort me. I missed my cats and our beautiful canal boat, moored under quiet willows where kingfishers dived. I missed Bob's reliability. Before long, I became ill. Bob returned to fetch me back.

Our relationship had changed totally. I was no longer a virtuous, retiring wife. I quarrelled and fought, shaming him by shouting my defiance in public. I took lovers when I fancied them, disrupting their lives in my search for casual sexual pleasure. I knew I would leave Bob again, permanently, before long. I planned to emigrate as soon as I had finished my doctorate. Bob became ill and depressed. Within a year, I moved out for good. Our marriage was not strong enough to survive my lack of commitment.

Sexually deprived in my marriage, I had felt deeply unwanted. My lovers showed they wanted me – for a while, at least. They found me exciting. They brought enthusiasm to sex and I responded by getting much more turned on than I had with Bob. This is why affairs can present such a threat to vulnerable marriages.

It wasn't just *my* marriage that fell apart when I discovered sex. A whole series of marriages collapsed like dominoes. I went through a phase of seeing every man as a sexual object and going to bed with all those who were both willing and passably attractive. Some were married but I saw that as their responsibility, not mine. I didn't want to deceive their wives or destroy their marriages; in two cases, I discussed my desire openly with the man's wife and was given permission to go ahead. But this tolerance was based on illusion. Only a tiny minority of those marriages survived the husband's infidelity.

Eventually, I realised that I was putting at risk my lovers' established relationships and I ceased to have sex with men I knew to be married. Freedom, I recognised, had to be coupled with responsibility. Even so, my disruptive influence continued; sometimes I discovered a man was married only when I heard his angry wife's voice on the telephone.

My casual attitudes caused a lot of pain both to the men whom I loved briefly and discarded and to their wives. I regret that; I never intended to hurt anyone. Despite the crucial part that sex with other men played in destroying my own marriage, I just didn't believe it could have such a powerful impact beyond this. Anyway, I rationalised, marriages that were so vulnerable to infidelity couldn't have much going for them. To some extent, with hindsight, I think I was right. Marriages usually do recover, and often become stronger after the stress of an affair discovered – but only if both partners recognise that the impetus to stray is generated by problems that they are motivated to solve.

I became a free woman, active in the rapidly-growing women's movement, seeking liberation from the attitudes that had constrained me. Talking with women in consciousness-raising groups, reading Germaine Greer, Betty Friedan and the seminal feminist authors of the early seventies, I discovered how much I shared with other women, how often my feelings and experiences ran parallel to theirs. I began to step aside from the judgements of the culture into which I had been born, to respect myself as never before.

I learnt that I could not ask others to *give* me freedom: freedom is a state of mind which I had to find for myself. Reared to serve and look after others, I had suppressed my self and my desires. In the importance I attached to duty, I had lost sight of what I wanted, looking only to find the little I imagined I needed. I had castigated myself for failing to be what I believed I should be. In reality, my failure was to appreciate what I actually was.

This was a time of intense questioning, when I examined both personal and social values and morality, seeking fundamental truths by which I could make the crucial decisions of my life. I had begun that process in adolescence, but it had almost stopped during my years as Bob's wife when I had lost confidence in my own judgement. Now, as a single woman once more, I was thinking again about philosophy and ethics.

The challenge was to become true to myself. That remains a great challenge: it requires that I truly know myself. The process of discovery never ends. Uncovering the boundaries of my sexual self was one of the challenges I set myself, and it is largely because this was a conscious search that my experiences were unusually wide and varied. I wanted to find out through experiment – for the curiosity of the scientist remained a strong aspect of my personality – what different forms of sexual experience felt like. I wanted to discover whether lust required love, whether I was truly heterosexual, and which of the many variants of sexuality would turn me on. I wanted to find out about sex with people from different cultures, different backgrounds. In the seventies, a time when casual sex for women was a new and exciting idea, there seemed to be no reason why I should not experiment. I could see no inherent value in limiting my sexual experience; quite the reverse: by broadening it, I would learn more about myself and other people.

For the first few years of living with Colin, my conscious search for personal liberation continued. This, in large part, was what working on *Libertine* was about. Philosophy and politics were – and still are – very important to Colin. We spent many happy hours talking about ethical issues. To us, individual freedom included sexual freedom: the freedom to share sexual pleasure openly and without guilt, with whomsoever we pleased. We had an open relationship and lovers posed no threat while we were certain of the strength of our love for one another.

There was a lot of pleasure during those years. If I fancied a man, I would tell Colin and, if I had the courage, I told the man too. One Christmas holiday, we called on Brian, a mutual friend, in Cambridge. It was late and we decided to stay overnight.

Brian asked me what I wanted to do, where I wanted to sleep. Shyly, I admitted that I would like to share his bed; then, gathering courage, I said that what I really wanted was to share a bed with both Colin and Brian. To my delight, Brian agreed without hesitation and we had a marvellous time discovering the delights of troilism. Two cocks were undoubtedly better than one from my point of view – and the men obviously loved it too.

In the morning, Colin went downstairs to make tea and

toast while Brian and I returned to a slow and sensuous fuck. As we were recovering, Colin appeared at the door – just in time to hear me say, 'But Brian, I had no idea you were gay!' Colin nearly dropped the breakfast tray. Brian admitted he had fancied Colin since the day they had met but the previous night was the first he had ever spent with another man; he hadn't dared come out and openly acknowledge his homosexuality.

The three of us had an extended and mutually pleasurable affair. I was fascinated – and privileged – to watch Brian making love to Colin; I learnt a lot from that! For a while, we all shared a London flat, until Brian left to move in with the man who had been his long-term fantasy object. With our connections in the gay publishing world, we had been able to introduce them. It was a great pleasure to have dinner with these two contented lovers a couple of months later.

Our bed in London was huge, quite big enough for three to sleep comfortably together. Sometimes we shared it with another woman, sometimes with a man. While our life was exciting and varied, outside lovers only added to our enjoyment.

But as the years wore on and we were forced out of publishing, the situation changed. Within our relationship, trust was ebbing slowly away. When I had lovers, Colin was envious, miserable that women did not find him as desirable as other men found me. Poverty had changed his life; without money and a flourishing business, he had lost power and influence and saw himself as much less attractive to women. My repeated assertion that the sort of women who interested him weren't likely to care whether he was rich or poor simply didn't fit in with his experience.

Then we discovered Aids. I read in the *New Scientist* about a strange new syndrome that was beginning to afflict gay men and drug addicts in the United States. Fascinated, I spent weeks in medical libraries reading all I could find about it. We pieced the puzzle together: it had to be a new type of virus, transmitted in body fluids, and capable of causing severe damage to the immune system. It was not long before our hypothesis was confirmed. The Human Immunodeficiency Virus was isolated and described. It was a new sexually transmitted plague, incurable, undetectable in its early stages, dreadful in its effects.

We understood the implications. Our sexually free life style – now more theoretical than practical – had to change. Only monogamy would be safe.

But monogamy leaves much to be desired. I found it difficult to fancy men and not act on my lust. Sex with Colin had become dull but it seemed there was no alternative if I was not to expose him, as well as myself, to the threat of Aids. Safe sex wasn't a safe option: if contraceptive failure can lead to pregnancy, then it must also be capable of exposing us to Aids.

Eventually, I succumbed to temptation. We had booked a skiing holiday but an injured shoulder forced Colin to drop out. In Austria, I met Johann; fourteen years my junior, he was too gorgeous to refuse. Johann was a local boy who lived in the basement of his mother's large guesthouse in Mayrhofen; his twin passions, reflected in his slim, energetic, muscular body, were skiing and sex. I loved his sudden grin, the way he would laugh and promise to fuck me as I had never been fucked before. We didn't talk much; his English was halting and my German virtually nonexistent but that didn't matter. We shared days and nights of overwhelming lust, fucking till we were too sore to continue, then skiing till we had recovered sufficiently to start all over again. I felt marvellous, rejuvenated, a young woman once more. I returned home to face Colin's fury. He could not accept what I had done. His rage erupted in violence. I could no longer ignore the bruises or deny my unhappiness in the relationship.

Suddenly I was forced to acknowledge that infidelity was dangerous in more ways than one. When we had reacted to the threat of Aids by deciding that we should not have affairs, we had changed the basis of our relationship. We had made a new commitment to be exclusive sexual partners and I had broken that contract. Colin's anger was predictable, understandable.

Most couples accept a commitment to mutual fidelity as soon as their relationship becomes important to them. Marriage almost always implies such a commitment. Although at least half of all married people have affairs at some point, this does represent a break with the contract that they made with each other, and anger, resentment and jealousy are almost inevitable consequences when the affair comes to light.[1]

People tend to have affairs when the marriage feels dull, confined. When sexual energy bubbles over because it's not being expressed within the partnership, both men and women find other partners. Infidelity may seem casual, but even casual affairs have a way of becoming involving, emotionally fraught, the focus of resentments. Inevitably, we compare spouse and lover; marriage comes to represent all that's boring while excitement lies outside. In the early flush of lust, sensible people lose their senses and put long-term relationships at risk, relationships that may be much more valuable to them than they realise.

Maybe the affair is unexceptional. In that case, it's not worth the risk or the bother. But if sex with your lover is wonderful, it can tear you apart. I lay in bed longing for Johann, unable to get his face – a face that seemed to come straight from the paintings of Classical Crete – out of my mind. I would daydream of Johann, hoping to obscure the reality of Colin with fantasy. I remembered his light-hearted laughter, his slender golden body, his boyish delight in uncomplicated sex, his eager cock. But I couldn't pretend Colin's body was Johann's, or Colin's cock Johann's. The closer our physical contact, the more I wished it was not Colin. Our sexual pleasure – what there was of it – was undermined, our touching disrupted by the phantom of the youth for whom I yearned.

No one individual can be everything we want; no single person combines the beauty and energy of youth with the wisdom of age. No single person can provide the variety that Confucius called the greatest aphrodisiac. This is the fundamental dilemma of monogamy, the test of will that Colin and I had imagined we could avoid.

My desire for sexual pleasure remained but my ability to achieve it with Colin had died. I could no longer permit myself to feel lust, lest it lead me to another man's bed. I coped by shutting down my feelings; even in my dreams, I refused sex, became disinterested. The inner flame went out.

Inevitably, we began to discuss separation. If I stayed with Colin, I thought, I was condemning myself to half a lifetime without sexual pleasure. I resented him deeply. We could scarcely talk without conflict; he found fault with everything I said, even the way I spoke. Whenever he spoke, it was to voice yet another complaint. What was the point in continuing?

On Christmas Day 1988, Colin and I went walking on the beautiful Pembrokeshire coastal path. Unseasonable wild-flowers bloomed under a cool blue sky. Colin was angry, as usual. I was crying, as usual. It seemed impossible to bridge the gulf that had opened up between us.

We were no longer working together. After writing eight books jointly, we couldn't do it any more. He was too viciously critical of my work. I wanted to edit the words he wrote out of existence: cold, cynical words, aloof words, patronising words that reflected his male arrogance. I would write my woman words: no man would tell me what they should be.

Nevertheless, we shared too much to part easily. I've seen friends turn into shadows of their former selves after separating from their partners. Grey-faced and thin, they crumple in on themselves, suffering dreadfully from a process that they quite often initiated, even welcomed – before they knew what it would feel like. You think, without that creep I'll be free from the nagging, the pressure, the rows; you never imagine the depth of the pain that can ensue.

Its extent will depend on the number and strength of the bonds that have formed between you. These ties take many forms: economic, cultural, philosophical, moral, religious, social, domestic, sexual; when you cut them, you must expect to bleed. Only if they have already withered away will you escape unhurt; and when this is the case, you have already suffered the pain.

For me, separating from Bob was relatively painless because, by the time it happened, there was little left to break. With Colin, there were many ties: our flock of gentle Dorset sheep and our dogs, whom we both loved; the volumes of writing we had created together; the ideas and ideals we shared; his children, who, though now grown-up, were very dear to both of us. Neither of us could look after the sheep alone, and neither of us wanted to desert them. I couldn't just walk away from our home, our joint mortgage, our mutual obligations.

Anyway, I kept thinking of the words of Colin's oldest son, Mark, to whom I had confided my unhappiness. 'If you leave Colin,' he warned me, 'you'll only find another one who'll probably turn out even worse.' I recalled the failed relationships of my younger days: how the men so quickly came to seem boring, superficial, trivial in their outlook; how often courtship would turn to patronising and bullying; how sex would deteriorate within weeks. I remembered how close Colin's philosophy was to mine, and how rare such a conjunction was.

But living with Colin had become so difficult. I felt utterly miserable, seeing only unhappiness with him and unhappiness if I should leave him. How ugly Colin seemed then! How frightening, how cruel! We had loved each other once; now that time seemed so far away, it was incomprehensible. A lump lodged somewhere in my diaphragm, hard and painful. I felt chronically exhausted, washed out with tears.

Illness struck us both then, when we were emotionally at our lowest ebb. An intractable tooth abscess dominated my inner world. The only creature who cared, I felt, was my faithful tomcat, Chicken-Egg, who never left my side as I tossed and turned in pain and fever. Then Colin went down with flu, quickly followed by pneumonia.

Suddenly he was weeping, vulnerable, and I was caring for him again. We had so nearly given up on our relationship, but not quite, not totally. We struggled to talk without fighting. We made an appointment with a marriage counsellor. I don't think what the counsellor said was crucial, so much as the fact that we had both gone to see her, both hoping that somehow our relationship could be salvaged. After fourteen years together, we weren't quite ready to let go. Her diagnosis was that I needed to become more assertive. If I were less passive, she said, Colin would stop bullying me. And he had to make an effort to curb his critical tongue.

There was hope. We both began to work on ourselves. I had to summon up the courage to tell Colin the truth about how I felt – especially how I felt about sex. We had to stop blaming each other all the time, come to terms with reality, start taking positive action.

It's difficult to break the habits of a decade. Our pattern of interaction had to change radically; we had to think before we spoke. I could no longer hide behind what I thought Colin wanted, acting the martyr and feeling resentful. I had to work out, for myself, what I actually felt, and act on that. I had always seen myself as honest. Now I recognised that I had not been true to myself. And Colin finally acknowledged that taking his anger with the world out on me just couldn't continue: he didn't kick his dog, why should he imagine he could kick me?

What had happened to our love? Was there still a spark, smouldering under the layers of routine and resentment? Could it be rekindled? Could we find the keys to love again? Crucially, did we care enough to make the effort?

The process of rebuilding our relationship took years. It's still going on, four years after that miserable walk along the Pembrokeshire cliffs. It has been difficult, painful and scary; but through that process we have grown up and grown together.

I had a clear vision of what I wanted. It was a relationship that was sufficiently satisfying, rewarding and exciting for me to feel that fidelity was not only possible but desirable; a relationship that I genuinely felt could last till death; a relationship with no dark secrets; a relationship that moved forward, to greater understanding, greater heights and deeper depths. I saw sex not so much as the central experience of this relationship, but as an indicator of its quality.

When our partnership was close to breaking-point and I had lost all sexual desire, I made a decision: if my feelings about sex with Colin were still negative two years after the New Year that I pinpointed as rock-bottom, I would leave him. I would do my best to make things work during the time; but if I felt, when the time for assessment came, our relationship had not improved sufficiently for me to want, and enjoy, sex with Colin, I would withdraw from it.

Those two years were the hardest of all. I sought and found help, first in an assertiveness class, which proved very revealing. One of the tasks which our leader, Gwen, a strong and positive woman, set the group, was to draw up a list of all the things we had not been able to say to particular people. I had imagined, before I wrote my list, that it would reveal communication problems between Colin and me – but to my astonishment, it didn't. There wasn't actually anything I felt unable to share with Colin. My list included a whole lot of frustration in my home life that didn't involve Colin at all.

At that time, we were living in a housing co-operative, sharing a Gothic mansion with a group of other people. Colin was unhappy both with the house and the co-operative, but I had been maintaining that it suited me. My list of unresolved niggles showed that a lot of my frustration was associated with Kevin, another co-op member. I felt unable to tell him how irritated I was about his attitudes because he threw a tantrum whenever I disagreed with him.

Suddenly I realised that I, like Colin, was not happy living in a co-operative. This unrecognised tension had been adding to the everyday stress in my life. Leaving the co-operative would significantly reduce the strain on both of us, and, I hoped, improve the relationship between Colin and me. Within a few months of this realisation, we had bought our own farm. It was a great relief.

It was then that I began to meet regularly with Charleen, my counsellor, who worked through my problems using psychosynthesis. Each session with her led to new insights and long discussions with Colin. I can't count how many hours we spent talking, seeking new understanding of ourselves, learning to share feelings I hadn't even realised I had and persuading him to trust me enough to share his own feelings. Sometimes it felt like a hopeless struggle, but more often there was a sense that previously locked doors were opening for us. Our relationship had much more potential than we had realised.

We were learning about ourselves and the way we interacted. We were opening up to one another, discovering depths that had been hidden under the weight of assumption and imagined obligations. And from these depths emerged a new fullness of passion, a love that endured the harshest test. I no longer seriously imagine that I will have any other lover but Colin, despite the fact that others continue to populate my fantasies; he is all the lover I need.

Once changes had been set in motion, they were progressive, their effects cumulative. We shook ourselves and like the patterns in a kaleidoscope, our mingled lives fell into new arrangements. Change tends to be painful at first: think how your muscles ache when you change a habitual pattern of behaviour and begin using your body differently; think how it hurts to move to another level of physical competence.

Just as the body deteriorates when you fail to expose yourself to physical demand, so emotionally we lose our strength when we don't dare to stretch, to feel the intensity of which we are capable. Rebuilding myself has taken effort and determination. But since I went through that process, my life has made more sense and I can understand myself and the dynamics of my relationships much better.

I am forty-four, Colin fifty-three. Middle age is a time when many people look at themselves, their relationships, their place in society. The mid-life crisis hits when the terrain of our lives stretches featureless ahead, too bleak to accept and too difficult to change. Is this what it's all about? Is this all?

I wanted to combine comfort and stability with stimulating conversation and bliss in the bedroom. I imagined – when things were bad – that I couldn't make it happen because the old routine dominated my life, my thinking. I had to overcome my fears, take risks; I recognised that my relationship with Bob hadn't gone anywhere because we had been scared of change, afraid to look too closely at ourselves, afraid to move forward into uncertain territory. With Charleen's help, I was able to tap into the courage that I needed to change my life.

I have changed. Colin has changed. I don't believe anyone is ever too old to change. All you need is the desire for something better and the determination to leave no stone unturned in the search for a fuller, more satisfying life. Sometimes my courage still fails me, but the setbacks are temporary because I know that we will go on moving forward and overcoming difficulties.

I have learnt that I can – indeed, I must – be true to myself and honest with Colin; that repressing and denying unhappiness is futile; that confronting reality in a relationship brings long-term closeness with a partner, even if it's often painful at the time. I have learnt to take responsibility for my life and feelings and to deal with problems before they overwhelm me; I know how to handle situations that I was unable to cope with when I was younger. The next section of this book explains how we have succeeded up to now, and how we continue to make progress.

I look at Colin sometimes with innocent delight. To me, he appears so handsome, so desirable, so sexy that I want to fall on him, to kiss and caress him, hold him in my arms, to surround and be surrounded by him. How lucky I am, to be living with a man as warm, as perceptive, as intelligent as this! At last I'm able to acknowledge his true value to me, and to value myself as never before. And now I appreciate him, he appreciates me too.

Finally, we have found each other and ourselves. We're in love all over again.

Part II

Rekindling The Fire

5

Sex is Multidimensional

When I was young, I imagined sex to be somehow different from the rest of my experience. There was normal life, and then there was sex. Life required thought, work, determination; sex just happened. If problems arose with sex, I tended to assume that they were due to what we did, or didn't do, in bed, and how we felt at the time. I didn't consider the context in which our sexual relationship existed.

If I didn't feel much in bed, I assumed it was because sex wasn't the marvellous experience it was said to be. Later, when I had discovered ecstasy, unexciting sex meant simply that the man wasn't a good lover. It didn't occur to me that the roots of our problems might lie outside the bedroom.

Although, if challenged, I might have acknowledged this ten years ago, I didn't really understand what it meant. Without realising it, I still accepted the cultural myth that sex was separate from the rest of everyday life. Too often, sex means the mechanical and technical sexuality that scientists study in their researches into arousal and orgasm; or the sexuality of sex magazines and blue films, portrayed independently of social or psychological context; or sex as discussed by doctors and sex educators, an act shorn of emotional content.

Now that I know more about fluctuating desire, I understand how sex can shift from wonderful to boring and back again. It has to do with the state of the inner furnace that fires sexuality. Many of us think of the intensity of our sex-drive as a more or less constant feature of our make-up. As we grow up, we come to recognise those friends who are sexually obsessed and those who are cool; we imagine we can sense the intensity of another person's sex-drive. There are those who feel randy all the time and those who seem unconcerned about sex. The level of drive grows in adolescence, to fall, we assume, with increasing age.

But the randiest among us can switch off at any age, and the coolest can flare into incandescence. What controls those flames is only partly the hormone-controlled power of human sexuality. All other aspects of life, from work to health, from social interaction to self-realisation, feed the fire.

In my recent efforts to rekindle sexual desire for Colin, I had to look at the whole of our life together. The blocks, I discovered, could lie anywhere. I have learnt not to make hasty judgements or opt out by accepting easy explanations. I had to see beyond simple propositions – 'He can't satisfy me'; 'It's his/my age'; 'He's/I'm/we're no good in bed'; 'We've done it so often, of course it's boring' – to the complex dynamics of reality. Our interaction, both inside and outside the bedroom, came under close scrutiny, and the problem was tackled on many fronts at once.

Why desire fluctuates

I should have learnt early on in my relationship with Colin about the influence of outside forces on sex-drive. His desire for sex plummeted when we had been together a mere three years. Suddenly this consistently randy man wasn't interested in me. Night after night, he would pick a quarrel at bedtime. Not understanding what was going on, I felt very hurt. I thought that he had fallen out of love with me, that I wasn't good enough, in some ill-defined sense, for him. It took me some time to realise that he was worrying about his business, and that I wasn't to blame. This was one of the difficult periods in our life together, when Colin was losing confidence and we faced uncertainty and the prospect of poverty.

Colin's reaction was typical of men in similar situations. Work-stress, potential or actual unemployment, and a sense of personal failure are all potent turn-offs. Men, more than women, tend to derive much of their self-esteem from the sense that they are successful at work; when they feel they are failing, their confidence plummets and one result is loss of interest in sex. One of the unrecognised effects of economic recession has undoubtedly been a widespread loss of sexual desire for a great many couples: the cause may be outside our control but we suffer the consequences in a very personal way.

When both partners turn off, the pressure is reduced. They can accept the situation, though they may not like it; if they care for each other, they ride it out. Every couple's life has nasty bumpy phases. Friends asked me why I didn't leave Colin when his business collapsed and we lost our home and our possessions; I said simply, because I loved him. Anyway, I was pretty low myself, struggling to cope with sudden adversity, and I certainly didn't feel randy. At those times, you know you have to stick together, to support each other, even if you aren't having much fun in bed.

Sexual pleasure returns when happiness blossoms in other parts of life. Without deliberate effort, sex becomes delightful when body and mind are in harmony. There's nothing like success for enhancing sex-drive, sex-appeal and sexual pleasure. Success is exciting because it doesn't happen all the time; if it did, it would become part of everyday functioning: unstimulating, neutral.

When everyday life is uneventful, creating sexual pleasure and harmony enhances colours and contrasts outside, improving confidence and the ability to cope. Good sex makes us more creative, more willing to take risks, more energetic, more *vital*. It is, after all, the very essence of life.

Identifying underlying problems

Colin and I have phases when we make conscious efforts to create a more exciting sex-life. Usually, the healing process begins when I realise that I haven't had a good fuck recently and have stopped thinking about our sex-life – or when Colin makes his frustration obvious. Then I consider the problem. What aspect of life is causing this? How do I feel about trying to deal with it? Am I generally turned off, or just not interested in sex with him?

When the problem is the other way round and Colin doesn't want sex when I do, I seek answers to a mirror-image set of questions. It may be possible to persuade Colin to think about them, but I can't *expect* him to do so; I have to want to do it myself. But even if I think it's his problem, I have to look at the context, and the way I may be contributing to it.

I consider the factors that are most likely to contribute to our problem. Unresolved conflict, anger and resentment are the most important and the most common causes of long-standing loss of desire. These negative emotions undermine affection and trust, leading to the creation of barriers between partners. Nagging resentment surfaces, crushing desire, at those critical times when loving feelings could develop. These are serious issues that must be aired if their destructive influence is to be curbed.

Total loss of desire is a frequent reaction to one partner's discovery that the other has been having an affair. Anger and loss of trust have to be resolved before desire is likely to return, and this can take a long time. But couples who persevere with working to improve their relationship and rebuild trust can rediscover love. As trust returns, so does desire; and the bond between the partners often ends up stronger than before.

The process of change need only start with one partner. If one changes, the other will also change, creating a new balance in the relationship. I have learnt that while I cannot *demand* that Colin changes, or try to change him directly, I can create the effects I want indirectly, by changing myself. But I still need to understand the underlying reasons for the problem that has emerged between us, so that I can work out what sort of change is necessary.

Finding the answers to such questions can be difficult. We don't always *want* to answer them honestly. Sometimes it's hard to see our way through the confusion of feelings that arise. Often my interpretation of the situation mirrors my own underlying difficulties, at least at first. Often, too, the problem on which we focus is merely a symptom of deeper unresolved issues; this is particularly likely to be true when couples are working through the aftermath of an affair. It's important to work at the problem for long enough, and think about it in sufficient depth in order to come to conclusions that have positive implications and point towards remedial action.

Take the situation where Colin seems to have lost interest in me. If I'm feeling unhappy with myself, I'll probably assume that he finds me unattractive. While there may be some truth in that, it surely won't take the simple form of my self-rejecting thoughts: that I'm too ugly, too fat, too flabby, or too old to be desirable. My intellectual self knows perfectly well that such features are of little importance after years in a partnership, but another part of my mind, the part that succumbs to the pernicious messages of our culture, remains vulnerable. Because I am neither young, model-girl slim nor girlie-mag buxom, because my skin is neither smooth nor tanned, I sometimes feel unappealing. But if I am unattractive at such times, it is that feeling within myself, a feeling reflected in my posture and behaviour, that makes me so.

When I put my insecurities about my body aside for long enough to look at the whole situation, I see a much more complicated picture. There are innumerable reasons why he may not fancy me at any particular time. Some will relate purely to his situation: he may be exhausted, disappointed by something quite apart from me or our relationship, preoccupied by a thorny problem or overwhelmed by a draining emotion such as grief for a lost friend or lost opportunity. He may be unwell, depressed, distracted by pain or obsessive thoughts.

Perhaps I am contributing to the problem by hiding my body under shapeless layers of practical clothing, boring him with incessant discussion of ewe obstetrics, turning him off with a lingering smell of disinfectant, sheep and manure. Perhaps I am not taking sufficient time to treat him in a loving way, not responding to his needs or the messages he communicates.

We can all think of patterns of behaviour that drive us away from our partners. For some women, the smell of engine oil, greasy hair and perpetually black fingernails become total turn-offs. Such cues may carry the message that machinery is all that matters; relationships come second. For others, the turn-off is piles of paper brought home from the office, a cue that says 'Don't bother me, I'm working,' when the other partner, longing for closeness, wants to talk or cuddle. Turned away too often, we turn off in anger and self-defence; we may not even realise it's happening until suddenly we notice the cold core within us, or our partner wants to know why we don't want sex any more.

Perhaps the reason is that your sexual interaction is no longer enjoyable or satisfying. The easy answer is that your partner is a lousy lover – especially if you've had other partners with whom sex worked better. But look deeper: you may have problems communicating your needs and desires clearly, so your partner doesn't know how to please you. Perhaps you need to find ways to encourage your partner to do for you what you most enjoy. Perhaps you haven't thought enough about what you want. All these things were true for Colin and me when our sex-life wasn't as much fun as it is now. Once the initial heat of passion died down, we became more critical of each other, more dissatisfied. When we simply judged each other to be unexciting lovers, our relationship went downhill; but when we learnt to stand back and look for ways forward, we began to create the reality we desired.

The immediate problem may seem insoluble: you may not be able to do anything about unemployment, poverty, illness or grief. But you can look at your own interaction, the ways you help or harm each other, the ways you react to your partner's behaviour. I have learnt that, whatever our external circumstances, it is always possible to work on some aspect of our life together so that we enjoy each other more. The crucial step is to recognise that you *can* do something, and to decide that you *will* take action.

With a multidimensional problem like loss of sexual pleasure, there are many things that can be done to improve the situation. For me, the process has taken years. I have had to look at myself and the influence of my background and early years; I have had to accept responsibility for my own sexual feelings, to discover what turns Colin and me on, and what turns us off; I have had to learn to talk much more openly with Colin, and to overcome the fears that interfered with my ability to communicate. These themes, and more, are the subject of the rest of this book.

Sexual pleasure is much more complicated, delicate and far-reaching in its effects than I ever realised when I started bonking twenty-five years ago. Understanding that, and acting on my understanding, has taught me to appreciate sex as I never did then. I hope my experience will help others to appreciate it too.

6

Learning All the Time

One of the many delights of life is that even when you think you know it all, there's still more to discover. When I thought I knew Colin as well as anyone could know another person, I suddenly came upon hidden facets of his personality, reactions that I hadn't predicted. I thought I had explored every aspect of my sexual self, only to discover that there was far more to learn. When there's always something new over the horizon, life can never get boring.

Not only do we continue to learn about aspects of ourselves that may have lain unrecognised or dormant for years, we are also changing all the time as we go through the varied experiences of our lives. Partnerships, too, mature and change: they are dynamic, and both partners have to be willing to adapt. An emotional relationship only becomes static when it's dead.

Early in a love relationship, we want to know all about each other. The process of discovery is rapid, stimulating, sometimes a little frightening. We're finding out about each other and our reactions to this other special person so fast that we can't make sense of all the information. There's a lot of uncertainty, a compelling desire to find out more, touch more; feelings are intense, experiences heightened by novelty. It's all part of the excitement.

After years of living together, the excitement fades but it

only disappears if we close our minds to exploration within the relationship. I made a lot of assumptions about Colin and our life together which I later found were unjustified, and which contributed to the sense of staleness between us. When we broke through some of those assumptions, we found we could get much closer and we began to feel happier together.

Psychologists often portray learning on a graph which charts speed or accuracy of performance against time. Whether we're learning a relatively simple skill like shooting at a target or a highly complex one like making love, the shape of the learning curve is basically the same. It accelerates sharply at first, when we learn quickly, then gradually levels off. Then it stabilises on a series of plateaux, jumping off from each with an unexpected steepening of the curve as we learn a new facet of the activity, to level again at a higher point.

The more complex the behaviour we're learning, the more of these plateaux and discontinuities we experience, but they become rarer and usually less dramatic as time goes on. Yet we can never be sure when they will occur, nor when one crucial jump will lead to a rapid series of others. Sometimes the learning process is never finished. That's how it is with relationships.

There are periods in the life of every relationship when we have to learn fast. One such point is the birth of the first child, which puts new demands on both partners and sometimes leads to the emergence of totally unexpected aspects of their personalities. The early years of child-rearing can create emotional crises that shake relationships to the core. Other periods of sudden and demanding change – loss of a job, moving to a new and unfamiliar place, taking on new responsibilities like an ageing relative or a farm – force us to learn and adapt. The more far-reaching the change, the more stressful the adaptation will be.

These phases of life can be so demanding that weak relationships crumble. But if we can support and encourage each other at such times, sharing those intense experiences will strengthen and enrich the partnership.

All the time, as you go through life together, you're getting to know your partner better. This is just as true of shared erotic experience as of any other aspect of life. Learning about making love and relating to a sexual partner is so complex that nobody can expect to know it all. You may imagine you can always predict what your partner is going to do, it's so *boring* – but you'd be wrong. I have thought that, often; but when I stand back from the immediate happenings, I know it's not true. He may indeed do what I anticipate, but in reality I don't know him totally. I don't know how he will behave when he's stimulated in a different way, or by a different person; nor can I know the parts of him that aren't apparent to me.

Colin and I get into familiar situations, predictable routines. Sometimes we don't seem to be learning anything new. But that's because there's lots of me and lots of him that isn't fired up by our interaction. Perhaps it could be. There's more to each one of us than we ever imagine. To find it, we have to explore – individually and together. We have to open doors in every aspect of our selves and our lives together, gaze through at whatever lies beyond, not leave them closed, our selves shut down and defended. Every time we say 'We never talk about that, we never do that, I couldn't say that to him, I couldn't do that with him, I can't even *think* about that,' we are refusing to open a door, afraid to face the consequences of confronting something.

Opening doors can be risky. I have often been afraid to express myself, my feelings, my desires, especially in relation to sex. I am afraid of rejection. So is Colin. When he says I am insensitive and clumsy, I get scared to experiment. When I don't react as he hopes, he gives up trying. Stalemate.

We generate the illusion between us that we are bored with each other, but in reality we are afraid. We each create an image of our self and the other that focuses only on certain features, ignoring or denying others that we may initially find difficult to handle. These diminished images limit our freedom of movement, of understanding, of interaction. Together we accomplish boredom.

It takes only one to untie that knot. As soon as you react differently to a previously predictable situation, you are changing the pattern, breaking the boredom. Your partner may take a while to change – that depends on many things, principally the degree of difference between what you're doing now and what you usually do. But change there will be, for both of you. Whatever the change, we learn from it.

The happier I am, the more new discoveries I make. I'm more open to new things when my confidence is high, countering fear and anxiety. That positive cycle starts with a decision to do something differently, to find new ways to live my life and express myself. Making that crucial decision to achieve a more rewarding relationship led to a great many changes.

Anxiety and fear have the opposite effect: they interfere with my ability to perceive what's happening and to learn new ways of coping. Focusing on things that scare me is almost always dangerous and counterproductive. To learn most effectively, I need to be relaxed but motivated, alert and open-minded. I have to put fear aside.

The First Rule of Bicycle Riding

I call this realisation 'The First Rule of Bicycle Riding' because it was when I learnt to ride a bike that it really became clear to me. The First Rule of Bicycle Riding is a simple statement: *Always focus on where you want to go.* I have it posted on the wall above my desk and I remind myself of it whenever I'm feeling scared or stuck.

As a girl, I never learnt to ride a bike. My mother believed bicycles were so dangerous that I might be killed if I had one. I tried a few times to ride a massive boy's bike on our back lawn; this convinced me that my mother was right – bikes were very dangerous things and impossible to ride anyway. I focused on my fear of falling off the bike, and sure enough, I fell off.

When I was nineteen and a student, I saw that those who could ride bicycles had more fun. They could go anywhere, even where there were no buses, and for nothing. I decided it was time I learnt to ride a bike. So I bought a small-wheeled bicycle and tried to master it. Bob assured me it was easy. It wasn't, not for me.

I couldn't keep the thing balanced. I ran into the pavement, fell off and bruised myself painfully. I couldn't turn corners without overturning. I couldn't even get started, unless I was pointed downhill, in which case the bike would terrify me by trying to run away while I struggled to get my feet in the right place to pedal. It was a relief when someone stole my bike. I knew by then that trying to ride it only led to bruises and humiliation.

Fifteen years later, my growing ecological conscience, together with a recognition of my desire to get fit and my novice writer's poverty, conspired to make me try again. I soon proved my total inability to balance on two wheels. This was only to be expected, for I have great difficulty with anything that requires any degree of co-ordination or sense of balance.

Colin wasn't having any of it. He was determined to prove that I could, and would, ride a bicycle. He explained the theory of it repeatedly. He filled my head with meaningless statements like 'you balance with your bum'. It didn't help. Still I failed.

But this time I refused to give up. The four-year-old next door was learning. Surely, if Lisa could do it, I could! I wondered if I should have stabiliser wheels like hers, sticking out either side. Colin compromised by fixing the seat so low that I could easily put my feet on the ground.

Then, struggling down the shady lane by the river where we lived, I suddenly solved the problem. It was wonderful, a joy, a liberation. I sang to myself in delight. I can ride a bike, I can ride a bike! It was a marvellous sensation, the wind in my hair, the bushes whizzing past on either side.

Once I concentrated totally on the road stretching ahead, my bike took me there! When I looked to the right, I turned to the right. When I looked to the left, I turned to the left. I finally understood that I *could* ride a bike – if I focused on where I wanted to go. No longer did I head uncontrollably for every boulder, every ditch along the way. I had discovered the corollary of the First Rule: *Do not concentrate on that which you want to avoid.*

When I forgot the First Rule and looked too closely at whatever hazard was nearby, I went into it. One day, after I had been practising for a couple of weeks, Colin and I went for a ride alongside the disused canal in the Swansea valley. Failing momentarily to concentrate on the narrow towpath, I found myself and my bike in the water. Colin, turning back when he noticed I wasn't behind him, was terrified to see the handlebars of my bicycle just protruding from the water – no sign of me. But all was well; I was way downstream, festooned with pondweed, chasing the shopping as it floated away in its plastic bags.

The First Rule of Bicycle Riding goes far further than it might at first seem. It's a general Rule of Life, crucial to improving relationships, creating a good sex-life, building self-confidence, writing books, and almost everything else.

It's very illuminating, learning such basic skills late in life. I am doing it all the time. If I hadn't grown up such an emotional cripple, forming happy relationships would have come naturally to me and I wouldn't have had to work at understanding how it's done. But it's a pleasure to be learning these things now; it takes the fear out of growing old when you know you're growing wiser. I shall return to The First Rule of Bicycle Riding many times in this book. I wish I could always remember it when it's most needed!

Relationships go into intensive learning phases at intervals. Most of the time, we're just trundling along and our behaviour is conditioned by habits, assumptions and experience. It depends on what else is going on in our lives. Sex becomes less important when Colin and I are preoccupied with other things; during lambing, for example, virtually all our energy, emotional and physical, is devoted to caring for sheep. At such times the sexual learning curve tends to go flat. Then – because every reaction provokes a reaction – things change after lambing, when we realise that we haven't been putting the energy into our relationship that it requires.

Having and rearing babies is a bit like lambing, and not only because lambs bring out the mother-instincts in their shepherd. It's a time when most mothers are so absorbed with the new life they are nurturing that the father may feel neglected, and begin to see the baby as a rival for his partner's love. Both parents have to cope with learning about parenthood and to handle needs in each other that hadn't been apparent earlier. This is a time when the new mother usually isn't particularly interested in sex – just as I lose interest during lambing – which is a common cause of strain in the relationship. Understanding is essential on both sides. Nobody's capacity for loving and nurturing is unlimited.

As the children grow, a new set of problems may emerge. Parents frequently worry that their children will hear them making love, or that they will be interrupted. They may find it difficult to relax together. Financial pressure, lack of space in the home, the lack of opportunity for spontaneous sex and disagreements about child-rearing can add to the strains on the relationship during this period, and sex is usually less frequent than before the first child arrived.[1] Adjustment – itself a learning process – takes time.

When Colin and I are concentrating on our relationship, as we eventually must when one of us is dissatisfied, we talk and learn. I find it difficult to raise issues that bother me – and sexual and emotional problems are the most difficult – because I get scared that he might react negatively to what I say, and that broaching a delicate subject will lead to a row. This is when I have to remind myself of the First Rule of Bicycle Riding and ask myself what I really want to achieve. Focusing on what I would like to accomplish ensures that we work towards a positive outcome, and that I don't simply criticise or complain.

After discussion, we may feel we've achieved a breakthrough, that we can now cope with some situation that hadn't really been satisfactory before; then we tend to sit back, let the new understanding consolidate, and integrate it into our lives. But as life settles into a routine, we are again at risk of stagnation and boredom and – almost before we know it – we're fed up and quarrelling again. Living with Colin is a continuous process of change and adaptation and change again. It has to be so, he gets bored very easily and I neglect myself and him equally easily.

When I'm comfortable, I find it all too easy to forget the importance of actively nurturing our relationship. We run into problems both when life is difficult, because we tend to take stress out on each other, and also when it's humdrum. So we have to actively seek learning experiences, to be open to novelty, searching together for the unexpressed facets of our natures, tasting the excitement of discovery in partnership.

Colin is very different from me, both in his background and in his personality; he doesn't think in the same way as I do, nor are his priorities the same as mine. To keep our relationship alive, we have to exploit these differences rather than allow them to become irritations or no-go areas; we have to appreciate each other as curious, sometimes incomprehensible individuals, keep communicating, and never stop trying to understand each other.

Learning new ways of behaving is always quicker and easier if you're rewarded in some way for changing. To encourage someone to continue doing something that you like, show your appreciation. Comment on what's just happened, as soon as possible after it's done. Tell your partner how much you liked it. Then, you increase the probability that it will be repeated.

Trying to teach somebody to change through criticism doesn't tend to work. Instead of learning to do what you want, they are likely to get upset and learn to fear and avoid the situation. Psychologists call this a 'conditioned emotional response'; it's the way all animals react to distressing experiences. So remember that First Rule: aim for what you want, and when you get it, smile, give him a hug, reward him with affection.

It's harder to unlearn bad habits than to learn good ones, but often we have to do both. Shaking off old, unwanted reactions is easier if you can replace them with totally different ones, and that in turn is easier if other aspects of the situation are changed.

Sometimes, working out new ways to do things requires a bit of lateral thinking. The crucial change may come at an earlier point than the beginning of the unwanted behaviour itself, so that you prevent the whole sequence from starting. For example, Colin and I got into a routine where he would lie flat on the bed, passively waiting for me to demonstrate a positive interest in sex, before he would make any move towards me. I came to find this situation threatening, so any flickering lust was killed by my anxiety. Telling him I didn't like the way he would lie there evaluating my actions made no difference; he explained that, after a long period when I had been passively putting up with sex, he felt he had to know my lust was sincere before he could act.

We got out of this unhappy pattern by changing our pre-bed routine so that he wasn't lying there waiting for me. When we take care to demonstrate our feelings unequivocally *before* going to bed, the problem doesn't arise.

We still have a lot to learn – but we're working on it. And that's the most important thing: never give up.

7

Value Yourself!

I have always found it difficult to feel confident of my own value. All too often, I feel worthless, useless, hopeless. I've been working on this problem for many years, searching for ways to feel better about the peculiar individual that I am, and while I have improved, I still have some way to go. I think this remains the hardest change to make.

My feelings vary tremendously from day to day and from week to week. I shuttle between a total lack of self-respect and great confidence in myself and my abilities. Sometimes I'm a lioness, striding proudly into the room, turning heads, happy to be the centre of attention. At such times I'm very attractive, very sexy. That's when my sex-life with Colin is at its most exciting.

When I feel worthless, my personality fades, I become less of an individual. Everything about me becomes less distinct. There's no vibrancy, no power, no decisiveness, little pleasure. I turn into a shuffling bent-shouldered depressive, avoiding everyone's eyes. Sex? Forget it. My fire is out, I am cold.

Problems like mine are very common. Perhaps my reactions are more extreme than most but I'm not convinced of that. Most people don't allow us to see their despair. Women hide behind make-up, blank out their feelings as they automatically carry on with their work-roles, push misery into dark corners of their minds while they act quietly normal. When people feel down, they tend to deny their feelings. They put on a brave show, hiding tearful eyes behind dark glasses. Forcing a smile for acquaintances, they lie: 'I'm fine, thank you.'

At home, we can't hide. Colin recognises my real feelings, sees me cry, knows my demolished self. I see him sometimes in a similar state, when he feels hopeless. Neither of us feels sexy at such times; each turns the other off, bringing the other down. The effects of losing one's sense of self-esteem can be dreadfully destructive.

As if our individual tendencies weren't bad enough, it's also a strange, sad fact that our culture seems designed to undermine our sense of our individual value. Women are particularly vulnerable. Settling down with one man, feeling like his property,[1] severed from the support of other women and faced with the ceaseless demands of nurturing a family, our female strength is sapped away. Those who don't go out to work but are tied to the home by young children, suffer most severely from a loss of appreciation of their personal value.

For a long-term relationship to succeed, we have to be true to our individuality. We have to have the courage to be real people. Anything else is not only false, it's ultimately boring. Acting a circumscribed role is limiting and predictable, it doesn't allow space for the expression of personality. Strength within a relationship demands a strong identity, but starting off with a weak sense of self I found it all too easy to lose that identity. My partners exploited my anxiety, by teasing me, appearing to put me down, encouraging me to feel stupid and incompetent. I made things worse by trying to placate, to be what I imagined Bob or Colin wanted me to be. That failed. I ended up feeling that the real me wasn't desirable, and I couldn't become what I thought I should be. Once again, I was in the all-too-familiar double bind.

The tendency of women to hold themselves responsible

for problems in relationships, and especially for sexual problems and loss of desire – whether it's his disinterest or her own – means that we take on an extra burden. Women who are sexually frustrated, who don't have orgasms or who experience complete loss of desire, all tend to believe it's their own fault. In Sheila Kitzinger's words, 'The overriding conviction they have is that *they* are failures.'[2]

It's important to the majority of women to make their partners feel good, but we often go about trying to achieve this in ways that will ultimately fail. When we deny, or ignore, or lie about our feelings in the hope of avoiding stress in the relationship, we are devaluing ourselves; and in the longer term, it is unlikely that our partners will appreciate our self-sacrifice. We end up feeling we aren't valued – because we haven't put a sufficiently high value on ourselves.

Coming to terms with your unique self

Women today are constantly reminded of their failure to meet cultural expectations. The media bombard us with images of lithe, beautiful, unlined creatures in sparkling homes, dressed in clothes we can't afford, achieving success beyond our abilities. We compare ourselves with these images and inevitably find ourselves wanting. Under constant pressure to achieve a culturally correct version of perfection, we fail to recognise our unique value within the context of our own real lives.

We learn these negative ways of reacting from an early age. As children, learning to cope with our first social challenges at school, we are faced with a double bind. Children reject uniqueness, so when one stands out, she stands alone. Yet we are encouraged by teachers and parents to compete, to make ourselves stand out as The Best. I clearly remember the conflict I experienced at school. Everybody wanted to be like everyone else, but when I did try to make myself the same as the rest, I lost my sense of personal identity. I couldn't win.

Learning to feel better about myself required gradual progress towards self-acceptance. It was easy to accept those aspects of my self that were valued by the culture in which I lived: the good girl; more difficult to come to terms with the bad girl, the bits that were not applauded. Yet these are nevertheless crucial parts of my identity. Recognising and accepting my whole self is a continuing challenge.

My counsellor, Charleen, taught me to recognise my neglected and rejected selves and integrate them into the whole person that is me. Learning to appreciate the parts of myself that I used not to like has been crucial both to my personal development and to the development of my relationship with Colin. For me, psychosynthesis was a process of exploration that led to growth, improved understanding and self-acceptance.

One lesson I have learnt from my personal voyage of discovery is that I don't fit into any simple category. I no longer think of myself as a single, coherent entity whose attitudes and behaviour are always consistent. I have many facets, many states of being, some of which may seem to be in conflict with others. I'm part teacher, part eager pupil; part judge, part playful child; part mother/shepherd, part sex-goddess; part passive, accepting, part active, achieving. Different aspects of my personality come to the fore at different times. All have their own value.

I'm not practical *or* mystical: I'm both. I'm not emotional *or* rational, physical *or* intellectual, active *or* slothful, dependent *or* independent, sexy *or* frigid. I'm all these things, just as everyone is a mixture of different aspects which express themselves in different patterns at different times. When these aspects of the self seem to be in conflict, it's because a balanced relationship has yet to develop between them.

Because I wanted to be strong, I suppressed what I saw as my weak self. I pretended it didn't exist. When it emerged, I fought it. And so that side of me became more and more battered, more neglected, more unloved, dragging the rest down. After a while, I just couldn't ignore it. I broke down repeatedly, unable to withstand harsh words from Colin because one part of me collaborated with him in condemning another part of me. The situation was unsustainable. I became weepy and hopeless. Weak. Ineffectual. Exactly what I didn't want to be.

When I learnt to recognise the child in me that cannot cope with everything, and allowed myself to be kind to that part of myself rather than condemn it, I stopped punishing myself and began to challenge Colin when he demanded more of me than I could give. I believe that weak child is growing up, growing strong in a new way. Colin treats me better, and I am better able to cope when he reverts to what I now see as unreasonable behaviour.

The crucial change was to find that beaten child and comfort her. Instead of condemning her, I had to help her to stand up for herself and not allow Colin or anyone else to kick her. But first I had to accept that the weak child was part of me, a part I had to care for, just as I would care if it were another young child. The child needs to grow and she cannot do that if she is deprived of love and sustenance.

I came to understand these truths with Charleen's gentle guidance. We can all benefit from such help when we're stuck in some unpleasant rut, and while people with Charleen's skills and perception are rare, I'm convinced that searching for help is worthwhile. Sometimes the most unexpected people come up with precisely the wise comment I need to hear, just when I need to hear it. But to find guidance, we have to be open to it. We must have sufficient humility to be willing to share our problems and seek help.

Every individual is a unique mixture. Other women will recognise parts of themselves that are like me; other aspects will be different. Not better, or worse: just different. We all have aspects that we neglect and aspects that we value, in the individual pattern that makes up our personality.

In the past, I used to try to suppress the parts of my self of which I felt ashamed. I denigrated or failed to acknowledge my desires, pushing them aside until they burst out with an irresistible force which undermined my intentions. I would end up achieving the opposite of what I intended. My dieting history showed this pattern clearly. Heavily influenced by the sixties fashion for boyish thinness, I condemned my feminine, rounded body as too fat. I suppressed my appetite by force of will. For a while, I lost weight, but eventually the conflicting pressures inside me became too great. I began to binge in secret on the most fattening foods, hating myself all the while. My whole relationship with food became distorted. Eventually, I found it difficult to judge whether I was actually hungry or not, or what I wanted to eat. I felt guilty about eating anything more fattening than an apple, and eating in front of other people, whom I imagined would judge me as harshly as I judged myself, made me terribly anxious.

It took me years to accept my shape for what it is, to acknowledge my need for food and permit myself to enjoy eating. I can now see myself as a fine example of a woman perfectly adapted to the damp, chilly Northern environment which produced me.

When I saw myself as fat, I was less attractive and less able to relate to other people. It was a slippery slope to depression and sexual apathy. How could I delight in the pleasures of my body if it disgusted me? And how could I imagine that my body could delight a man when I saw myself as repulsive?

There are thousands of women who feel the same way as I did, who are ashamed to let their partners see them naked. One typical survey of British women[3] found that 85 per cent of respondents wanted to lose weight. One in four try to avoid letting their partners see them in the nude.

I know how destructive that is. Even now, occasionally, my confidence drops and I slip into old, self-denigrating patterns of thought. The simple pleasure of taking a hot bath dissolves into a distressing confrontation with an expanse of pink flabby thigh. I find fault with myself, I don't feel comfortable in sexy clothes, I can't display myself. If

Colin approaches me, I cringe and withdraw from him, imagining he is as critical as I am. I turn away, rejecting him because I reject myself.

So many women are unable to enjoy their bodies because they believe they are too fat. Time and again, I read their sad stories in magazines, their words quoted in sex-therapy manuals; I recognise self-disgust in their choice of totally concealing clothing. They make themselves sexless because they don't want to call attention to their bodies. For some, getting fat in the first place is a symptom of fear of social situations involving men. If you're fat, you won't be expected to perform, you can opt out of the sexual rat race.

Self-criticism is a total turn-off. I understand all too well the woman quoted in *New Woman*[4] magazine who said, 'If we're making love and I look down and catch sight of my dimpled thighs or a roll of tummy, that's it. It kills the passion for me instantly.' It's impossible to tune into sensation when you're thinking about how undesirable you are. When I was at my fattest and most depressed, I didn't even want Bob to touch me lest his fingers sink into the mass of flesh that was my body. I went to bed first, hid under the covers, turned away from him.

Where does this weight of self-disgust come from? Christian religion certainly contributed to my feelings. 'Forgive me, Father, for I have sinned,' I intoned throughout my impressionable years. I criticised myself for real and imagined crimes, believed I was unworthy of love. I scarcely needed the specific antisexual attitudes, the condemnation of lust and the glorification of celibacy, for my sexual fires to be truly damped down. The general rejection of human desire is enough.

Simply being female can induce lifelong guilt in women reared in cultures controlled by male-dominated religions. Judaeo-Christian religion condemns Eve for corrupting Adam, and a succession of powerful clerics have regarded women as dangerous because they tempt men away from institutional priorities by reminding them of their humanity. Even now, such attitudes are used to justify hideous attacks on women. The ritual mutilation of girls' sexual organs in some Islamic cultures must do dreadful damage to their sense of inherent value as women.

What the process is about – whether it is personal suppression by parents or social suppression by priests and Imams – is controlling people, keeping them subjugated. My conditioning was designed to turn me into a nice quiet little girl. To become whole, I had to discover and awaken the wild thing that slept inside me: the passionate me, the me that knows her own needs, asks her own questions, makes her own decisions and cares for herself without looking over her shoulder for approval. I had to discover my inner strength and power.

Valuing yourself: the key to feeling good

When you value yourself, you can get in touch with your capacity for pleasure and for pleasuring another person. That has undoubtedly been my experience: the more I value myself, the more I get out of my sex-life. It means knowing what you want and believing that you deserve it.

Valuing yourself makes you desirable to others. You don't burden them with your need for reassurance: you can give out freely, make your own choices confidently, without holding back through defensiveness or fear of rejection. Admittedly, some people are scared of self-confident, assertive women; I've seen men with desire in their eyes, who ran away when I openly offered them what they so obviously wanted. They need to learn to value themselves too.

Sexy people are people who value themselves. They walk with easy grace because they feel comfortable with their bodies; they talk without hesitation because they're saying what they want to say; they listen with quiet interest because they don't need to interrupt to prove how clever they are. They make love without fear because they know what they're doing. They can be adventurous and flexible because they don't feel deeply threatened if something doesn't quite work out as they intended.

Some may protest at my blanket assertion, pointing to the arrogant creeps who are so full of themselves that they dismiss or ignore anyone else's feelings. My response is that the people (usually men) who override others' feelings are those who are out of touch with their social, loving selves. They are lonely too. At some level they imagine that, were they to stop and wait to see if you cared for them, they might find themselves ignored or rejected. So they don't give you a chance to challenge them. In the end, of course, they do get rejected. They get shut out of the warmth of the love of others.

It's always the same. The best way to ensure that you will be rejected is to fear that you will be; the way to be loved is to know that you're lovable. When I feel good about myself, I feel desirable. I'm the same size, the same untidy person as I am when I'm feeling down, but I give out different signals and people respond positively to me. They see me differently.

I remember being astonished, shortly after I left Bob, at the number of people who commented on how good I looked: 'You've lost weight!' they'd exclaim, or 'You're looking gorgeous – what's changed?' I hadn't lost weight; what had changed was that I now saw myself as desirable. I no longer judged myself as Bob had seemed to judge me, as someone who wasn't particularly exciting, attractive, or sexy: I looked at myself in the mirror and smiled. And other people smiled at me.

But when I feel uncertain of my value, I take on board other people's critical judgements all too easily. Colin, like Bob, has phases when he puts me down frequently; when my poor self-image encourages him to agree with my own assessment of myself and find fault with me. That's when I become a victim.

The destructiveness of put-downs

One of the reasons I lost interest in sex with Colin was because I lost belief in myself as a consort for him. He used to put me down so often that I came to see myself as useless, and this self-concept spread from the home and farmyard, where it was nurtured, to the bedroom. I came to feel that I was an unexciting lover and I withdrew. Colin told me I was boring, described me as a sexless sack of potatoes. My lack of belief in myself was confirmed.

He wanted to provoke me into proving that I wasn't boring, but the effect was that I turned off as I struggled to shield myself from the pain of what he was saying. He regarded many of his put-downs as jokes, most of the rest as helpful criticism. But that wasn't how they felt to me. I tried to take his comments in the spirit that I believed they were intended – but often, I couldn't. They hurt more than I admitted. And that unacknowledged pain became one of the blankets that smothered the glow of my sexuality.

Seeing the links between his comments – witty or justified as they often were – and my sexual feelings was crucial to motivate both of us to change the pattern. When I began to point out how much he put me down, and show him how it affected me, he started to think before he spoke; not just about a clever way to say something, but about the underlying message and the way I might react to it.

He still makes jokes at my expense sometimes, though not so regularly. I may writhe as the barbs strike home but I'm getting better at responding directly at the time. Instead of cringing and feeling worthless, I try to acknowledge and share my anger or distress, telling him immediately how I feel when he says something that hurts. That helps me to grow stronger so that I'm more often able to laugh at his jokes without internalising unintended pain.

Men put women down, criticise them and point out their failures, far more often than vice versa. Many men are scarcely aware of snide comments about women: these are the norm. Woman is often synonymous with incompetent – as in 'woman driver'. But they are quick to question those relationships in which the situation is reversed, where the woman regularly insults and denigrates the man. 'Why does he put up with it?' a man of my acquaintance mused about a colleague whose partner consistently refers to him as an idiot. When I pointed out that he had heard Colin make similar comments about me time and again over the years, all he could say was, 'That's different.' Yes, I know. He thinks it's okay for me to be denigrated because I'm a woman. But it isn't any different. Whoever does the putting down, it's destructive.

Colin and I have to remain aware of the destructive power of careless criticism. This is a shared danger area for us. But that's how it is with any relationship. The work you put into it doesn't cease; your particular dragons never die, they just become easier to control as you come to know them better.

Learning to act for yourself

Learning to accept myself without expecting perfection meant acknowledging that I must make my own choices, set my own goals, rather than trying to follow anyone else's lead. A thought that often helps to abolish unrealistic expectations and the inevitable disappointment that they create is one Colin shared with me years ago: Only the mediocre are always at their best. It's not necessary to shine all the time, and feel a failure because you can't. It's enough to make steady progress in one's chosen direction.

Focusing on my own goals helped me to conquer the sense of inadequacy induced by the feeling that I was failing sexually.[5] This meant putting aside damaging critical assessment of myself as a sexual performer. It meant ceasing to ask myself, Am I sufficiently responsive? Am I capable of being orgasmic? Are my sexual turn-on systems working correctly? Am I doing the right things? All the time I am judging myself, seeking out faults and magnifying imagined problems until they become real, I'm turning myself off.

This is the First Rule of Bicycle Riding in operation. Focus your mind on what you want, and you tend to make it happen. It's not a new idea. Other people have called it positive thinking; it's the basis of some forms of witchcraft; it's ancient wisdom. But it's terribly easy to forget. I have to keep reminding myself, when I'm being pessimistic, or feeling hopeless or undesirable, that I'm breaking the First Rule. And then I make the effort to think about what I really want and what I need.

As I recognise and acknowledge more varied needs and goals, the range of my personality and my interactions with others inevitably grows. Like a rope, the more intertwined aspects I have, the stronger I am. I become multidimensional, more stable, more whole. If I define myself in a narrow way – as I did when I saw myself as an academic and nothing else – there's nowhere to go if that door closes. I had to find more aspects of myself before I could see that there were other options, other opportunities.

There's no conflict between humility and valuing one's self. An inflated ego that resists the role of pupil reflects a lack of self-acceptance just as surely as the diminished self that imagines it has nothing to teach another person. We can continue learning, continue developing, continue growing in wisdom and understanding for as long as our minds remain alive.

Losing that crucial sense of personal value is often a result of failing to attend to your own needs; regaining it requires that you discover what these are, and give yourself time to act in your own best interests.

I don't always know what I need. Needs emerge that I didn't know about. Needs change. Circumstances, and the way my needs are met, change. People and creatures on whom I relied, die or go away, out of reach. Adjustment can be painful. At such times, I have to go through a process of healing and re-evaluation. I may lose certainty and feel depressed. Confidence fades. I cease to feel sexy.

Although depression is a state in which I lose touch with my sense of self-worth, I've found that it's foolish to strive simply to rid myself of these feelings without first trying to understand their full meaning. I learn about my neglected needs from these journeys into pain.

Depression is not all bad: it's a necessary part of life. Out of pain comes forth poetry. Without depression, what is elation? What is joy, if you don't know sadness? Before I understood that depression could teach me something, I imagined – encouraged by doctors and their use of drugs as the primary means of treatment – that my brain had gone spontaneously awry. I blunted my feelings with drugs, closed my mind to unwelcome and unpalatable knowledge. I tried to escape in every way I could. Only my concern for my family prevented suicide, the ultimate escape.

The idea that you have no value is central to depression. Indeed, you may feel – as I have – that you are worse than useless and the world would be a better place without you. This is a cop-out. It assumes you cannot choose to live in a way that is valuable in your personal terms. It allows you to abdicate from responsibility for what you do.

Assuming responsibility can be scary but the rewards are tremendous. When I take my courage in both hands and acknowledge that I am at least partially responsible for my own happiness, I begin to move away from depression.

Each time I sink into depression, I force myself to question my way of life, my assumptions, the choices I make, my relationships. Often there's a strand of deep and unrecognised anger underlying the depression, as there was when I was living with Bob. I have to find out why I'm angry, confront my situation. I have to rediscover my own path through life, the path that matches my personal needs and values. Self-esteem returns naturally when you know you're on the right track.

When you remember that you *do* matter, that your personal problems matter because they are at the centre of your life, you will begin to move out of depression. It's important to use whatever time, energy, and money you have to deal with whatever is pulling you down into the mire, and not to struggle on regardless. Something has to change, either in the way you live or in the way you perceive your situation. The challenge is to discover what change is needed. That's when a perceptive counsellor can help you to explore yourself, your needs and your strengths.

Attending to my personal needs is a strategy I use to nurture my sense of my own value. This may seem selfish – and I was brought up to abhor selfishness – but in reality, everyone benefits when I look after myself. I cannot be a whole person and relate to others fully and unselfishly unless I care for myself. The concept of selfishness, which developed in the context of material scarcity, has become over-extended to cover all personal behaviour. Giving pleasure to one's self, purely for one's self, is only morally questionable when it actually damages someone else's interests.

Deciding what I need and concentrating on achieving those things helps me to develop a positive focus and distracts me from ways of thinking that undermine my confidence. And when I do identify neglected aspects of myself, concentrating on bringing them into balance makes me feel stronger. This is a process of maturation, becoming a whole person, a multifaceted individual.

Finding a new standpoint

Often it's helpful to look at problems in a new way. To return to the common problem of feeling fat, I can react to a flabby reflection in the mirror in one of three ways. I can ignore the image and kid myself that I really don't care. That doesn't work for long because I do care and I can't lie to myself indefinitely. Or I can wallow in self-disgust and harangue myself, telling myself that I must give up eating so much because I'm letting myself go, and if I carry on like this I'll get enormous and my health will suffer.

Alternatively, I can take the positive view, recognising that the reflection in the mirror tells me I haven't been attending to my body's needs. I need to give myself more time for fun, for dancing, walking, cycling, badminton and all the physical activities I enjoy; I need to make myself nourishing meals, not grab snacks because I can't be bothered to look after myself. When I think positively, I stop moping about the house, guiltily scoffing biscuits and flopping in front of the TV because I can't get in touch with my energy. As I begin to look after myself better, I become happier with that image in the mirror.

When Colin lost his business and no longer had the options that money could buy, he coped by finding a new way of looking at his situation. Living in a tumbledown cottage became an opportunity for developing his survival skills in the face of adversity. When we needed a new septic tank and had no money to pay for it, Colin gathered three thousand bricks from waste-tips and dumps. He dug out a septic tank with hand tools and built it himself. He created a productive vegetable garden and kept the house warm with waste wood from skips. Coping in such ways assured him of his resourcefulness and gave him a lasting sense of achievement.

Poverty both produced strains and stimulated achievement. Sometimes we were miserable, sometimes happy. Both Colin and I discovered new strengths and abilities and pleasures we had never anticipated. Life felt good and our relationship blossomed when we concentrated on what we could do, rather than on those things that were out of our reach at that time. There's no point in regretting what we are not, or what we cannot have. To sustain our sense of personal value, we have to maintain a positive outlook, and while we should acknowledge and work on our failings, it does no good to focus on them.

I find I become vulnerable when I expect myself to be superhuman instead of appreciating what I am. Sometimes I imagine I should be wonderfully vivacious, I should have a perfect body; I should never be forgetful or careless or make bad decisions; I should be tidy; my accounts should be up-to-date and totally in order; my sheep should be supremely healthy; my neck always free from grime. Reality is uncomfortable: in the real world, I struggle and muddle along. I find it difficult to permit myself to fail to meet the standards I set myself or that our culture seems to set for me. And when I do fail – as inevitably I do, again and again, in every area of life – I'm prone to blame myself.

The irony is that I usually have just as much scope for self-congratulation as self-blame. But self-acceptance is neither of these extremes: it's acknowledgement that the whole person I see in the mirror is me, a unique package. The parts fit together. To feel whole, I need to stop focusing on the wobbly bits (too flabby, too pale) or the acceptable bits (nice waist) but instead acknowledge that the whole person in action is me as I am. No comparison with ideals – what are they but one particular cultural stereotype? – this is what *is*. This me is *alive*.

Yes, it is hard to dismiss cultural stereotypes. It is hard to believe that I am not inherently inferior to the leggy models in the magazines. I reassure myself by looking at my sheep, for whom there are no clear-cut cultural ideals. I look at my plump Dorsets with their woolly faces and short stocky legs and find them delightful; then I look at my leggy Mules and find them delightful too. Neither is better than the other: they are different, that's all, just as men and women are different though neither is superior, neither inferior. And I am different from every other member of the human race.

That difference, that uniqueness, underpins Colin's love for me. If I were a Barbie doll, he would not be interested. Every feature would be predictable. How dull that would be!

The character of my face reflects my personal development. I do not fear the passing years. At each birthday, I look back and remind myself of the ways I've progressed, the things I've learnt in the year that's gone by. I find then that I do not envy the raw teenager, the naïve young adult, nor even the me of two years ago, who couldn't cope with some of the challenges that I can deal with now.

Our youth-oriented culture makes it all too easy for women to imagine that personal value diminishes with age. Confronting the loss of physical beauty can be terrifying when so much importance is attached to outward appearance. Who wants a crone? Self-respect can ebb away, leaving women victims of the depression that is so common in the years after the menopause, and particularly after retirement.

It need not be so. When we keep our minds alive and open, we grow in wisdom and understanding; years of experience can give older people a perspective that simply isn't available to the young – so long as they resist the temptation to allow their views to fossilise into blind dogma. Age can have its own intrinsic value.

I know that I look and feel attractive when I can smile at my reflection in the mirror. It doesn't matter that my once-red hair has faded and white strands have appeared at my temples; it doesn't matter that my figure is not quite as firm as it used to be. What is important is the inner spark, the sense of my own value. That gives me a strength, a vibrancy that makes me feel sexy and causes Colin to desire me.

Just as the answer to the problem of ageing is to look at yourself in a positive way so that you can see the virtues that balance the losses, so the general answer to feeling worthless is to look at the underlying issues and yourself again, from a new standpoint.

Finding that new standpoint is part of discovering your individual path to the future you want to create. Progress implies directed movement, deliberate change; it's liable to be very haphazard until you know where you're going. I won't underestimate the difficulty of working out one's aims in life; it's a question to which I find myself returning again and again. But even if you don't know, at the moment, what direction to take in broad terms, you can focus at least on the goals you desire in the short term.

The longer Colin and I stay together, the less our deviations from ideals or norms seem to matter. What he really wants is for me to develop into the most magnificent form of me, nothing suppressed, all my facets in unique interplay. And that's all I want of him: I want him to live and experience his own life to the full, to experience his capacity for enjoyment to its full extent. Often, our pleasure and stimulation comes from interaction with one another, but our mutual dance develops from the richness of individual experience.

8

Trust

'How can I ever trust him again?' I heard that plaintive refrain so often over the years from my dear friend Suki, and I never did have an answer. How could she trust her husband not to stray when he'd been unfaithful so many times before? Eventually she couldn't stand it, couldn't live with the lies. She gave him the final ultimatum: It's her or me. Give up the other woman or leave. He left.

She was devastated. She turned into a shadow of her former self, lost thirty pounds in weight. Only her commitment to their two young children stopped her from committing suicide. David was, had always been, her only love. To her (and to too many other women) David was the sexiest person on earth; yet when she finally ceased to trust him, she couldn't feel desire any more. For years she felt empty inside, grieving, broken.

They continued to see each other – it's difficult to avoid seeing the father of one's children – and slowly, painfully, they began to rebuild their relationship. Neither could let go of the other totally. Neither could quite come to terms with divorce. Suki and David separated; he went to live with the other woman, had another baby with her, and the same problems arose . . . the other woman tried to stop him ringing Suki, she didn't trust him either. He would sneak off to public call-boxes to talk to his wife, the wife who'd thrown him out.

Eventually, they were communicating honestly. Trust returned, slowly, and with trust came lust. After seven years, David returned to Suki's open arms.

'What happened, that you trust him now?' I asked.

'I know what he's capable of doing,' she replied. 'But I don't think he'll do it any more because it hurt him as much as it hurt me. I didn't believe that at the time. He lied because he didn't feel he had any alternative; now I give him an alternative. I gave him such hell before, I didn't make it possible for him to come back. I was totally confused; I thought that if I could get him out of my life, that would resolve the situation. I couldn't stop loving him, although you know how hard I tried. I started to feel desire again when he started to talk to me – when I let him say what he really felt without screaming at him.'

Trust, fidelity and desire

Trust is crucial to long-term desire. Few people feel able to abandon themselves with a partner on whom they cannot rely, and when the very essence of committed partnership is mutual reliance, lack of trust undermines its foundations. If you can't believe what your partner says, or if you feel convinced that he's hiding important things from you, how can you know where you stand in relation to him? How can you relax completely with someone who could be lying to you?

For many people, trust is inseparable from sexual fidelity: they feel they cannot trust someone who has other sexual partners. Fidelity is a crucial part of the often unspoken contract between almost all couples. It is part of the conventional wisdom of our society that men and women must be faithful to each other if their partnership is to last. Yet only a minority of couples are actually faithful to each other. Most people who have been married for five years or more have secret affairs. In her American sample Shere Hite reported figures for extramarital affairs of over 70 per cent for both men[1] and women;[2] ironically, almost all the people she quotes believed that their partners did not also have affairs.

Sexual abandonment requires the ability to hold your partner without the intrusion of fear, without being tormented by the idea that tomorrow he could be in another woman's arms, or that the woman whose bed he shared yesterday was more exciting than you. Comparing yourself with another person – someone from the past or a potential threat in the future – can be a total turn-off.

Secret infidelity, once discovered, kills desire, for it's impossible to feel secure when unfaithfulness is compounded by lies. Naturally, the partner who finds out that the other has been breaking their contract in secret, will feel angry, let down, and then, often, depressed. Those negative feelings intensify the problem. The situation often goes from bad to worse: the individual whose perceived lack of responsiveness may have led the other to seek sexual solace elsewhere is likely to become even less responsive, even less open to sexual approaches, when the affair is discovered.

I find it difficult to make sense of this situation, where the behaviour of the majority so clearly conflicts with the cultural ideal to which they cling. Personally, I never could be confident that I could promise to remain faithful for ever. I knew that there was always a possibility that someone would cross my path who was just irresistible; that any vow of fidelity could be broken. Equally, I felt sure that few men were capable of ignoring the pull of desire for another woman. So fidelity was not part of the contract I made with any man. If he demanded that, I said, sorry, I can't make that promise. And I won't be put in a position where I may find myself lying about it.

Even now, Colin and I don't promise each other eternal fidelity; I know that if Julie Christie were to turn up in the farmyard, he'd be off like a rocket – if she'd have him. For that matter, he recognises that I would be tempted beyond endurance by a single touch from Bill Levy. We trust each other because we both feel sure that, afterwards, we would return to each other. Our relationship is too deep to be threatened in that way.

Although we have always trusted each other on this level, the issue of trust has been relevant to our relationship. There have been times for both of us when we felt we couldn't trust the other to *care*. I have felt unable to trust Colin to meet my need for love and affection, not to hurt and reject me when I felt vulnerable. And he has felt the same way about me. At these times, we are unable to trust each other enough to experience desire.

Trust and lies

Colin and I try hard not to lie to one another because we know that lies destroy trust. Lies can be passive – being economical with the truth, failing to admit to the way we feel, covering up. Or they can be bold: pretending you're working late at the office when you're actually in bed with your lover. I was a passive liar, but I pretended – to myself as much as to him – that I was truthful. Fear of his reaction to the truth led me to conceal it.

Few people find it easy to lie to those they love. Usually, lies are constructed in self-defence, because you want to hang on to love but you're not confident that your relationship can withstand the truth about what you really are, what you really feel. David used to lie to Suki because he believed she was insanely jealous – as indeed she was when she didn't know what was going on and she feared the unknown.

Most people express no feelings of guilt or regret about their secret extramarital affairs. Many even believe that their marriage benefits – so long as the truth is never discovered. For women, affairs make them feel appreciated; their hunger for affection, unsatisfied in their marriages, is met by their lovers. Men report that they learn about more exciting sex from their mistresses. But these positive attitudes are held in secret; it seems impossible for most couples openly to acknowledge the benefits of extramarital sex or to act on the lessons that could be learnt from it to the advantage of their own relationship.

We lie when we imagine that the consequences of telling the truth would be intolerable. You can discourage lying by not punishing your partner for being truthful. Even if the truth is unpalatable, at least you can work with it, come to understand it, adapt to it. It's very important not to judge, but to try to discover what motivates your partner to behave in a way you find unacceptable. Only then can you hope for constructive change.

The known is almost always less fearsome than the unknown. The more we talk about our real feelings – even if they seem threatening – the less dangerous they become. Feelings are usually complex, mixed; Suki had to come to realise that David never stopped loving her despite his actions, but she wouldn't listen when he tried to tell her this: she imagined that because he had fallen in lust with another woman, he could not love her. She over-simplified the situation and by doing so, caused tremendous pain to everyone in the family. And he, too, over-simplified: he allowed himself to ignore the reality of his love for his children, who would inevitably get hurt by his actions; he allowed himself to imagine that passion was all-important, prudence insignificant. He paid for his delusions with years of depression when he realised he had lost the family that mattered desperately to him.

Prudence versus passion

The conflict between prudence and sudden passion becomes greater when there are strains within the partnership. If one partner is angry with the other, or feels rejected or lonely, the lover's lure becomes all the greater. Why should I be faithful to Colin, if Colin is nasty to me and the other man is charming? Why should he be faithful to me, if I'm a miserable hag and a smiling woman beckons?

The reason for fidelity is to safeguard the future of the relationship: but that only makes sense when the relationship seems worth saving. And sometimes, in truth, it doesn't, at least until the tensions within it are resolved. Why be prudent, if prudence brings no joy? 'Prudence versus passion,' wrote the great philosopher Bertrand Russell, 'is a conflict which runs throughout history . . . To the man or woman who, by compulsion, is more civilized in behaviour than in feeling, rationality is irksome and virtue is felt as a burden and a slavery. This leads to a reaction in thought, in feelings, and in conduct.'[3]

We can't expect ourselves, or our partners, to be virtuous all the time. It's unrealistic. And if we cannot accept or forgive occasional lapses from the standards we set, we risk sacrificing relationships that are too valuable to relinquish so readily. Suki knew that David was a passionate and impulsive man – that was a large part of what attracted, and still attracts, her to him. To reject and punish him for being the person he was, was not rational. But of course, she is passionate too: and she was as passionate in her condemnation as in her love.

Long-term relationships require a combination of prudence and passion, which can be difficult to achieve. If you and your partner were totally prudent, you could have total trust – but then you would have a sterile, passionless relationship. The combination of total trust *and* passion just isn't on life's menu. Focus too much on prudence, on rationality and on relating in a sensible way with one another, and passion will fade, to recover only when you allow your emotions freer rein, accepting the risks. Because uncontrolled emotions are risky, and passion, by its nature, cannot be controlled.

Sometimes the balance between prudence and passion is held within the relationship. When one partner is more prudent, the other more passionate, each can complement the other. My parents' long and happy marriage was built, in part, on just such complementary roles; my father represented the prudent core which allowed my mother to express her passionate self.

In reality, there is no such thing as absolute trust or absolute honesty. Trust is conditional within a framework which changes from time to time. Absolute honesty requires that you know yourself totally, and that your thoughts, feelings and beliefs are entirely consistent and unchanging. Nobody is like that. Human beings are complex, inconsistent, and to that degree, inherently unreliable.

Rebuilding trust

When we accept what we are, and we are as open to one another as we are able to be, trust returns. Colin and I rebuilt trust by talking about the way we really felt, without allowing fear to block communication. Trust and communication (see Chapter 14) are intimately linked. The promise we've made to each other is that we will carry on talking honestly and listening to each other, and that we will do our best to help each other to face up to, and cope with, feelings that could be important to our relationship.

He can't promise never to hurt me, nor can I promise never to reject him. We've had to come to terms with that. It's better to face the truth about each other than try to pretend we're more perfect than we are, or to demand unattainable perfection. If we can't accept each other, we invite deceit.

Trust and confidence

It's easier to trust another person if you have faith in yourself and you recognise the special qualities you bring to your relationships. One reason Suki felt so threatened by David's infidelity was that she felt inferior to the other woman. Her image of herself was so uncertain that she couldn't imagine that she was worthy of lasting love. She wasn't confident that he could ever find her more attractive or more interesting than other women. How could she expect him to stay with her under such circumstances? And unable to believe in a future with him, she threw him out. Living alone was better than living with the torment of uncertainty.

The years on her own changed her. She discovered that she could cope without David. Following her own interests, she found that she was talented, intelligent, and attractive. As her confidence grew, she began to believe him when he told her that he did love her, had always loved her. And as she grew stronger in herself, she was able to listen to him when he told her how he felt about other women. Of course he fancies them: he adores women. But that doesn't mean he doesn't love her, or that she isn't lovable. Ultimately, she matters to him more than any other woman. David may have another foolish fling; he probably won't but if he does, he'll come back and she'll accept him again. After twenty-five years of marriage, she recognises the truth and he feels no compulsion to lie.

Learning to trust

When you accept that trust cannot be absolute and people may let you down despite their love, the nature of the issue changes. It's no longer a question of whether the other person is sufficiently trustworthy, but more whether you yourself are able to tolerate the degree of uncertainty that relating to another imperfect human being involves.

There is always uncertainty, even in the most committed relationships. Uncertainty is an unavoidable feature of the world we live in: it's one of the fundamental laws of physics. The only certainty we have about the future is that, eventually, we shall die. We make plans based on probabilities, and probability has to be sufficient because it's all we have. We can make judgements about each other, predictions about our partner's behaviour, but we can never be certain that we're right. So we work on the best assumptions we can come up with.

We're back to the First Rule of Bicycle Riding. When you focus on where you want to go, you're trusting yourself to get there and trusting your bicycle to get you there. By doing that, you maximise the probability of achieving the outcome you desire.

It may not work out: your bicycle may break down and throw you into the gutter – but that's life: we pick ourselves up again. It hurts when you fall off, but you recover. In your rage and pain, you may want to throw your bike into the nearest river, vow never to ride the damn thing again; but that phase passes. Bicycles, like relationships, are usually repairable. If you don't give up, if you find out why your bicycle let you down, repair it, and do what you can to prevent a similar problem arising again, trust will return. And then you're ready to explore, to enjoy the world again together.

9

Desire

When Colin and I first lived together, the desire I felt for him was totally overwhelming. I was obsessed. I thought about him all the time, to the exclusion of just about everything else. I wanted to make love to him every minute of the day and half the night. When I was alone in my flat, I used to lie awake imagining him beside me, inside me. With that level of ambient desire, I used to reach orgasm easily with unsophisticated, energetic fucking and nothing more. On one occasion soon after we had first met, an extended kiss was enough to make me come, so strong was my lust.

Desire and responsiveness remained high for the first couple of years. Then, gradually, the pleasure faded and my orgasmic potential declined. I didn't know what was wrong, why my feelings had cooled. I turned off progressively until, after fourteen years, I didn't want him at all.

Nevertheless, I longed to relive the excitement of the early stages of lust: that feeling of warmth and excitement that suffuses my whole body, the weakness in my knees that makes me want to fall with my lover on to the nearest convenient bed. When I feel like that, I have a desperate need to kiss and caress, to be kissed and caressed; my cunt throbs with a hot ache that can only be soothed by fucking. This is the lust that makes me irrational, prompts me to ignore conscience and take risks with my lust-object, the sort of desire that culminates in frantic, abandoned sex – and fades instantly if sex proves disappointing.

I call this experience 'falling in lust'. It's happened to me so many times, I know it doesn't last. When I decided that I would not have any lover apart from Colin, I learnt to resist the promptings of lust, to keep sufficient distance between my body and tempting potential lovers, to keep the pressures controllable. I wanted to feel desire for Colin again, although I knew it would not have the same quality as it had in our first months together, but it was some time before I discovered how to make it happen.

Of course, hot lust isn't meant to be controlled. Remove a few layers of inhibition and clothing, forget rational decision-making and social conscience, and the brakes come off. Drugs like alcohol and dope make it easier to take risks, to ignore the reasons for holding back, to imagine it's just impossible to maintain control. I've learnt not to get stoned when I'm alone with a lust-object. It's much too dangerous to take the risk of exposing my delicate yet precious relationship with Colin to the pressures of sex with other partners, or of contracting and spreading sexually transmitted disease.

I used to confuse lust with love. The myths of our culture encourage this: descriptions of passionate love fit intense lust. It's a dangerous confusion. Many people marry their lust-objects, only to discover their basic incompatibility when the heat haze of lust no longer exists to obscure the reality of their differences.

Love is a long-lasting emotion, caring that doesn't fade when sexual interest loses its intensity. Lust may be wonderful, but love is the basis on which we can build a lifetime together. Lust is pure sexual desire; love is multidimensional. Love is a meeting of minds as well as bodies, where values, beliefs and attitudes correspond sufficiently to nurture mutual respect and close friendship as well as desire. In a loving relationship, partnership develops through dialogue on many levels.

I have often felt lust without love, although at the time I was not always aware that my feelings were purely sexual. My mother used to believe that a woman couldn't enjoy sex without love but I found that was only half true. When I don't feel loving, I don't enjoy sex, but I can get very horny and highly orgasmic with total strangers whom I don't know well enough to love. When I did fuck with such men, it was recreational sex in its most uninvolved form: sex where their bodies were just substitutes – with luck, superior ones – for my vibrator, dildo and imagination. Such experiences taught me to see through the romantic illusions of Western culture.

After years of partnership, seeing each other every day, making love whenever we want to, lust tends to fade. We become so familiar with one another that the chemistry that first attracted us loses much of its magical charge.

I suspect the driving force of lust is primarily to do with chemistry at the basic, biological level: it's a reaction to a particularly attractive set of pheromones, the natural sex-chemicals which we smell and taste on our lovers. But these pheromones cease to set our bells ringing when we smell them every day. We become habituated, failing to react in much the same way as we cease to notice trains rattling by when we live by a railway line. Yet just as we can choose to become alert to the sound of those trains if they take on a new significance, so we can focus on the attractions of a familiar partner and continue to respond.

After nineteen years, my desire for sex with Colin comes and goes. I can't honestly say that I ever feel the way I did in those first few months, although very occasionally I do feel a slight tremble in the knees when he's being particularly lovable. But the sad truth is that the intense, insistent lust has gone.

For all that, I do still get very turned on to him. Sex with Colin can be brilliant, all-consuming, better now than ever before. But I'm slower to get going, more reactive to what's going on around me. We're not likely to want to fuck in the branches of a willow tree, as we once did. I don't experience desire as a desperate need for sex; if he's not enthusiastic, it's easy to say, okay, there's no pressure, I can wait till you want it too.

At the beginning, the merest look, the slightest whiff of his natural body scent turned me on because I'm pretty much turned on all the time when I'm in lust. I was impatient for sex.

It took me a long time to realise that I needed extended tenderness to rekindle the feelings that had once been so strong. I imagined that what had been sufficient to delight me when the fires of lust were burning high should still be sufficient. Now, I'm thinking of so many other things – work, worries, everyday life – that it takes a while to shift my thoughts away from the mundane to the prospect of sex.

My level of desire is affected by many influences: my own internal cycles, Colin's behaviour, our domestic situation, outside pressures. Each varies in importance from time to time. Sometimes I'm excessively sensitive to one distraction or another; at other times I'm unaffected by things that would normally turn me on or off. All right, I'm unpredictable and unreliable. People are like that. It makes partnerships difficult but more interesting.

As far as I'm concerned, warmth and affection is now the most effective stimulus for desire. When Colin smiles and gives me lots of spontaneous cuddles, it can make me feel I'm the luckiest person in the world. He's generous with his love. For me, knowing I'm loved, feeling loving carries no risk of rejection. I snuggle closer to him, closer and closer . . . After all, what is sexual desire but a longing for ultimate closeness?

Colin is Leo, ruled by the Sun. When the sun shines, I bask in its warmth. When his face turns hollow and drawn, the sun hides behind storm clouds and I feel no desire for sex with him. I do care, I still love him, but I've been conditioned, over the years, not to feel desire for him when he is unable to show warmth. Grey face in the morning, shepherd's warning. He's too likely to turn on me, to snarl dangerously like a lion in pain. So I have grown wary. I watch and wait, seeking cues in his body-language, hoping to find ways to ease his distress.

During our most difficult years, it was hard for me even to get in touch with that deep love. There was too much accumulated resentment, so many issues we had to resolve. However he behaved, I felt no desire. It was necessary to work through the layers of anger, learn to express my real feelings and talk about the fears that had built up, before I could experience again my potential for sexual pleasure with him.[1]

Touching, stroking and caressing inflame desire. These gestures of tenderness tell me more clearly than words ever can that I am precious to him. I relax, tension soothed by his hands; I can feel my skin becoming warmer and softer, more responsive. I don't like direct genital touches without preliminary stroking elsewhere on my body or my face: I tend to react by feeling pressured to respond sexually before I'm ready and that turns me off because I don't anticipate sexual pleasure if I'm being rushed.

Men tend to be more directly genitally focused than women; they have to learn to treat us gently and allow enough time for our feelings to catch up. But they, too, need the tenderness that convinces them that they are loved and desired.

Some people – more often men than women – express their need for love and closeness through increased sexual demands.[2] If a man's partner is turned off, the demands can escalate and change to frustrated rage. This turns the woman off even more. Finding a route out of this negative cycle requires action on many fronts – learning to communicate more effectively, learning to touch each other again, learning to deal with conflict. These are topics of later chapters in this book.

Building lust

Lust is a whole-body sensation, and anything that makes my body feel good encourages it. I like Colin to brush my back in the bath till I tingle; I love it when he strokes my back, fondles my bum, rubs his body – clothed or naked, but especially naked – against mine. I feel a hunger for his skin, sometimes, a desire to feel as much of him as possible in contact with me. Best of all is the full-length horizontal cuddle, arms tight around each other, hands stroking and kneading, noses nuzzling skin. It doesn't take much of this before I turn my attention to his cock and welcome attention to my cunt.

One of my sexiest woman friends imagines herself as the heroine of a romantic novel – telling herself the phrases that she finds erotic: he kissed my breasts and I felt my nipples harden . . . he bore down on me, gently parting my thighs . . . She revels in such fantasies as she lies in bed, relaxes in a bath, or when she's driving home, knowing her husband will be there to greet her. They turn each other on with lewdly worded conversation; talking about plumbing, they'll take an idea like sliding pipes into holes and change the context, making it suddenly sexual. 'Shall I put it in for you? Do you want it?' he might ask, with a sidelong look and a suggestive smile. Suddenly they're not talking about plumbing, but about sex. At other times, they build lust through eating together: being fed and putting morsels into another person's mouth can be intensely erotic.

Anticipation of pleasure is the greatest aphrodisiac. This makes a familiar partner, who knows better than anyone else how to please you – after all, you've been practising for *years*! – more desirable than the most handsome stranger. I remember how marvellous sex with Colin has felt in the past, and I'm confident that it can be just as good again. In fact, maybe this time it'll be even better, because although we hit high peaks together not so long ago, I've no reason to believe that we have reached our summit. Last month it might just have been the Matterhorn – Everest, here we come!

I consciously build desire as I relax in a hot bath, anticipating lust-filled hours with Colin, recalling the sensations his fingers, his lips, his tongue, his cock have induced in me. Sometimes when I masturbate, I imagine Colin joining in, making me come so intensely that I long for his cock to feel it too; when he's with me, he picks up my desire, replacing fingers with his engorged cock, fucking till consciousness clouds.

I acknowledge that it's not always possible to anticipate wonderful sex. During those years when sex with Colin gave me little pleasure, I didn't anticipate excitement with him. That was one reason, I'm sure, why my desire for him fell to such a low level. We had to relearn how to delight each other, discover that it was possible to enjoy sex together again, before desire returned fully. This is something of a chicken-and-egg conundrum: when you don't feel desire, sexual pleasure doesn't develop; and when there's no pleasure, desire fades.

During the process of reviving sexual pleasure, while we were learning to trust each other again and teaching each other what we enjoyed, all I could anticipate was progress. At the time, that was not enough to induce lust; but as we went further, sexual desire returned. It is a delicate feeling; it gets knocked back, all too easily, by disappointment and criticism. But it can recover, fade and return again more strongly. When things are going badly between us, I hang on to the knowledge that our relationship is capable of improving again and, when it does, that desire will return.

I have to be careful to distinguish between anticipation and expectation. If Colin perceives my anticipation of sexual pleasure as pressure on him to perform, that's likely to turn him off. He has to feel he has freedom of choice, just as I must. Knowing I have the option and the opportunity for sex is exciting but I never want sex if I feel it's expected of me, whether I like it or not. Anticipation of pleasure must be mutual.

Anxiety is the worst turn-off. If I'm suffering from thrush

or any other condition that makes intercourse painful, any desire I might feel won't develop and flower into lust because I worry that sex will hurt. I have to sort out the problem first.

As we get older, health problems that can make sex uncomfortable or frightening become more common. We have to make allowances for creaking hip joints and aching backs, informing each other about what might hurt and choosing positions that work for us both. I've learnt never to keep quiet about discomfort and not to put up with it; that can cause lasting problems with desire.

Trust is crucial, and open communication enhances trust. I know I can trust Colin not to do anything that is likely to hurt, so long as I have told him about it, but I cannot assume he will know how something feels to me. He will not, for example, try anal intercourse because I have explained that that is always painful for me and I tense up if anything is inserted into my bum. He knows I don't like painful bites, nor do I enjoy it if he sucks hard on my nipples. I may not always feel raging lust for him, but I can be confident that sex will bring pleasure not pain, and that is enough to sustain desire.

Talking about sex sharpens anticipation. Telling him what I like best makes me focus on pleasure. I love it when he tells me what he likes, too, at least when it's something I know I can do. That gives me confidence.

I love it when he tells me how much he loves me. Most people are the same, but some men seem curiously reluctant to admit to love for their partners; presumably, it makes them feel less masculine, less in control. My mother used to say that she might have stayed with her first husband if he had only told her he loved her.

Anticipation of pleasure gets me ready for sex. I feel my cunt grow warm and damp, swollen and sensitive as we extend that period of anticipation, stoking up the fires of lust until they're all-consuming. I enjoy knowing that we're going to go to bed together soon . . . but I like to give the anticipation time to build up, to wait till I feel I can't hold back any more. When I'm desperate for sex but still the waiting is extended while the temperature stays high, that's when I get most excited, when normally quiescent desire flows hot through my belly and I feel the greatest longing for him.

Building sexual energy

If there is to be delay between the initial surges of desire and consummation, it has to have a positive purpose, increasing the positive charge between us so that we can enjoy a greater intensity of discharge. It's not a question of self-deprivation or inhibition of desire: energy must increase not decline. To wait while energy fades away is to waste delightful opportunity.

It's important for both of us to get our energy levels right for sex. One problem we often confront is a discrepancy in the energy we can each muster for sexual excitement, and we have to seize the opportunity when we're both eager for sex. Desire demands energy; it doesn't well up when I'm tired. I rarely enjoy sex in the small hours because I cannot really participate when I just want to sleep. If we delay too long, desire corrodes into tetchiness and tension: I may need sex in order to relax but in these circumstances I'm not capable of contributing much. Waiting too long can be a recipe for trouble.

My energy levels drop too low for active sex when I'm working very hard or worrying too much; Colin's energy fluctuates tremendously with his metabolic state and his mood. I have learnt not to feel rejected when he can't cope with sex; he is learning to accept that admitting he's not up to it doesn't reflect badly on him.

Hormone cycles

My hormone balance is probably the most important determinant of my sexual energy. It changes markedly over the course of the lunar month. Lust increases steadily from a relatively low point when I'm having my period to a much higher level in the second week of my menstrual cycle. Desire peaks with ovulation. I can feel ovulation as a sharp near-pain in one side of my belly that comes and goes over the course of a single day in the middle of my cycle. That sensation is associated with a driving longing for sex. It's marvellous when my ovulation coincides with a peak in Colin's level of desire but frustrating when it doesn't. Often, I masturbate at such times to avoid putting pressure on him. It doesn't diminish my pleasure in sex if we do make love, but it stops me being irritable when we don't.

After ovulation, desire plummets quite rapidly. It's not that I can't get aroused, more that I don't seek sexual contact, I don't feel I need it. This is a very common experience; for some days in the second half of the menstrual cycle, most women report no interest in sex. The day before my period starts, I'm suddenly, surprisingly, briefly, randy again. Anne Hooper commented, 'If someone could market whatever it is that floats through my body the night before a period, they'd be the world's greatest millionaire.' She described such a night as 'one of those marvellous physical states where all my sensations were velvet . . . I really could have stayed being stroked and touched all night.'[3]

Many men find it difficult to accept the profound changes in the female internal state as we progress through our monthly cycles. Colin is no exception. Having no direct experience of it, he can get irritated, complaining that I'm either premenstrual or menstrual for ninety per cent of the month. In reality, the high points balance the low; unfortunately, if he doesn't feel sexy when I do, he may miss my peak and get frustrated and irritable when I'm not particularly interested for the next ten days.

Women vary in their responses to sex-hormone changes. Many don't share my definite peak of desire at ovulation. Almost half of the women who responded to a questionnaire prepared by Paula Weideger[4] reported their peak just before, during, or just after menstruation. Interestingly, however, women are most likely to engage in sex, and most frequently have orgasms, at mid-cycle. But this could, in part at least, reflect the fact that they avoid sex when they're bleeding, because it's messy or because some men find the blood offputting. And in some cultures, for example among Jewish people, sex during menstruation is regarded as unclean.

Each woman can get to know herself by keeping a diary where she records both the way she feels and how she acts, learning the best time for sex and helping her partner to understand how her feelings change. These fluctuations, after all, don't carry important long-term implications for the relationship; I may be tetchy when I'm premenstrual, but that doesn't necessarily mean that Colin and I are running into significant problems. Just that he'd better watch out!

In the week before my period, I am particularly sensitive to criticism. Although this can cause conflict, it is an opportunity to bring up issues that have been bothering me, but which hadn't seemed sufficiently important to resolve while my hormones made me more accepting. If I can keep on a reasonably even keel, the premenstrual week can be a good time for discussing problems and preventing them from building up.

By understanding my cycle, I can make best use of my changing moods. Deep-rooted problems have to be confronted when I'm calm and I won't fall apart if we delve into potentially painful areas of my psyche. We can discuss sexual issues positively when we're not feeling too frustrated or edgy; if either of us is irritable, discussion tends to degenerate into conflict.

At least three-quarters of women between adolescence and menopause suffer from some degree of premenstrual tension (PMT). It makes them more irritable, edgy and tense than they would otherwise feel. Loss of desire is just one of a pattern of effects ranging from a tendency to recall painful memories rather than happy ones, to a long list of unpleasant symptoms: depression, confusion, mood swings, irritability, fatigue, anxiety, accident-proneness; water retention and swelling, particularly of the legs and belly; breast pain, backache, abdominal pain, joint pains, headaches; sugar cravings and weight gain; and increased susceptibility to allergies and infections ranging from thrush and herpes to colds and flu. The defining feature of PMT is its timing: the syndrome occurs in the second half of the menstrual month. It varies from woman to woman, and from month to month, but the general pattern for each woman can become painfully familiar.

Understanding how my hormone levels change and how my behaviour is influenced by this helps to keep our relationship on a more even keel. When I get seriously ratty or depressed during the premenstrual weeks, I know I have been neglecting my own needs: for regular exercise, for a properly balanced diet that delivers all the vitamins and minerals I require, for rest when I'm sinking into exhaustion.

At its worst, PMT can lead to murder or suicide. It puts tremendous strain on partnerships. My premenstrual misery used to last from three days after ovulation until the second day of my period, causing hideous disruption in our household when I became murderously angry or weepy with nameless dread. Such drastic effects can be prevented by taking plenty of exercise, eating nutritious food every three hours or so, and avoiding exhaustion. Food supplements – particularly B-group vitamins, magnesium and evening primrose oil – can make a tremendous difference but they're no substitute for a nourishing diet.

Most important, I've learnt not to restrict my food intake and I never, never diet when I am premenstrual, even if I can't fasten my jeans! I eat when I'm hungry (and sometimes when I'm not), choosing organic wholefoods and avoiding sugar. I need plenty of food for energy and stability, and by keeping my energy levels high, I can ensure that I remain sufficiently active both to stay generally fit and to prevent premenstrual and period pain.

Colin now understands these things – he's read my book on hormones[5] – and he encourages me to get out on my bike, go for long brisk walks or bounce on my mini-trampoline when I seem to be going downhill. He's learnt that he benefits when I'm functioning well. I may even feel like making love despite being premenstrual if I get the balance right!

Turning on to a sexy partner

Colin's presence alone can be enough to turn me on when he's active and feeling good. I enjoy watching his physical power in action, the way he moves when he's chopping logs or knocking in fenceposts with a heavy hammer. I love the ripple of muscles, the fluidity of motion, his strength and control. It's very sexy. His scent after he's been working must be laced with a whole cocktail of pheromones because it affects me at the most basic level. I don't like the smell of stale armpits or the sweat of mental stress, but male sweat produced by recent muscular work is quite another matter. I've asked him to take his baths in the morning, rather than wait till evening when we may want sex, so that this smell is still on him.

Natural body smells can enhance desire for both men and women, but they can also inhibit it. Colin says I have a unique perfume that he enjoys, but my cunt juices get stale and fishy quickly so he prefers me freshly bathed. My hair takes on the smells of the environment very readily, which is fine if I'm surrounded by perfumed smoke or pine forests but not so good if I've been in close contact with sheep. Environmental and internal pollution cause unpleasant body smells because poisons can be excreted through our pores, in our sweat and in our breath; Colin and I are convinced that fresh country air keeps us both smelling sweeter.

My mind must be receptive if I am to respond with desire to sexually arousing stimuli. I know that my hormone balance plays a large part in creating that receptivity, but external influences are important too. I have to be free from the distraction of worries, unresolved conflict and all anti-erotic mental preoccupation. If I'm preoccupied, I'm not open to sexual stimuli at all, whatever their nature. They bounce off me, unnoticed.

Even thinking can undermine desire. Rationality conflicts with my sexual nature. When I lived almost entirely on the rational level of my being, as I did in my late teens and early twenties, I was out of touch with my sexual self. I had to learn to let go of the thinking part of my mind and allow myself to *feel* instead of analysing.

Of course, not all feeling is consistent with sexual pleasure. I won't dwell on depression here: there was enough on that in Chapter 7. I won't dwell, either, on anger; that's the subject of Chapter 13. It is enough to say that feeling low, whatever the reason for it, is anti-erotic.

Up-feelings enhance desire: optimism, joy, relaxed energy, sensual delight. Like the way I feel when I bask under a warm sun, or swoop down a sparkling mountain on skis, breathing chill champagne air. Like the way I feel when I've just showered after an hour's badminton, when we've had unexpected good news or hard-earned success, or when Colin's wit leaves me helpless with laughter.

Excitement is part of desire, and when I'm primed with excitement – whatever its source – I feel sexy. The excitement of success is best of all; according to endocrinologists, it produces a rush of androgens, the sex hormones that underpin desire. Women have androgens circulating round their bodies just as men do, albeit in smaller quantities, and these sex hormones are produced as much after the menopause as before. That's why older women can still feel sexy.

The lure of novelty

Novelty is exciting. It can be difficult to create novelty within a long-term relationship, but if Colin turns up with a pleasant surprise, my first instinct is to hug him and kiss him. Immediately the opportunity for desire is there. I rack my brains to dream up surprises for him; sometimes they take the form of unexpected insights, sometimes unasked-for culinary delights, or simply my appearance in the sitting room wearing nothing but a sexy black swimsuit and high heels. Occasionally, delightfully, he responds. But even if he doesn't react immediately with kisses and caresses, he will usually smile, and that's a start.

When we've been separated for a while, coming together has a novel aspect. Separation raises the sexual temperature; once, when we were apart for over three weeks, I missed him so much I used to sniff his clothes and I became desperately frustrated. So randy did I feel, in fact, that when he rang and suggested I find myself some pleasure elsewhere rather than moping at home, I decided to take him at his word. I headed for the seaside and wandered around a boatyard where I could watch men at work and play.

An afternoon's flirtation (no fucking, thanks!) with a desirable man will revive my spirits and allow me to return to Colin with my inner flame once more alight. A brief separation, a little novelty, an encounter that reminds me of the sheer physical desirability of the male body, can work wonders.

Holidays can enhance desire for many reasons, and going away together is often a good way to start to revive a fading sexual relationship. Holidays are play-time, when normal pressures and inhibitions can be shed and we concentrate on enjoyment. Holidays can bring exposure to new people, sexy bodies seen if not felt, a new ambience to remind us of the joy of living. Even a trip to the city can be enough to break stalemate for us country-dwellers. When we went away for a few days to London, Colin and I were able to break through blocks that had seemed impassable at home; free from the everyday demands and habitual patterns of life on the farm, we were able to talk more easily, to touch more readily, to reach parts of ourselves that had been hidden at home. We brought the benefits of that improved communication back with us when we returned.

One advantage of going away together is that we can explore feelings with reduced risk. If our trip is successful, we return with the fruits of that success; if not, the change of scene is enough to prevent negative feelings from persisting for long. Problems at home stay with us longer than difficulties experienced in a different context; it's easier to experiment somewhere else, when familiar patterns are broken.

Gaps and breaks in the everyday pattern of life enhance desire, allow sexual juices to flow once more. And a resurgence of desire does more than just permit the possibility of revived sexual function; it makes sex enjoyable by creating lubrication and priming me for orgasm.

Orgasm

Desire and orgasm are intimately connected. With the resurgence of desire, I began again to have regular orgasms with Colin after a long period when orgasm was elusive. If desire isn't fully there, my inner fire stays damped and I don't usually come; when it returns, I can come to orgasm again. I don't expect to come as easily now as I did in our first years together, but I have recently become multi-orgasmic again. This reflects the progress we've made not just in our love-making techniques, but more crucially, in our relationship generally.

Books about sex usually portray female orgasm as a rather mechanical reaction that can be induced purely by suitable physical stimulation. If this continues for long enough, the assumption is that the woman will come. Not true! I can be stimulated till I feel desperately tense but I can't come if I'm feeling anxious or upset. Even if I am using that most potent of orgasm-inducing devices, my vibrator, I won't reach orgasm when my mind is preoccupied and I can't relate fully to what's happening to my body. It's true that the right kind of stimulation makes orgasm more probable, but that's as far as it goes.

If my mind is tuned to sex and I'm mentally turned on, my cunt produces lubrication and gets warmed up ready for sex without any physical stimulation. The merest touch can bring me to the edge of orgasm and a few thrusts of a much-desired cock can make me come. But if his cock is not really desired, Colin can thrash away for as long as he likes and I won't come; instead, what lubrication I have produced dries up and I get sore and miserable.

When I wasn't having orgasms, it was primarily because I felt confused and ambivalent about Colin. Often, I wasn't conscious of the problems that undermined my ability to lose myself totally in sexual pleasure. It took a while to realise that I wasn't able to relax completely because I didn't trust him not to turn on me and hurt me emotionally.

Alone using a combination of masturbation and fantasy, I was usually able to come quite quickly and easily, but I couldn't do it with Colin or in his presence. It didn't matter how expertly he stroked my clitoris, or how long he worked on my body, or even if I stimulated my clitoris with my vibrator in exactly the way I enjoy doing it on my own: if Colin was there, my mind blocked orgasm.

So I wonder about those women who report that they are unable to come during intercourse. Is it really because the relevant bits aren't getting stimulated? Would additional fingerplay on the clitoris, or a different position, in fact solve the problem? Is it really because they don't have the necessary sensitivity within the vagina? I doubt it. I suspect the problem goes much deeper, as it did for me. You can be equipped with all the sexually sensitive organs you need, but they may not function if your relationship is going through a tense and troubled phase. Emotional problems have to be sorted out before improved sexual technique is likely to be helpful.

Nevertheless, discovering what types of touch turn you on and learning to get the most from sex, is immensely valuable. Colin and I have spent hours talking about sex and discovering more about what we both need and enjoy. We no longer make the assumptions about each other that we once did; now that I'm not floating on a cloud of lust, I am no longer content to accept the sort of plain fucking that seemed delightful eighteen years ago. I want more than this!

I want to do all the things that take me – and him – into the heights of ecstasy, to explore all that I'm capable of feeling. That's where technique comes in. That's why I ask him to lick and suck me for as long as I can take it, why I want his fingers stroking me where they create maximum delight. I work on him till he's moaning with exquisite pleasure because that delights me and makes me feel outrageously sexy. All these things contribute to the intensity of my orgasms and the more we do them, the greater my level of desire.

Achieving orgasm is something that many women have to learn gradually, patiently. Anne Hooper's delightful book, *The Body Electric*,[6] describes the groups she initiated where women learnt to discover their erotic potential; many were able to achieve orgasm for the first time with Anne's sympathetic encouragement. She doesn't deny the importance of underlying tensions in relationships; it wasn't unusual for the women in her groups to discover that these were the factors that inhibited their orgasmic capacity.

Anne Hooper discusses masturbation in detail, for masturbation is the most effective way to unlock orgasmic ability. Most women masturbate; I have phases when I do so quite frequently. It's a good way to relax and relieve tension, to indulge in pure, harmless pleasure, to take time out from the pressures of life.

I am unable to masturbate to orgasm with my fingers alone. I use a soft-tipped vibrator against whatever part of my clitoris feels most responsive, moving it slightly as the focus of sensation changes. When my vulval area begins to feel hot and to throb, I insert a well-lubricated dildo into my vagina with the other hand, searching inside for a reactive spot and pressing hard when my climax begins.

For me, clitoral stimulation alone is not enough. I'm one of those relatively unusual women (yes, we *do* exist) who cannot achieve satisfaction without vaginal stimulation. So I keep a dildo by the bed to imitate the pressure of a stiff cock inside me when I'm approaching orgasm. Take heed, you 'experts' who assert that women don't use self-penetration during masturbation! We have many sexually responsive parts, some of which are hidden inside the vagina.

I used to feel anxious about the way I masturbated. I believed I should be able to bring myself to orgasm without any aids, just with my fingers, in what I saw as the 'normal' way, the way I've seen other women do it. I imagined that my need for a vibrator meant I hadn't been able to overcome my inhibitions enough to enjoy my own sexuality. But now I think, what does it matter? If I prefer – even need – to use a vibrator, so what? That's the way I am.

Other women have their own preferences and these cover a great range of activities. While most women stroke the side or shaft of the clitoris with their fingers, some like to stimulate the clitoral area with jets of warm water from a shower-head, others rub themselves against anything from pillows to teddy bears, while yet others lean against a vibrating washing machine. Some like to penetrate themselves, others do not. If you read *The Hite Report on Female Sexuality*[7] you'll discover hundreds of different methods of masturbation that women use.

Masters and Johnson, that well-known team of academic sex researchers, were the main proponents of the myth of the clitoral orgasm, the idea that female sexual response begins and ends with clitoral stimulation. They, and many who followed them, became so obsessed with the clitoris that they seemed to want to explain every nuance of female sexual responsiveness in terms of clitoral stimulation. If intercourse turns us on, they maintained, it's because it pulls on the tissue around the clitoris and that's what actually responds. If penetration doesn't turn us on, it's because the clitoris isn't getting sufficient stimulation. The fact that the women they studied were selected for their ability to reach orgasm through clitoral stimulation by the fingers alone would inevitably have distorted their conclusions.

Sexual responsiveness is not that simple. It has many more facets than such mechanistic research acknowledges.

How anyone can really imagine that the vagina isn't sexually responsive is beyond my comprehension. What a strange failure of design that would be, if Nature had failed to equip us to enjoy the action that the whole process is designed to lead up to! But Nature did not fail us. I – like most women – respond to a variety of forms of direct vaginal stimulation.

Inside my vagina, on the front wall just above the pubic bone, there's an area that Colin can reach to drive me wild. This is my G-spot.[8] He tells me he can feel a highly responsive strip of tissue that's quite distinctive and easily recognisable. It swells with stimulation just as a man's cock swells, as blood accumulates in the specialised tissue behind the walls of the vagina. For my part, I experience the most exciting sensation when he massages my G-spot with his fingertips, a sensation quite unlike anything else.

I was amazed when he found this point. Having read about the G-spot, I had tried to find it myself and failed; I can't locate it. It seems to produce its most dramatic effects when my clitoris is being stroked at the same time. What it does is make me absolutely desperate for fucking; it brings me to the edge of orgasm and holds me there till I'm begging for his cock. I've warned Colin that he must hold back from touching my G-spot if he's not ready to fuck: once he's been stroking me there, I am not willing to hold back. I have to be filled and filled deep.

I have come to the conclusion that the function of my G-spot is to induce an urgent desire for penetration. It can be no accident that it's readily accessible to a man's finger, but not to my own. I believe Nature designed women to want to take sex all the way, to want to feel a man's cock inside them, and to feel the greatest pleasure that way. What else should we expect, after all?

I feel sad that such experts as Masters and Johnson should be so sceptical about the G-spot, or, indeed, about the responsiveness of the vagina generally. So what, if 'less than 10% of a sample of over 100 women who were carefully examined had an area of heightened sensitivity in the front wall of the vagina'?[9] To me, this merely suggests that the women they studied were not sufficiently aroused to enjoy the sensations produced by this area. This is not sufficient evidence to justify dismissing its existence – and it certainly does not justify putting people off exploring the pleasure that the vagina is capable of inducing.

Deep penetration does something else to me. It makes me come, if I'm ready. If I were to believe Masters and Johnson, I shouldn't feel that way. According to them, 'The vagina has relatively few nerve-endings. As a result, the inner two-thirds of the vagina are relatively insensitive to touch or pain.' Furthermore, 'The cervix has no surface nerve-endings so it experiences little in the way of sexual feelings.'[10]

More nonsense! Whatever the state of my nerve-endings, I most definitely do experience sexual feelings inside my vagina; when I'm aroused, I experience a desperate ache, a longing to be filled that's located deep within me; and – again, when I'm fully aroused – I adore the sensation of a thrusting cock hitting my cervix. I can feel it all the way, feel the head as it moves against my velvet membranes, feel the movement in his cock when he comes. The whole area comes alive with sexual delight, not just the outer third.

Nor am I alone in feeling this way. Why else should novelists like Erica Jong write phrases like 'He pounded her so hard she was about to come again', and 'he rocked from side to side, touching parts of her insides she could have sworn were untouched before'?[11] She is describing the sheer delight of hard, deep fucking, fucking that seems to fill a woman, fucking that's on the edge of being painful, the sensation is so intense.

Freud and his followers denied the importance of the clitoris, condemned clitoral orgasm as immature, and asserted that women should be satisfied with vaginal intercourse only. Masters and Johnson, and their followers, on the other hand, understate the importance of the vagina. But I know from my experience – and I'd like every woman to discover, from her own experience – that sexual pleasure can involve every part of our bodies. It's absurd to denigrate or deny any of it.

Naturally, women vary in their sexual preferences. Some, doubtless, have more sensitivity inside the vagina than others; some enjoy hard fucking more than others. I've found very little information about these variations, far more about the differences in women's clitoral responses. But since some women find the clitoris can become so sensitive that direct touch is painful, and others reach orgasm with intense stimulation right on the sensitive tip, I believe that there is bound to be equal variability in other parts of our sexual anatomy. That's why each individual woman must show her partner what *she* likes; her partner will never have met anyone quite like her before, and no manual will tell him about her particular tastes.

But the most crucial organ of all is unquestionably the mind. When my mind is ready for sexual delight, my body responds readily; when I'm not mentally prepared, I don't respond. Desire is the key, desire focused through tender touches, cuddles, kisses, affectionate conversation; desire aroused, perhaps with the help of fantasy or erotica; desire reciprocated, making me feel wanted and loved. Only when that process is complete can lust be fully unlocked and the body experience the fruits of desire fulfilled.

10

Dreaming

Everyone dreams. Dreams, those creations of our subconscious minds which the ancients believed were messages from the gods, can fulfil many functions: they can express our fears and preoccupations, give us solutions to problems and insights into issues that concern us in our waking lives. Both night dreams and the daydreams we call fantasies, are stuff of the imagination: tinged with memory and desire, they are syntheses created by our individual minds for our amusement, pleasure and future survival.

Dreams and fantasies affect desire, sexual expression and relationships. But we are not passive recipients of our dreams: we can consciously direct them, through fantasy, in ways that help keep love alive and add to the fun of loving relationships.

Freud, and generations of psychoanalysts who followed him, linked dreams and sex, interpreting dreams in terms of sexual symbolism. But I'm not going to go into Freudian theory; he was a product of his particular time and circumstances and I have never found his work helpful or convincing. Analysis, with its focus on problems, goes against the First Rule of Bicycle Riding.

Nevertheless, I have found that dreams can reveal my inner (subconscious) self to my conscious mind. Although I sometimes have bad dreams, even terrifying nightmares, many of my dreams are expressions of desires. But even dreams are inhibited by culture, upbringing, and the myriad of taboos that control our behaviour. 'I would never dream of . . .' and 'beyond my wildest dreams' are revealing expressions in our language.

Permitting yourself to enjoy sexual fantasy, and, through fantasy, opening the doors to more sexual dreams, could allow you to experience pleasure that you may never have imagined possible, but which should not be beyond your wildest dreams.

All this came together for me a couple of years ago, when I realised that fantasy was the crucial component that was missing from my sex-life. Without it, desire and responsiveness were suppressed. Colin and I had been working on improving our relationship for well over a year. We'd been talking through our problems, dealing with anger, rebuilding trust, moving closer together – but still my desire for him remained obstinately low, even though I felt sure I wanted to be with him. Something was missing, some part of the pattern still eluded me. I couldn't work out what it was.

He wanted sex, he loved and desired me. I felt I loved him, but I just couldn't turn on. I initiated sex rarely, responded feebly. The situation was making us both tense and unhappy and I began to despair of ever finding a solution to our problem.

Then a publishing firm rang to say they'd had an idea for a new book, and they thought I would be just the person to write it. It was to be called *The Good Sex Diet*. I reacted to the proposal with secret horror. The very idea churned me up inside. How could I write about Good Sex when I wasn't having it?

My knowledge that I *should* be able to write that book made matters worse; it threw our problem into stark relief. I'd edited a sex magazine, hadn't I? I'd written reams about diet and my previous book had been about sex hormones. If anyone could create a Good Sex Diet, it should be me.

I signed the contract, accepted the deadline – and panicked. I realised there was only one way that I could do it: by getting myself to the point where I could write, as I have to write, honestly, from the heart. Anyway, I did so much want an exciting sex-life. I wanted to feel the warmth of desire surging again. I wanted to discover aphrodisia, in whatever form it existed for me. This book, I felt, could save our sexual relationship – if I could only write it.

I consulted Charleen in the hope that she would be able to help me identify and overcome the blocks that prevented me from starting work. After some hours with her, I began to understand the problem. I had been waiting for Colin to light my fire – but I wasn't allowing it to happen, I was keeping the dampers closed. I hadn't been imagining myself as a sexual being.

Thinking about good sex, I began to remember my sexual self: how it used to feel when sexual feeling surged through my being, the excitement I'd experienced with previous lovers. The book started to emerge. I wrote about meals I'd eaten with past lovers, the dishes we'd shared before making love. I spent hours daydreaming about erotic encounters. And as I dreamt, desire returned.

Dreaming revived my interest in sex. Daydreams followed by night dreams; dreams of men I knew and men I'd never met; recollections and fantasies combined, elaborated – and recorded. As I fantasised, I created menus to share with Colin, dishes based on aphrodisiacs from a variety of cultures. I cooked, we ate, and later, we made love.

Suddenly, I was enjoying myself. That book was such fun to write! Every day I spent at my word processor I'd dream myself into a sexual frenzy, taking breaks to masturbate when I couldn't think clearly enough to write. Then I'd share my lust with Colin, who was delighted to assist.

Every aphrodisiac we tried worked like magic. I knew by then – as I acknowledged in the book – that the magic was in our minds. Cooking meals with potentially aphrodisiac ingredients released our sexual potential, not through any physiological effect (although that may sometimes contribute) but through the psychological effects of thinking about sex, thinking how to get the sexual juices flowing, anticipating excitement.

Each time I cooked a special recipe for Colin, I was making a statement: we'll have fun together tonight. Believing it, we made it happen. We were focusing on where we wanted to go, the effects we wanted to achieve. And so what we wanted to happen, happened.

The Good Sex Diet[1] started out as a collection of recipes but it became a work of erotica. It turned me on and it turns readers on by stimulating their dreams. Through fantasy, I discovered aspects of my dream-self which had been neglected for a long time. It was as though I'd put that part of my being into a cupboard and shut the door firmly. Writing the book motivated me to open that door, to find the fire in my core, to discover that the flames could leap again.

Fantasy: the real food of love

The difference between a wonderful sexual encounter and one that's nice, but nothing special, is that you're on edge with excitement, your senses become super-receptive, your feelings incredibly intense. The least touch sends a tingle down your spine. A brief look can melt you. That's how it is when you're in love. But it's your own imagination that has this powerful effect, and fantasy can unleash this power even if you've been sexual partners for decades.

Consciously harnessing subconscious lust is sometimes derided as 'thinking dirty thoughts'. It's surprising how deep this prohibition can be: you may believe you're not that sort of person; you've learnt that such indulgence is despicable. We are all sexual beings, but when crude lust has run its course, we may have to motivate ourselves deliberately to achieve the effects we want.

Sexual fantasies are about pleasure, nothing else. Fantasising helps prepare the mind for a more exciting and rewarding reality. Most of us have now junked the old hang-ups about masturbation, and fantasy is its mental equivalent. The physical and mental are inextricably entwined: perhaps you need, as I did, to liberate yourself from prohibitions about sexual fantasy.

Fantasies don't have to be novel creations. Some people enjoy making up stories but we're not all equally imaginative. I'm not particularly creative; I identify with songwriter Fran Landesman, whom I once heard saying on the radio that she wrote from experience because she didn't have enough imagination to create poems any other way. Fantasies can be memories, lovingly rerun, stories you've read or seen on film, or experiences you'd like to have. The crucial thing is that you let them unfold in your mind, lingering over them, exploring details, tasting sensations in your imagination.

This gets easier with practice. But first you must decide you want to use the power that is within each one of us, to feed that inner fire of sexual vitality. Take time away from all distractions to indulge in fantasy, and you'll find your sex-life will become more exotic, more exciting in reality.

In *The Joy of Sexual Fantasy*,[2] Andrew Stanway gives detailed instructions on how to indulge in this most personal of pleasures. He emphasises the need for complete relaxation, beginning with slow, deep breathing. Each breath you take in should fill the whole of your chest with air. As soon as you feel you've drawn in as much air as possible, let it all out; then immediately breathe in again, right to the top of your chest. Twenty or so deep breaths taken in this way can produce deep relaxation.

Once you feel calm and relaxed, he recommends that you visualise a favourite scene – a garden, perhaps, or a beach, lingering long enough to imagine the flowers, the birds, the colour of the sky, the sounds and the smells.

When you are relaxed and you can feel and see these things in your imagination, go on to create an erotic fantasy. He suggests you start by remembering a video, book or encounter that turned you on. Imagine your sexual organs becoming larger and hotter. Then add your favourite sexy scene. Again, repetition is the key to success.

Most of my fantasies are based on memories. I'm lucky that my varied sexual past provides me with a treasure trove of erotic material. I can select from a range of recollections: showering with a tall, muscular, smooth-skinned African, his erect cock purple as an aubergine; Brian and Colin together, proving I could take two cocks with ease when sufficiently turned on; fucking with a beautiful artist in his New York loft, delighting in the contrast of dark flesh moving against white; and best of all, Bill Levy sucking me to ecstasy in Amsterdam.

All those gorgeous men! Those wonderful masculine bodies! The perfect nights and days of delight! When I was turned off, I didn't allow myself to remember. Now I permit myself to savour and develop my erotic fantasy-life. New people come into it, men I know and like, men I could imagine becoming my lovers if our circumstances were different. I have them in my imagination: Jim, bound hand and foot with silk scarves, spreadeagled so that he can't escape, cannot help but respond to my hands, lips and cunt; Jonathan, whose hugs and restrained kisses always turned me on, unrestrained in my fantasies, his hands roaming over my naked body and mine over his; we danced, once, with such togetherness that I know sex would be marvellous with him. And dear Alan, his animal power and raw energy focused on sexual pleasure. I'd make love to them all, if I could; but since I have no intention of actually doing so, I indulge in fantasising about it.

Fantasising in this way will turn you on. I usually get so excited by deliberate fantasies that I'll masturbate; sometimes I fantasise as I lie in bed, waiting for Colin to come and join me – especially if I know he's eager for sex. I'll appreciate him all the more when he arrives!

Stimulating erotic dreams

Fantasy can unlock a wealth of erotic dreams. Daydreams emerge, apparently spontaneously, when we relax and let them come, following the flow of their internal logic. Other dreams unfold as we sleep. More plentiful when my sex-drive is high, my dreams reflect a waking delight in sex. The more I fantasise about sex in the daytime, the more I dream of sex at night. Waking with an orgasm puts a smile on my face that can last the rest of the day. Which is all the more reason for giving myself time to indulge in fantasy.

Linking conscious and unconscious

I've discovered I have to give myself permission to have delightful dreams. If my daytime thoughts turn me off, I'm turned off at night too. Taboos – even quite new taboos, like the ones I've adopted in the wake of Aids – reach right through into the dreaming mind. Tuning in to dreams can tell us about our unconscious fears, anxieties and blocks, issues that we may need to address when we're awake.

Actually, I find it reassuring that we can shape our unconscious through conscious thought. It means we are more in control of our destinies. When we make up our conscious minds about something, the unconscious mind gets the message too. If my dream-self insists on safe sex, for example, I know that the temptation to behave foolishly won't be overwhelming when I'm awake.

Some dreams have clear meaning, which I've learnt to heed; others may just be fun. One night, I dreamt I was in bed with Michael Heseltine, a man I can't imagine choosing in waking life! There was, I recall, a problem; my dream Heseltine didn't come prepared for safe sex and we didn't fuck. In my dreams, I've refused sex with many a gorgeous stranger because neither of us had a condom.

Learning from fantasy

Although these dreams don't seem to have much significance, the fantasies we create when we are awake do. In particular, they reveal sometimes unrecognised sexual preferences. Some fantasies reflect hostility which you may need to work through with the help of a counsellor; fantasies about damaging or hurting other people, in particular, reveal anger and deep distress which will have to be resolved before you are likely to be able to enjoy a satisfying sex-life.

It was by thinking about my fantasies that I realised what sort of sex-acts I like best, in what contexts, and in what positions. I observed that there was a recurring pattern. I imagine a man – always someone I know, often an ex-lover – kissing me, nuzzling and stroking my breasts and body, and then starting to lick my clitoris and the surrounding area. When I'm coming close to orgasm, I imagine his cock, erect, its tip swollen and hot, sliding into me deeper and deeper, pushing inside me, filling me up, massaging me inside, then thrusting hard as if battering down the door to my womb.

It's all very straightforward. But I realised that these fantasies revealed definite preferences which were relevant to the way Colin and I made love. In particular, I thought about the way the fantasy man licked me, and the positions of our bodies. So after years together, I finally knew what I wanted and I told Colin. Now he makes love to me in the way that most turns me on. I accept that our preferences differ, and we also do what he likes best; but there must be a balance which doesn't favour one of us at the expense of the other.

Acting out fantasies

If I'd been more relaxed about sex, I'd have known what I preferred and would no doubt have told Colin years earlier. But I find it hard to decide what I want, even harder to tell someone else. Oughts and shoulds and assorted anxieties get in the way of desires. I'd been brought up to regard the fulfilment of desire as selfish; I felt I should always be thinking about the needs of others.

Looking at my fantasies, spending time with my dreaming self and thinking about the themes that recur in my waking fantasies and my sleeping dreams, informed me about my desires. Telling Colin how I felt allowed reality to come closer to my dreams, and he was delighted with the positive energy I was putting into our sex-life. At first I was tentative; it was like learning to walk again after years of immobility. But before long desire had returned, liberated by fantasy.

Whether you share your fantasies is a personal decision; they may be entirely for your own pleasure. They may involve people or animals who aren't, and cannot be, available as sexual partners. That doesn't matter: the delight of fantasy is that it doesn't ever have to become reality, unless you want it to.

Fantasies can never be totally recreated in reality, because you're dealing with other people, who will feed in their own desires and interpretations and their personal style. This is no disadvantage; the unpredictable element of that input can bring an extra fillip of excitement. However, we have to be selective about which fantasies we try to enact: some, like rape, are obviously unsuitable for real life.

Living out fantasy roles – strict mistress and submissive lover, teacher and schoolchild, nurse and patient, Tarzan and Jane, Catherine and Heathcliff – can be tremendous fun when both partners enjoy the parts they play. Weaving a story together, you share the building excitement. Even playing out a fantasy in your own mind – imagining yourself as Carmen or Madonna or an accomplished concubine – can release parts of you that you never realised existed, with delightful effect for both partners. Playing roles frees you from some of the inhibitions that surround your self-concept. You can find yourself acting in novel ways. Role-playing is a wonderful antidote to sexual boredom.

Reading feeds my dreams: Anaïs Nin, Erica Jong, and of course, Bill Levy, ex-editor of *Suck*, that amazing sex paper created by Heathcote Williams, Germaine Greer, Jim Haynes, and Dutch artist Willem de Ridder. Bill keeps my dreams alive with his erotic stories, stories that trigger memories of the night I fell in love with him. We both dream of writing another chapter together, some day . . .

For a while, I was anxious that fantasising about other men, like Bill, who could become lovers in real life, might break my determination to remain monogamous. Colin was reassuring; if you can imagine it happening one day, the fantasy is all the more exciting, he said. Don't spoil the fantasy by worrying about reality. I know he's right; turning off fantasies turns me off generally. I need to dream on, so I do. It's better for both of us.

The more I fantasise, the more I masturbate, the more I enjoy sex. In Nancy Friday's words,[3] 'It is the mind that carries the genesis of sexual life, inhibits us from orgasm or releases us. Masturbation gets its fire, its life from what is sparked in the mind.' Fantasy complemented by masturbation keeps my sexual fires burning, my cunt lubricated, my orgasm muscles strong. It doesn't turn me off Colin, quite the reverse; it keeps me ready for him, ready to appreciate him and the emotions and sensations he can induce that I cannot match on my own.

What makes a man a wonderful lover is the gloss my imagination puts on his actions. What he does is important, of course; but my mental readiness, my psychological commitment, my rose-tinted vision, is crucial. When my dream-self is in total accord with reality, reality becomes extraordinary. So I nurture my dreams to keep desire alive within me, and as Colin and I kiss and cuddle and fondle each other, he becomes my dream lover.

Dangerous delusions

Just as enjoyable fantasies can liberate us, so depressing fantasies imprison us. Unleashing the fantasy that Colin will reject me, or hurt me, or ignore me, will turn me off just as surely as my fantasy of him as dream lover turns me on. Fantasies of disapproving mothers or rejecting ex-lovers are well-recognised turn-offs;[4] Anne Dickson refers to these figures as 'personal prudes'. But we can, with some effort, switch our attention away from these fantasies, or deliberately change them so that they do not interfere with our pleasure. For example, the ex-lover who made you feel an idiot could be gagged, tied to a chair and left to squirm while you enjoy yourself. Sharing such demons with your partner may help you laugh at them together and thus remove their power.

Telling Colin about my fears has certainly helped. He tends to be kinder and more demonstrative to me because he doesn't want to cause me anxiety. Sometimes I have to remind him that I'm vulnerable; sometimes he tells me that he's afraid of being ignored or rejected, and then I'm more gentle than I might otherwise be. We fluctuate from day to day; some days, pleasant dreams and memories appear in our minds, other days we're unhappy; life's like that. But we can exercise some power over the way we feel, by choosing to dump depressing fantasies and looking for more enjoyable ones.

Let the music play . . .

Music, with its unique ability to heighten emotion, is a potent adjunct to sexual fantasy. It touches parts of the mind that nothing else can reach. Music can stimulate the subconscious, guide, shape, and enhance feelings. It's a universal key to our primal selves. After a day of turmoil and tribulation, the irresistible emotional broom of Tchaikovsky or Beethoven will clear space for the emergence of desire. Music is emotional, intellectual, and spiritual, and it's so wonderfully and easily available, we need not deprive ourselves of any aspect of the pleasure it can bring.

For me, the sexiest composers, singers and performers are the most passionate. Many different types of music affect me deeply: Beethoven, whose multi-hued emotions come so clearly through his music as it moves through rage and despair to delight and on to ecstasy; Annie Lennox, singing songs of compulsive longing; Hendrix, the immortal 'Voodoo Chile'. Colin's tastes are different from mine: he tunes into the emotion of Tchaikovsky, the complex rhythms of jazz, the power of rock.

Music affects the whole body, urging us to move, to break free of the barriers in our minds. I feel the insistent beat of rock as a driving sexual force, one that demands the release of dance. I identify and flow with Annie Lennox singing to a Caribbean rhythm and let the lyrics carry me away: 'I'm so full of desire, you set my head on fire – I need to be right by your side . . .'

For me, dance is a form of physical fantasy. When I dance alone, I feel the power of the music deep inside, radiating from my belly through my limbs, soothing my mind, releasing me from tension, focusing sensuality, warming me from head to toe. I am in touch with my primal self. Dancing with a man I desire, I communicate that feeling, inviting him to come to me, come into me.

I believe that dreaming and dance are especially important for women, allowing the vague patterns and feelings in our minds to coalesce into pictures, giving us access to our inner reality. We must dream to get in touch with our deeper selves, the selves that can become crushed under the burdens, obligations and assumptions of everyday life. We have to make sure we don't neglect our dream-selves, our deep selves; we need space just to be with ourselves. When we give ourselves the opportunity to drift with the current of our dreams, we gain insights and understanding that might otherwise elude us.

Many native peoples speak of dreamtime, a state of knowing and accepting the wisdom of natural forces. The dreamtime concept gives their lives a larger context, connecting them with their ancestors and the mythology of their existence. It validates and sanctions their being and the relationships upon which humanity depends by bringing all the essentials, including love and sex, into a common matrix of belief and expression as part of a universal whole. In turn, the wholeness of individuals and their social group is maintained.

Dreamtime is something many people lose as the pressures and sterile provisions of civilisation occupy and channel their thoughts. But dreaming together brings us closer than any tangible bonds ever could. Spend time with your dreams, and they will become a creative and continuing part of your relationship. Dream it – then be it!

11

Contraception and Sexual Feeling

Contraception might seem an odd topic to address in a book about desire in long-term relationships. Sex counsellors don't usually bother about contraception: it's something the couple (usually the woman) deals with in the same sort of matter-of-fact way as a visit to the hairdresser. But contraception is, by its very nature, a barrier between male and female: either a physical barrier, or a barrier of a more subtle type which acts by disrupting the delicate reproductive systems of the body.

For me, that barrier has at times been physical, sometimes psychological. I tried a whole range of contraceptive methods, all of which interfered with sexual pleasure both for me and my partners for many years. Finding the right way to avoid pregnancy was an important step towards building a more enjoyable sex-life.

Most of the time, for most people, sex is not about procreation. This is especially likely to be true for those who have been partners for a long time; usually, babies arrive relatively early in the life of a relationship. The last child is usually born within seven years of the date of marriage.[1] If a couple have the children they want in their twenties, as most do, the woman confronts three decades when she is potentially fertile yet she has no intention of getting pregnant again. For most of the years when men and women live together, sex is about closeness, enjoyment and excitement. Pregnancy is not a desired outcome, and contraception is therefore very important.

I have never been able to enjoy sex when I feared it could lead to pregnancy. On the very rare occasions when I have had unprotected sex – something that only happened during the part of the month when my fertility was low, and only with Colin's assurance that he would withdraw before ejaculation – I couldn't relax, couldn't suppress the anxiety I felt. I knew that withdrawal was not completely safe because there are sperm in pre-ejaculatory fluid; so even though I trusted Colin implicitly, I believed we were taking a risk that I found unacceptable. There was no point in going through with it.

Colin and I are one of the four per cent of couples who choose to remain childless, though he has children by a previous marriage. In my view, childlessness has many advantages. Rearing children takes a great deal of time and energy, it's expensive, it would interfere with whatever else I might want to do, and I have always been conscious of the ecological damage done by too many babies on a planet where resources are diminishing.

All these issues loomed large in my mind, for I had been warned repeatedly about the way unwanted pregnancy can disrupt a woman's life. My mother, forced to marry the father of a baby conceived by accident, made very sure that the same thing would not happen to any of her daughters. Proudly, she told us about the way she took her portfolio of drawings to the Principal of the Slade School of Art, and how he was so impressed that he accepted her immediately as a Fine Art student; and then how her life was made miserable by what we now call date-rape, followed by pregnancy. Her family, being pillars of the Church, insisted that she marry the father of her child; she wept as she walked up the aisle, praying to God that He would ignore this enforced marriage.

The painful birth of my sister Judith was followed by

years of marriage to a man my mother would not have chosen, made harder by his drinking and violence and her sense of being trapped, penniless and hungry, with dependent children. Unable to cope, she took an overdose of barbiturates. She should not have survived; it was a miracle that she did. My mother told this tale many times over to her three daughters. She discussed contraception openly with us during our teenage years: she was realistic enough to know that forbidding us to have sex was pointless, but she warned us to protect ourselves from the potential consequences. Her warnings were effective. In our combined reproductive lifetimes, my two sisters and I experienced only one unwanted pregnancy, and that was caused by contraceptive failure.

But I haven't been lucky with my experience of contraceptives. Over the course of a dozen or so years, I tried virtually every type of reliable contraceptive available. Every method interfered with my sex-life in one way or another. And whatever form this interference takes, it is bound to add to the total sum of pressures that detract from sexual pleasure and desire in the long term. According to Sheila Kitzinger, my experience is not unusual. She spoke to three hundred women, who described 'what amounts to an obstacle race to be able to control fertility.' Women have simply not admitted to all the inconveniences and discomforts of contraception: we put up with unsatisfactory methods, coping as best we can, but often to the detriment of our health and sexual pleasure.[2]

Contraception is very much a woman's problem. Women have the babies, women predominantly look after them. Women carry the burden; they are ultimately responsible. Few men even mention the subject, although they contribute equally to the creation of a baby.

Because this is a woman's problem, the male-dominated medical establishment shows little sympathy. Contraceptive problems tend not to be taken seriously, any more than premenstrual problems or the menopause. Male doctors disregarded my experience again and again, ignoring clinical evidence in favour of their own assumptions.

My first experience was with the Pill. Twenty-three per cent of British women were using the Pill in 1991;[3] although it is less popular now than it was fifteen years ago, it is still the most frequently chosen contraceptive method. I went on it when I was eighteen and still a virgin, in anticipation of sex with Bob. It seemed fine at first, an excellent answer to a difficult problem. But after a few months, I began to deteriorate both mentally and physically; within two years, I had lost interest in sex. Many women find that sexual desire and pleasure diminish when they take the Pill. 'I never felt like sex except during my period' (the week when she wasn't taking the Pill), one woman told Sheila Kitzinger. 'It put me right off my husband as well as sex,' said another. Yet another commented, 'It depressed my interest in sex and my ability to feel *anything* during sex.' It's ironic that the pharmaceutical advance we hailed for its liberating effects should be capable of turning us off in this way.[4]

When I started taking the Pill, in 1967, it was still relatively new. Nobody worried about side-effects. Few people knew anything about the side-effects of drugs at that time, and most of the Pill's hazards had yet to be discovered. So it never occurred to me that my increasing problems with weight-gain, depression, headaches and recurring thrush might have anything to do with the pill I took conscientiously every night.

I took the Pill for the best part of four years. During that period, as already mentioned, I went in and out of the university sanatorium, suffering from depression, treated for month after month with anti-depressants and tranquillisers, migraine tablets and fungicidal pessaries. I finally took a year off university because I was too confused and depressed to think.

Then, belatedly, a suspicion came into my mind. I had never suffered from depression and all those other miserable conditions before I began taking the Pill. Could the two be linked? It had to be worth finding out. I stopped taking it.

Within two days, the whole world changed colour. Suddenly, the sun shone again, everything looked brighter and I felt quite different deep within myself. It was as though for years I had only been half alive and now I was whole. It was totally unexpected, utterly wonderful.

I vowed never to take the Pill again, but that was before I discovered the drawbacks of other forms of contraception. My mother had only warned me about their unreliability and the obsessive care I should take in their use; but I found there were many other problems. When a family planning doctor assured me that a new, low-dose formulation of the Pill would cause no side-effects whatever, I wanted to believe him. He was wrong. This low dose was enough to bring back the depression and the headaches. It was like suffering from premenstrual tension the whole month through. My libido disappeared.

In 1977, I tried again. This time, the family planning clinic gave me progestogen-only minipills. They assured me that my problems with combined pills (which contain a mixture of oestrogen and progestogen) were caused by their oestrogen content.

I was living with Colin by then, travelling back and forth to Bergen, a resort town in Holland, to produce a reader-written magazine call *Love*. It was a beautiful magazine, a strange mix of blurry photographs of readers, with baroque borders and ornate frames surrounding unedited, often crudely written, letters from ordinary people about their sex-lives and fantasies. *Love* offered sexual reality, warts intact, in a bouquet of elaborate artwork. It didn't sell well.

The last time I went to Bergen to work on *Love*, I was taking progestogen-only minipills. My memories are confused but sharp with anguish. Searching my mind, I pick up a feeling of living on a roller-coaster, running out of control. I became paranoid. I suspected people of laughing at me, insulting me behind my back. I couldn't relate to any of the friends with whom we were staying. I began to hate some of the people in the house, though they did nothing to deserve it. I snapped viciously at Colin.

What a waste of weeks in Bergen! There was I, unable to enjoy or appreciate anything in this charming sunny town where sparrows perched confidently on café tables, tidying up crumbs of Dutch applecake. A short stroll through perfumed pinewoods took us to the nude beach, while the multifaceted pleasures of Amsterdam were just a couple of hours' drive away. I was miserable. My mind had gone haywire, twisted.

The episode ended with Colin throwing my pills away. I fought against that. I'd become too irrational even to acknowledge the possibility that they might be causing my problems. Once again, the world changed colour. I woke as if from a bad dream.

I learnt my lesson. I cannot afford to dose my body with powerful sex hormones, even in small quantities. When I do, I lose my sanity.

The Pill is not the only form of hormone-based contraception, though all work on the same principles and all have broadly similar side-effects, affecting both mind and body. We hear most about the cardiovascular hazards of the Pill; depression, headaches, loss of libido and weight-gain are regarded as minor side-effects. But when the statistics show that women who take the Pill are significantly more likely to commit suicide than those who do not, I believe the mood-changes it can induce should not be considered trivial.

Contraceptive injections have even more dramatic side-effects than taking the Pill – and women who have them have to wait for months before these wear off. I suppose this is better than rearing unwanted babies, but I had to find a better solution to the contraceptive problem than messing about with hormones.

I am aware that many women feel fine on the Pill and some even feel the better for taking it. I acknowledge, too, that it is a very convenient form of contraception, and that the early type that I took in the sixties contained much higher doses of hormones than those that are used today.

And while I feel uneasy about interfering with such a delicate system as hormone balance, especially for teenage girls, taking the Pill is almost always better than risking unwanted pregnancy.

A small minority of Pill-users suffer even worse side-effects than I did. I survived, after all, largely undamaged; but I have met women who have been crippled by strokes in their twenties, almost certainly caused by the Pill. I recommend Dr Ellen Grant's book, *The Bitter Pill*,[5] to those who want to know more about what we once regarded as the Perfect Contraceptive.

When I returned to the family planning clinic after I gave up the Pill the first time, I was fitted with a diaphragm (Dutch cap). This is a contraceptive method used by less than two per cent of women, despite its reliability and safety. Patiently, the doctor taught me how to use it, how to compress it between my thumb and forefinger and push it gently into the vagina, and then reach inside to check that my cervix was completely covered. Once I'd learnt to put it in correctly, I was shown how to smother it with spermicidal cream before insertion.

I found that the cap could be the most awkward device: springy and slippery with spermicide, it was prone to shoot through my fingers to gum itself messily on to the carpet on the other side of the room. Hooking it out six hours or more after sex – very carefully, lest it get pierced by a fingernail – I was confronted by a disgusting gungy thing that I would sling into a basin of warm water to wash as quickly as possible. But it had a unique advantage: it held back the blood when I had a period, so that I could have sex without staining the sheets.

It is essential to be fitted with the cap, because it has to be the correct size. Too small, and the thing doesn't work; too large, and it's uncomfortable. When mine was just the right size, I couldn't feel it, but when I lost or gained weight, as I frequently did in my obsessive dieting days, I had to get a new one. When I dropped a dress size, my cap had to be a size larger, when I grew fatter again – as I inevitably did – I returned to a smaller cap.

Once inside my body, the cap was safe enough for a few hours, and it ensured safety from pregnancy. When I wasn't using it, I washed it, dried it and replaced it carefully in its box.

I kept a pet ferret in my cap-using days, a most luxurious and playful creature. One morning, my ferret discovered the box containing my cap on the bedside table. Now ferrets particularly love to break into boxes, and this one, hiding its curious plaything, proved a total delight. I shall never forget the sight of that ferret dashing across the room with my cap held firmly in its teeth. When I found it eventually, behind a chest of drawers among the ferret's other toys – melon rind, chicken-bones, cutlery – it was riddled with small holes. I let the ferret keep it.

Fortunately, new caps are available without prescription from most pharmacists. You just have to know what size to ask for. But the cap does have drawbacks, even if you don't keep ferrets in your bedroom. One problem is that it has to be in place before you start making love, because going off to the bathroom and fiddling with the thing disrupts the pleasure build-up. You have to anticipate sex and consciously prepare for it. I coped by putting it in every night if I was going to sleep with a man, just in case we would fuck.

Unfortunately, the cap has to be inserted with a copious covering of contraceptive jelly, otherwise it isn't reliable. I used to wash the stuff off my vulva, but as soon as my juices began to drip from within, the flavour of spermicide pervaded the whole area. And it doesn't taste good.

I couldn't enjoy cunnilingus knowing the man was getting a mouthful of spermicide; and I couldn't enjoy sucking his cock after he had inserted it into me, because it would come out smeared with gunge. Ugh!! Once again, my choice of contraceptive was disrupting my sex-life.

Some men dislike the cap; some say they can feel it. A couple of my lovers found it so off-putting that they insisted on using condoms instead; and in view of the way condoms interfere with sensation, the cap had to be pretty annoying! This reaction was unusual, however, and I wonder if it might be related to the particular shape or size of these men's cocks; one, I recall, was very large indeed.

Fed up with the bother of using a cap, I had an IUD (intra-uterine device, or coil) fitted. The IUD is the contraceptive chosen by five per cent of women. Its popularity has slowly declined over the years as more people have favoured sterilisation. I imagined that an IUD would be the perfect answer to my contraceptive problems: no interference with hormones, high reliability, nothing to worry about once it had settled down in my uterus.

No such luck! I had my first experience of really nasty period pain after I had the IUD fitted – itself an unpleasant experience, to say the least – and while the severity of the pain did diminish, it returned with every period.

Like most women, I was willing to tolerate some pain to gain protection from the risk of pregnancy, and I put up with my IUD. I should have known better; I should have heeded my body's protests. I knew perfectly well what it was objecting to. The IUD sets up inflammation within the womb, creating an environment too hostile for fertilised eggs to become implanted. But sometimes the inflammation goes too far and infection sets in.

After eighteen months, I developed pelvic inflammatory disease (PID). I recognised my symptoms: abdominal pain, a smelly discharge from the vagina, nausea, a low fever. I had a pamphlet that described exactly these symptoms in the context of gonorrhoea. I was penniless in Iowa at the time, and I went to a free clinic where the doctor obviously thought I was a drug addict complaining of pain to trick him into prescribing opiates. The doctor told me that pain was normal for a woman having a period. I protested that this period had lasted far too long, the pain was much too severe, and that years of experience of living in my own body left me in no doubt that this was very far from normal. But he was the expert. He sent me away without treatment.

I lay miserably in my sick-bed till the bleeding stopped but the pain grew worse, spreading to the bowel. Then I returned to the clinic, where a nurse took a swab from my vagina for analysis. This time, the doctor told me that I had gonorrhoea, and gave me an injection of penicillin. My pamphlet informed me that by the time my symptoms had progressed this far, a single injection of penicillin would not cure my illness; but no matter, the doctors were sure they knew best.

I dragged myself to a telephone and made the most embarrassing calls of my life, to tell recent lovers that I had been diagnosed as suffering from gonorrhoea. A few days later, the test results came through: the doctor had been wrong again. I didn't have gonorrhoea. They didn't know what had caused my illness.

As I had anticipated, that penicillin injection did not cure me. My symptoms worse than ever, a feminist from the local women's centre who by then was taking care of me, took me to the local hospital. There the doctors diagnosed PID and linked it with my IUD. It had to be removed before I would recover.

I screamed involuntarily when a medical student pulled on the string that hung from my inflamed womb, dragging out the IUD. In all my life, I have never known such agony. I was given tetracycline and sent home. Finally, under the gentle care of the Iowa women's group, I began to improve. When I was sufficiently recovered to contemplate sex again, I bought another Dutch cap and spermicide in a chemist's shop.

Back in England, fed up once more with the bother of the cap, I consulted a family planning clinic again. There, the doctor denied that there was any link between IUDs and pelvic infection – reassurance that my later reading showed to be totally unjustified – and persuaded me to have another one.

This time, I suffered recurring low abdominal pain and a stinking, chronic discharge. I felt embarrassed about the smell of my vagina, convinced that it must be horrible for the men with whom I was having sex. I became so concerned, in fact, that I was completely unable to enjoy being licked or kissed in that area: I didn't want anyone's nose or mouth between my legs. I didn't know what was going on in my body; I just felt it was bad.

The IUD damaged my sex-life in other ways, too. Some men could feel the string that hung through my cervix, especially when they thrust hard; Colin withdrew on one occasion, I remember, as though he'd been stung. There was a fine red line on the delicate tip of his cock – a line of inflammation left by the string. I know men who refuse to fuck with women wearing IUDs. Most doctors deny that men can possibly feel either the rigid structure of the IUD itself, or the harsh plastic string that dangles through the cervix. I prefer to believe the men: I've had too much experience of doctors denying reality, especially doctors who deal in contraception. They would rather listen to the manufacturers of IUDs than the people who use them.

Eventually, I saw another doctor, a charming and sympathetic woman who told me I should never have had another IUD after my experience in Iowa, and that because the recurring infection caused by the IUD had damaged my reproductive organs, I might be infertile. She fitted me with another cap.

After my dreadful experiences with the Pill and the IUD, it was a relief to return to the cap. At least it wouldn't make me ill! It was a nuisance, admittedly, but one to which I felt I could adapt. I prefer caps to condoms, though only condoms offer significant protection against disease. Condoms are the second most popular contraceptive method after the Pill, and their popularity is growing steadily. The main reason for increased condom use is probably the fact that they offer protection against sexually transmitted disease including Aids, and because of this they have been promoted heavily and are readily available in a much wider variety of outlets than any other form of contraceptive. The women who prefer condoms point out that they capture messy semen so that it doesn't drop on to sheets or down their thighs.[6] In 1991 they were used by sixteen per cent of couples.

I don't much like the feel of cock covered with condom. Even though condoms are lubricated, they don't slide in as well as a naked cock does. And the sensation is different, less silky. If I had any lover but Colin, I would insist that he used a condom; but I would rather it was not necessary. Sliding it on can be sexy, though: smoothing the condom down over an erect cock with delicate fingertips, holding and stroking, making love as we share the occasion. Colin recalls that one time when he used a sheep-gut condom, he had a double orgasm induced, he believes, by its tightness over the head of his cock. Condoms aren't entirely functional!

There are some barrier methods I never tried. One is the cervical cap, which is too unreliable to be satisfactory. Another is the female condom, with which I would certainly experiment if I needed contraception now. It is a sheath designed to line the inside of the vagina and, like the condom, it offers protection against sexually transmitted disease as well as contraception. It is available from pharmacists.

Neither did I try the rhythm method, avoiding sex during the mid-part of my cycle when I'm likely to conceive. Frankly, it's too uncertain to be safe. And, infuriatingly, it would mean I couldn't have sex when I most enjoy it, because that's when I'm most fertile.

My contraceptive problems came to an end when I was thirty. I was fed up with struggling with unsatisfactory methods of avoiding pregnancy. By this time I had decided that since I still didn't want a baby, I was not likely to change my mind; so I acted to prevent conception permanently. Unwilling to confront the hurdles I anticipated with getting sterilised by the National Health Service, I went to the British Pregnancy Advisory Service (BPAS) to enquire about having it done privately.

A BPAS counsellor interviewed me, asking about my reasons for wanting sterilisation and checking that I was aware that this was an irreversible operation. I made it clear that I had thought about the issue at length and that I was in a stable relationship and had never had any desire for children. Within a couple of weeks, I was given an appointment for an operation in a clinic in the Midlands. It was a relatively painless procedure, done under general anaesthetic. The surgeon made two tiny cuts in my abdomen and through these, fitted tiny nylon rings to my Fallopian tubes, blocking the route from ovaries to uterus.

I was sick and sore when I woke after the operation, but tremendously relieved to know that my third IUD – inserted because Colin was fed up with my cap – had finally been removed. The discomfort I suffered was caused by the gas that had been used to inflate my belly and separate the organs so that the surgeon could see the tubes on which he worked; the actual cuts didn't bother me at all.

Four out of the six women in the recovery room had had IUDs. We all reacted in the same way when we woke from the anaesthetic, searching our bedside tables for those hated objects. The clinic staff were obviously accustomed to this, for they returned them to us so that we could be completely sure they had been removed. Each woman threw away her IUD with relief and delight. Good riddance!

A week after I had been sterilised, the residual soreness in my abdomen had disappeared and I was ready to have sex again. It was marvellous to have no worries, nothing to get in the way of pleasure. Then, when my next period began, I was delighted again. There was no pain! I was finally free from pelvic infection, from smelly discharges, from messy spermicide, awkward caps, mind-twisting synthetic hormones and worry about pregnancy. I only wish I had had the courage to get sterilised earlier!

Sterilisation is becoming increasingly common. Twelve

per cent of women were sterilised in 1991, almost twice as many as fifteen years earlier. Every woman I have spoken to about her sterilisation has felt the same relief as I did. None has experienced any subsequent problems, after the initial soreness had worn off. Older methods of sterilization had caused long-term damage in some women; but with the development of tiny plastic devices to close the Fallopian tubes, the side-effect problem has effectively been conquered. I have two scars so minute that nobody would notice them if I did not point them out: one on the edge of my pubic hairline, the other in my navel. I'm glad they're there: they reassure me that I need never again worry about pregnancy.

Most men are equally happy about vasectomy; 13 per cent use this method. As with women, there is some soreness for a few days after the operation but it disappears soon enough. I have occasionally heard of men becoming impotent after vasectomy, and there is statistical evidence of a slight increase in the risk of testicular cancer, so I am not quite as happy about the sterilisation of men as of women. The choice really depends on the couple; if the man is happy to go through with the operation but his partner isn't, then let him have it; in our case, Colin could not come to terms with losing his fertility, while I looked forward to it. It was a decision that suited us both.

I find it regrettable that it's not easier to be sterilised on the National Health Service. After all, producing children – or, indeed, coping with the problems induced by unsatisfactory contraceptive methods – must cost the State far more than sterilising those who want to avoid pregnancy. I hope that one of the benefits of a market approach to medicine will be a realisation among policy-makers that a readily available, free sterilisation service would lead to financial savings.

Now that I have been sterilised, Colin and I can enjoy uninhibited sex at its best. I feel completely whole; sterilisation, if anything, enhanced my desire for sex because I was totally free from anxiety not only about pregnancy but also about unpleasant smells, flavours, and loss of sensation. If you have had all the children you want, or you don't want any at all, don't hesitate – get sterilised!

For some years after my sterilisation, knowing I couldn't get pregnant despite the fact that my body reacted as though I could, I took great pleasure in cheating Nature. Sometimes fucking has felt so intense that I have been convinced I would become pregnant; that feeling may be totally irrational, but it is quite delicious.

I have been told by women who really wanted children that sex is best of all when you are aiming for pregnancy – at least, while you're confident that you will get pregnant. I can believe that; your whole body and mind are totally in tune, everything working as intended. This is an experience I shall never have; but that's all right, I made my choice and I don't regret it.

12

The Other Half

The hardest part of living with Colin is coping with the fact that he is that strangest of life-forms, a male. Why can't a man be more like a woman? Professor Higgins's lament in *My Fair Lady* is the mirror image of my plea. Sometimes it seems more difficult to understand the human male than females of other species; he doesn't think, perceive, talk or act the way a female would. Males, in a word, are *weird*.

Sex differences and 'genderlects'

Human males and females followed divergent evolutionary paths way back in prehistory. Their roles in ensuring the survival of the human species were different. Women lived in gatherer groups with children and the elderly, nurturing each other, continually on the move as they collected food. Men – the hunters and scavengers – would leave the group and go off on adventures, killing wild animals and other men. The men could take risks because, individually, they were expendable: the children of the tribe depended on their mothers more than on the men, who provided a far smaller proportion of the food.

These complementary roles produced differences both in physiology and behaviour which persist to this day. Men developed metabolic systems designed to fuel heavy muscles for fast, demanding activity alternating with periods of inactivity. By contrast, women would have been active, if less strenuously, all day. Because of this, men have bigger livers, which act as fast-fuel stores, while women are designed to use their larger fat deposits. Men readily produce surges of adrenalin for running and fighting, while women remain on a more even metabolic level but have greater endurance.

Along with the physical differences, there are many psychological differences. Scientists are only recently beginning to discover the extent of these differences. They range from the superior ability of the male in visualising and manipulating three-dimensional forms, to the female's superior colour vision, her greater tendency to notice detail, and the earlier development of her verbal skills.

Many of these differences between the sexes seem quite small, and the range of variation between individual members of each sex is large; but taken together, they add up to a substantial and largely unacknowledged divergence between men and women. It is risky to make generalisations about the sexes, but I am going to take that risk despite the fact that the points I make will not fit all individuals. I realise that a general statement like 'men are larger and stronger than women' isn't true for a minority of large strong women or small weak men, but it is true of most people.

Gender – even biologically defined gender – is not totally fixed, nor are the boundaries between male and female completely distinct. Men have feminine traits, women masculine; there is a mix in all of us. Culture complicates the picture by defining some types of behaviour as suitable for one sex but not the other, and it can be very difficult to work out whether sex differences that emerge through the cultural distorting process are really innate, or learnt. Inevitably, this is a complex and controversial question, and the answers I offer can only be based on my own conclusions. Nobody can be sure of absolute truths in such an uncertain area.

The interaction between gender and culture produces differences in ways of speaking and use of language, and generates a great deal of misunderstanding. So great are the contrasts between men and women that sociolinguist Deborah Tannen writes of two separate 'genderlects', learnt in worlds so different that she comments, 'I had the feeling I was looking at two different species.'[1]

When I was a young adult in the late sixties and seventies, it was fashionable to minimise sex differences. Women – including me – were setting out to prove that they were competent in many areas of life that had been the sole province of men. But years of living in extreme circumstances with Colin have taught me that we are far more different than I had been willing to admit. We have a different pattern of strengths and weaknesses, different ways of viewing the world, different modes of perception, different reactions to similar circumstances. Recognising and coming to terms with these differences has been an essential part of adapting to living with a member of the opposite sex.

I used to imagine that the obvious differences between us were all that mattered. I couldn't deny our complementary genitalia: his cock and balls, my cunt, womb and ovaries. I couldn't ignore our different body shapes: my breasts, his broad shoulders, his greater height and weight. But I have become convinced that we think differently too, and recent scientific research supports my view.[2]

From the earliest days in the womb, a different pattern of hormones shapes the separate development of males and females throughout our lives. These hormones do not merely affect our bodies, they determine the way our minds function too. Male and female brains are actually wired up differently, and they continue to respond to a sex-specific mixture of hormones which influences our thinking, memory, moods, perception and reactions.

The underlying similarities between women's minds and ways of communicating means that we understand other women much more easily than men. Many things don't have to be said, they're obvious; and when we do talk, we can expect to understand each other. Men have a similar rapport between them. When pairs of men work together, they can manoeuvre the most awkward objects quietly and efficiently. In such situations, Colin and I start screaming at each other in no time at all. People of the same sex are better at predicting each other's reactions correctly; with men and women, it's more difficult. Even though Colin and I know each other more intimately than anyone else, misunderstandings are frequent.

The same words can mean completely different things to the two of us, or carry a totally different set of implications. When we talk about our thoughts and feelings, we anticipate reactions that we would get from another member of our own sex, not realising that the opposite sex will often respond differently. Even our body language has a sex-specific meaning; for example, women create trust and intimacy by looking straight at one another, while men avoid facing each other directly because they tend to interpret it as challenging, a hostile gesture.[3]

Acknowledging that we aren't as similar as we assume, and making efforts to check that we do understand each other, as far as we can, helps to bridge the gulf between the sexes. But the gulf always remains; inside the most committed of New Men there lurks a man's mind, and it's fundamentally different from a woman's.

Different sexes, different minds

The way I see it, Colin has only half a brain. I admit that his half-brain can be very sharp, a lot quicker, and often more logical than mine. But there is a whole area of feminine thought/emotion/intuition to which he has no access, and of which he has only second-hand knowledge.

The problem Colin has with me is that he thinks *I* have only half a brain. I just don't understand what he's talking about when he goes off enthusiastically into some of his masculine areas. I don't really see why swords, knives and other weapons should so fascinate him, but I recognise that these are the tools of the hunter and warrior, and are therefore fundamental to his nature.

When I get exasperated with him, I say to myself – and often as not, to him – what can I expect of someone who's only got half a brain? It's a continuing joke between us that began in my seaside landlady days during the mid-eighties. Living in a huge house only minutes from the sea, it seemed fitting that we should have a lodger. The local college found Ahmed for us, an enthusiastic Muslim teenager who had been sent to England by his father to learn about Western business methods. Every evening, as I cooked supper, Ahmed used to hang around the kitchen, telling me about the Koran and the Prophet Mohammed, whose word was Truth.

One night when we were eating, I asked Ahmed why women were never Mullahs, why the Imam had to be male, and why men dominated his culture so totally. He seemed nervous about answering, fiddling with his potatoes as though the answer lay buried on his plate. Finally, he found the courage to explain. According to the Koran, Ahmed told me, women are not capable of understanding religion, philosophy or mathematics. This is because they have only half a brain.

I nearly fell out of my chair with laughter – but then, to Ahmed's amazement, I agreed with him. 'Your Prophet was quite right,' I said, 'but he was a man, and he spoke from a man's perspective. From the woman's point of view, a man has only half a brain too.'

I picked up an orange and cut it in half to illustrate my point. Sliding the halves across one another so that they partially overlapped, I continued. 'This half represents the man's mind,' I said, 'and the other half, the woman's.

Where the halves meet, men and women understand each other readily; but where they don't, we are different. We may imagine that the part we don't understand doesn't exist, and we feel mystified by behaviour generated by that part. So some men see women as stupid and irrational, and women sometimes think men must be mad. It's because we don't recognise the half-brain we don't share.'

The Muslim culture is not unique in dismissing women's ability to think. It's not long since Christian societies held similar beliefs, and they still linger not too far beneath the surface. In Victorian times, and even in the early years of this century, it was generally accepted that if women were to exercise their minds in thinking about such matters as mathematics, their reproductive organs would wither. Women were designed by God (a male deity) to have babies and look after the home, not to think. Although such extreme sexist attitudes are now rare, vestiges remain in the still widespread belief that a woman's place is in the home and that mind-numbing housework is women's work.

Old beliefs take a long time to die. I have a cartoon in my kitchen showing a filthy sink full of dishes. The caption says, 'This is an equal-opportunity kitchen.' I still find myself doing far more than my share of the housework – but Colin justifies his attitude by pointing out that he does more than his fair share of building and shovelling. His body design is better suited to that sort of heavy work and I find it hard to argue when he points to the equal-opportunity chainsaw and the equal-opportunity concrete blocks! Though I don't recall him cleaning the lavatory when we lived in the city and there wasn't any construction or shovelling to be done.

Only a small minority of men actually share the housework equally, even when their partners go out to work for the same number of hours. Somehow it's nearly always the wife who has to cram the shopping into her lunch-hour and make the supper when she gets home. A 1985 survey of 6000 women revealed that 54 per cent of women working full-time and 77 per cent of those who worked part-time did all or most of the housework. Husbands were willing to do only the most onerous jobs. Many couples believe in theory in sharing housework; very few do so in practice.[4] Women all over the world work longer hours than men do. Maybe if the men took on a bit more of the load, they would find their wives less resentful and more eager to put energy into sex.

I have virtually given up fighting what I see as Colin's residual sexist attitudes. Perhaps I give in too easily, but I don't believe I am going to be able to change him so I have had to come to terms with his behaviour. I make allowances, but I tell him when something really bugs me.

Crucially, I have to make sure that he understands what I mean, and that I understand what he means, when we are trying to communicate. When dealing with half-brains, we can't assume it's obvious. In *Secrets About Men Every Woman Should Know*,[5] Barbara de Angelis explores ways in which some of these differences can affect relationships. She explains, for example, that men generally find it much more difficult than women to admit to being wrong, so it's hard for men to say sorry. They imagine they should always know what to do, and find it hard to ask for help. They find it difficult to cope with the intensity of women's emotions, and tend therefore to dismiss them; and they often express themselves sexually when they can't express themselves emotionally. When she wants a sympathetic cuddle, he's all too likely to offer a stiff cock.

I found that Ms de Angelis's book fitted my experience with Colin very well, even though there are some aspects of my behaviour that are more like her typical male, and Colin is sometimes more like her picture of women.

The challenge for both men and women is to cope with the fact that sometimes we seem like separate species. Women tend to talk more, rely more on feelings and intuition, on global impressions. We are more aware of what we don't know when information is incomplete, and that makes us more cautious in many of our judgements. Men, in general, see the world in black and white, whereas women operate with finely-differentiated shades of grey.

Women tend to see social relationships in terms of connection, as networks of equals aiming for intimacy and consensus, while men are more concerned with social hierarchies where they struggle to preserve independence and avoid failure. For women, talking is often primarily about interaction, togetherness; for men, it's exchanging information. Hence small talk – or twaddle, as Colin calls it: he long ago recognised my peculiarly female need for twaddle-breaks – is important to women, while many men see it as a waste of time.[6]

In recent years, many women have been trying to behave like men in order to gain advantage in a male-dominated society. Female power-dressing in the eighties revealed this approach clearly: the image of the female executive, with her broad-shouldered suit and svelte hips, was of a woman struggling to appear as near male as she could. She was fighting to climb the male hierarchical structure, and making herself more masculine in order to do it. I believe that rather than accepting male patterns that don't suit us or the natural world around us, we should use our feminine strengths to rebalance our culture so that female ways of seeing and working are respected.

More and bigger

The different patterns of male and female attitudes and perception affect our sex-lives both directly and indirectly. One common feature of the male world-view is that if something is good, more must be better. Men aren't usually as comfortable as women with concepts of balance and moderation. So they want more sex, bigger cocks, bulgier biceps; they tend to focus on plenty of seemingly uncomplicated sex rather than involved love relationships, and they don't always recognise the crucial interactions between the two.

Most men think about sex more constantly than women. They imagine they need more sex than they get, and because they believe they should be fucking all the time, they put pressure both on themselves and on women. Ask almost any man whether he gets enough sex, and he'll say no![7] Survey after survey reveals that the majority of married men feel sexually deprived. Like children at a party, continuing to stuff themselves with goodies even when they feel sick, they often try to grab more than they can manage. Probably the most obvious example of this aspect of male behaviour is the way many men abuse alcohol: a man is far more likely than a woman to drink himself into a stupor. Some men only know they've had enough when they've had too much.

Quantity is very important to men. This is tied up with the tremendous importance of male pride and display: they need to feel both dominant and admired. I believe that this is at the root of the common male tendency – displayed in differing degrees by both my long-term partners – to put women down. It makes them feel superior. And most men will try to dominate in the bedroom until women teach them that co-operation and sensitivity lead to greater pleasure.

The meaning of the male erection

Sexual potency is a crucial part of the masculine self-image. In male cultures – and especially among immature men – a ready erection is admired and envied. When the pre-human male stood up on his hind legs, his cock was exposed for all to see and compare. Because a man's sexual response is so obvious and so important for his ego, he's in trouble when he can't get it up. Most men are very afraid of that. Those who have experienced one or two episodes of erection failure can easily become impotent, for anxiety suppresses erection. Fear of failure is probably the most common single cause of failure.

Unfortunately, failure to achieve goals set for himself can be crippling for the male ego. This may go right back to the world of the primitive hunter, where failure could mean getting killed. It's certainly tied in very strongly with the male desire for power and his struggle for supremacy in hierarchical structures.

Men tend to be goal-orientated, they want to get to the point and appreciate the delights of the journey less than women. This makes it difficult for a man to solve the problem of erection failure; to do so requires that he stops concentrating on the goals of penetration and orgasm, and instead steps back to focus on pleasure and feeling. Men tend to rush into fucking, whereas women often prefer foreplay.

Ironically, a man with erection difficulties will be able to function more effectively in his uniquely male way if he can learn to behave more like a woman, appreciating the importance of emotion, communication, and the quality of the underlying relationship. Pleasure doesn't require a stiff cock; that comes as a by-product.

The male drive for success, and his problems with tolerating what he sees as failure, can add to the difficulty in solving sexual and relationship problems which require patience and compromise. He may try to avoid feeling he's failed by steering clear of risky situations or blaming the woman and refusing to consider how his attitudes contribute to joint problems.

Colin and I experienced this situation recently. After months when sex had been delightful for both of us, we ran into unexpected problems. He began to turn off when we were in the middle of making love and blame me for doing something wrong. He stopped, for instance, when I was really enjoying the sensation of his tongue on my clitoris, angry because I grimaced (he said), and that showed I had lost interest. I couldn't convince him that it wasn't true. Another time, he started pushing my head into an uncomfortable position when we were fucking and accused me of getting my hair in his face so he couldn't breathe. I was unaware of doing anything unusual.

Naturally, I found this very upsetting. I couldn't understand what was going on and I felt horribly rejected. After the pattern had been repeated a few times, with variations, I began to lose my desire for sex with him. I couldn't trust him not to pick on me when I was vulnerable. I didn't know why he had suddenly started to feel I was making so many mistakes when things had been progressing so well.

Eventually, he began to talk about it. He admitted that he was afraid he wasn't able to meet my expectations. He had been going through a stressful and depressing period in his work, and my demands on his prowess as a lover seemed to be increasing all the time, so he couldn't just relax and enjoy sex. The fact that I was writing about our sex-life added to the pressure: sex had become a public performance.

Pride had prevented him from telling me how he felt. So he protected himself by blaming me, making it seem that the failure was mine, not his. It wasn't easy for Colin to admit this to himself, let alone me. Once he did, we were able to deal with it. I reassured him that I didn't expect him to be a great sexual athlete all the time – how could I expect that when I'm unreliable too? – and he promised to tell me if he didn't really want sex *before* we got started, so I wouldn't put demands on him. He has found it difficult to acknowledge that he doesn't want sex all the time and that he can't always sustain an erection. That sort of admission doesn't do much for a man's macho self-image. It forces him to confront the disturbing knowledge that he's not as potent as he'd like to be.

Solving such problems demands humility, openness and communication without judgement. Colin, like most men, has difficulty with this. I was able to help when I told him honestly how hurt I felt, but then put my own sadness on one side so that I could encourage him to tell me about his feelings. We had to wait for a time when we were both calm; struggling to talk about these delicate matters when either of us is angry, depressed or frustrated achieves nothing.

Most men worry about their sexual performance. Many get anxious about whether they can achieve an erection, whether they can last long enough before coming and whether their cocks are big and powerful enough. Those who see sex as a performance find it difficult to lose themselves in pleasure.

Such attitudes are based on the assumption that technique is all-important. They reflect a male failure to recognise the importance of trust and emotion in female sexual responsiveness. Whilst sexual knowledge and skill in stimulating one's partner are valuable, they aren't enough if the emotional backdrop is wrong.

I have had lovers who seemed to do everything right, yet who left me cold; the worst were those who seemed like spectators. For these men, their own virtuoso performance was what mattered most; I was the object on which they proved their prowess. They seemed to think that if they stimulated the right parts in the correct manner for long enough, then I should come. If I didn't enjoy it or didn't respond, I must be frigid. The alternative explanation, for men who saw sex in this way, was that they failed to break through my defences because their sexual power was not sufficiently overwhelming. Predictably, macho-men prefer the former option.

Cock size

It's because of this performance/display orientation, coupled with the assumption that more is better, that men get so worried about cock size. The standard statement by 'experts' is that this is nothing to get hung up about. In *More Joy of Sex*, Alex Comfort wrote that 'Sex counselors who aren't, and don't wish to appear, unsympathetic, are just about fed up with answering anxious people's questions about penile size. We've spent years telling enquirers, correctly, that penile size is, functionally, wholly unimportant; . . . that the only difference between penises which are large and small when flaccid, a few rare conditions excepted, is that the large kind enlarge less on erection."[8]

I believe that this is misleading. The implication is that all cocks end up more or less the same size, which is untrue. I know from experience that penises, whether flaccid or erect, vary both in shape and size even more than other parts of the body. These variations definitely feel different to the woman and they produce different effects.

Having heard 'experts' frequently proclaim that cock size makes no difference to the woman's pleasure, I went to some trouble to find out whether other women agreed that it can matter. All those with fairly wide sexual experience did agree. Each experienced woman has her own picture of an ideal cock that fits her perfectly, and she can define that ideal in terms of shape and size. And while well-meaning counsellors may try hard to deny that reality, the prevalence of anxiety about cock size[9] reflects the fact that men know perfectly well that they aren't all the same, or anywhere near the same, in this respect.

Most women don't believe, as many men seem to, that bigger cocks are always better. For me, a whopper can be uncomfortable, especially in positions where penetration is deep; I have to be very well prepared to receive it, and if it fits too tightly I may not be able to tolerate it for long. At the other extreme, a tiny cock gets lost in a cunt that is not also tiny. I once had a man whose erect cock was scarcely larger than my thumb; it wasn't capable of stimulating anything as far as I was concerned.

Colin tells me that women also differ; some have great drive-in cunts, others are minute. Most, of course, are somewhere in the middle, like the majority of men. Like cocks, cunts vary from time to time, as the woman's level of arousal changes; and women who regularly exercise their cunt muscles by practising pulling in and pushing out, or learning the yoga method of isolating the column of muscles that runs down the front of the belly, can keep them taut and tight.

The point is that couples have to try to achieve a match between their sexual organs, and that may mean adapting styles of love-making to accommodate differences in anatomy. Great lovers come in all shapes and sizes; they are the people who know how to get the best out of what they've got. When I feel I'd like Colin's cock to be bigger, I do all I can to ensure that he is as aroused as possible before we start to fuck. The more excited he is, the more his cock grows: its size when erect is no more constant than it is when flaccid.

We also tend to fuck in ways which maximise the depth of penetration, because that's what I prefer. In general, these are positions where our bodies are at right angles to one another; if we're lying flat, one on top of the other, penetration tends to be shallower and usually less pleasurable for me.

One advantage of a small(ish) cock is that it's easier to suck. I remember trying to suck a seriously big one: I had to open my mouth so wide my jaws ached, and still I found it impossible to keep my teeth from scraping it. I had to adapt and limit my style to cope, licking rather than sucking. For anal intercourse, I think a big cock is a very definite disadvantage. On the other hand, a big cock can produce the most delicious sensation. I have found I can reach orgasm very quickly when I fuck with a man who has a particularly big one – so long as I'm completely ready for it – and have felt totally filled in the most satisfying way.

In general, the way to cope with a size mismatch is the same whether the man's cock is big or little: lots of love-making before fucking. If he's built like a horse, the woman has to be relaxed and very well lubricated to enjoy it. If he's on the small side, both partners need to get very turned on so that the woman is super-sensitive and the least touch is exciting. When I'm really desperate to fuck, Colin's cock feels massive. I doubt if it really is, but what does reality matter when the experience is wonderful?

While men can reach orgasm through fucking even when there is a size mismatch, the same isn't always true for women. It may be difficult to come without additional clitoral stimulation when the cock is too small to provide sufficient internal stimulation. One of my ex-lovers, whose cock was considerably smaller than average, understood this perfectly. Richard had perfected his oral and digital skills to such a degree that he was the acknowledged Don Juan of the university department, undisputed favourite among my sexually active women friends.

Of course, other facets of the relationship – trust, acceptance, the sense of being valued and valuing oneself – are far more important than cock size. Richard wasn't just a skilled lover, he was charming and sympathetic too, very good at making people feel relaxed and comfortable. He had social as well as sexual grace.

What matters most is the match between attitudes and personality, the way we treat each other, the depth of communication. I chose Colin for his personality; whatever the size of his cock, I would love him for his total self. This is what really determines the quality of our sex-life. If I cared only about the size and shape of his cock, I'd be better off with a dildo: I can't have a row with a dildo, it's always available when I want it and it's totally reliable.

Timing the fuck

As with cock size, many men imagine that the length of time they can fuck before they come is crucial to the woman's satisfaction. Seventy per cent of the men who contributed to Shere Hite's study of male sexuality[10] said they sometimes came to orgasm 'too soon' after penetration.

Many men don't seem to realise that prolonged fucking can get boring and uncomfortable for women. He can be heaving away like a demented carthorse while she runs through her shopping-list or works out the best way to redecorate the bathroom as she waits for the pumping to stop. I know – I've done it.

Older men generally require a longer period of stimulation before they come. For those who had hair-trigger tendencies in their youth, this can be a welcome improvement, but sometimes orgasm can get frustratingly elusive. It's usually better for such men to get more aroused before penetration, so that orgasm is not excessively delayed, unless the woman enjoys a really long fuck. Personally, I'm liable to get sore.

Colin and I often stop fucking after a while by mutual consent, sometimes changing to sucking or hand stimulation, sometimes stopping completely. We return to fucking later if we feel like it. As we get older, this is likely to happen more and more. Although he enjoys orgasm tremendously, he has discovered that he can sometimes enjoy sex without it, just as I can.

It doesn't make sense for men to try to draw out the length of time they can hold their erection without making sure their partners enjoy it. More is not necessarily better. I would hate to think that the man fucking me was deliberately thinking about something else in order to avoid coming too soon – I want him to be totally focused on the experience. Most sex therapists also warn men against doing mental arithmetic or otherwise distracting themselves: it doesn't work, and it doesn't make them better lovers.

However, premature ejaculation can be exceedingly frustrating for women, if the man doesn't do something to compensate for the short period of fucking. To produce maximum satisfaction for both partners, there's a happy medium for which we have to aim.

Premature ejaculation is, I'm told, a common problem, although precisely what 'premature' means can depend on your beliefs. I've only encountered it with two men, both of whom were highly stressed. My sexual relationship with each was very short-lived so I have had no experience of trying to cure it. There are well-researched methods for helping men to last longer, described in detail in books by sex therapists such as Masters and Johnson. Basically, these methods involve squeezing the penis, either at the base or just below the head, to delay ejaculation. If you want to learn to delay ejaculation, watch a sex-education video like Andrew Stanway's *The Lovers' Guide*: the section on sexual problems shows precisely what to do.

As with all sexual problems, dealing with the man's anxiety about his sexual competence is more important than the specific treatment technique. It's no coincidence that the two premature ejaculators I knew were tense, frenetic individuals who prided themselves on achievement. They were rushing for the finish in every aspect of their lives. Unfortunately, they missed out on a lot of pleasure along the way. They judged their own performance harshly too: having come too quickly (before penetration in one case, immediately after in the other), they both withdrew from me in shame. I was sad that they didn't linger, relax over a drink, and make love again until their erection returned. I suspect there wouldn't have been a problem if we had tried fucking a second time. But their sense of failure turned them off completely.

These men obviously hadn't taken the time to learn the First Rule of Bicycle Riding. They had ceased to focus on what they wanted – a good fuck. Had they shrugged off the initial difficulty and concentrated on pleasure, they would have had much more of it.

I wasn't much help, though: I was too naïve to know how to behave. If either of them were my lover now, I would do my best to prevent them from running away from the situation, and encourage them to talk about the way they felt – about me, about sex, and about our relationship. I'd spend time making gentle, undemanding love to them, helping them to relax. And if I were not willing to do this, I wouldn't share my bed with them. I was being selfish, trying to use them to assuage my frustration without considering their feelings.

Dr Andrew Stanway believes that 'premature ejaculation is a form of sex avoidance in many men, though they do not, of course, consciously realise it'.[11] If that is the case – and Dr Stanway has long experience of helping couples with sex problems – then reassurance, relaxation, cuddles and closeness are very important indeed for these men. Building trust in the relationship becomes crucial to solving the problem and increasing sexual satisfaction for both partners.

Learning about cocks

It took me years to learn how to relate to men sexually, to understand what pleased them – apart from access to my body. I used to be nervous; I didn't know what I should do, didn't know how to take an active role or how to help them feel comfortable. The possibility that men, too, might be anxious or shy didn't occur to me. Cocks scared me (apart from when they were well hidden inside me) because I didn't know how to handle them.

I first encountered an adult cock when I was nine. I met a flasher by the telephone box at the corner of the street where I lived, and told my parents, more in surprise than fear. They called the police, who asked for a drawing, which I provided without hesitation. I wondered why all the adults were so concerned – the man hadn't touched me, hadn't done me any harm. If any damage was done by that incident, it was because the message for me was that I should have been scared.

I *was* scared when I first saw an erect cock. My boyfriend and I were sitting on the back seat of a bus when he kissed me and unzipped his jeans. A horrible pink thing emerged. I couldn't imagine what I was supposed to do. For a long time, my relationship with cocks was very ambivalent; I realised that when they grew hard it was a sign of appreciation, but I saw them as threatening, demanding. Boys with erect cocks represented an unwelcome pressure on me.

I gradually came to understand that I was expected to handle the things. Nobody showed me what to do: boys seemed to think I should know, and that their cocks should delight me. They didn't. After a while, I discovered that boys seemed to like a firm grasp on the shaft of the cock, coupled with an up-and-down movement. But I couldn't maintain the strength of grip that seemed to be necessary. It's easier to apply that sort of force when you're approaching it from the owner's direction. It's more difficult for a woman, whose hands and arms are weaker, and who hasn't had cause to build up the appropriate muscles.

I came to feel something of a hopeless failure in relation to cocks. And lacking confidence so badly, it hasn't been easy to learn to approach Colin in the positive and forceful way that he sometimes wants. I still feel inexpert at doing hand-jobs, but I've come to terms with my limitations and no longer attempt to imitate the method that he uses – I just can't sustain it.

What I can do is caress and titillate his cock with my hands. This works better when I use a lubricant, but KY jelly is not ideal because it tastes nasty. If I should want to suck his cock afterwards I don't want it to have an unpleasant flavour. So I have invented perfumed cock oil, made from harmless aphrodisiac ingredients which smell and taste delightful.

Otherwise, I use natural lubricant from the tip of his cock – the delicious pre-ejaculate juice that he starts to produce when he's turned on. I squeeze hard at the base of his cock and slide my hand up to the tip to encourage the emergence of slippery drops of fluid. I love the flavour and I'm convinced it has aphrodisiac properties!

When my hands glide easily over the shaft of his cock, I stroke and smooth it and rub my palm over the tip. He likes me to hold the shaft as firmly as I can, moving the skin over the engorged cylinder of flesh beneath. I haven't tried doing exercises to increase the strength of my grip – if I were really dedicated, I suppose I should practise by squeezing tennis balls! It's important that I don't scratch – I have to be aware of my fingernails, making sure that only the fleshy pads of my fingers are in contact with his cock.

I work my way up to the most sensitive, most highly reactive parts: especially just below the tip (the frenum) on the side facing away from his body. Colin drew me a diagram to show me precisely where the sensation is most arousing; it's on the underside of the ridge around the head. Fingerwork on this area produces the best responses; he enjoys it most when I hold the skin back with one hand near the base of his cock and rub delicately with the fingers and palm of the other hand, over and around the head, particularly where it joins the shaft.

I have tried to describe some of what I do with Colin, but it won't be appropriate for all men. Sensitivity and preferences vary widely, and women need to persuade their partners to show them what they like best. Colin is circumcised; uncircumcised men are often more sensitive and may prefer a very delicate touch around the head of the cock. Each woman must let her man guide her, help her learn what feels most exquisite to him. We all need gentle instruction – nobody can guess right all the time, and no man should expect his partner to know intuitively what best pleases him.

Sucking

While it excites and delights me when hand-work turns Colin on, I find sucking more rewarding and more enjoyable. This, too, was something I had found difficult. When a man (who presumably had no inkling of just how innocent I was at the time) pushed my head down on to his cock, expecting me to know what to do, I had little idea. As so often before, I felt inadequate and nervous. And when I was faced with an unwashed cock, I felt sick.

Unlike other men, who insisted that I should suck their cocks without telling me how to do it, Colin explained what he enjoyed so that I was able to learn. Once I knew what I was doing, I came to enjoy it too.

Most men tremendously enjoy having their cocks sucked, although only about forty per cent are always, or usually, able to reach orgasm this way. But a disturbingly large proportion of Shere Hite's sample said that women weren't good at it, or that they felt women didn't like doing it.[12]

I think of cock-sucking as an expression of adoration. I see Colin's cock as precious, desirable, amazing. I want to suffuse his whole person with delight by communicating my feelings through his cock, and I use that most sensitive and adaptable part of my body, my tongue, to achieve the effect I'm after. I do it best when I'm kneeling between his legs while he lies on his back. In the 69 position, my repertoire is limited, I can't reach the sensitive areas comfortably, and I'm easily distracted by what he's doing to me. Virtuoso cock-sucking has to be a solo performance.

Sucking is actually an inappropriate word for what I do, but the proper word, fellatio, seems too formal, almost medical. A sucking action doesn't produce particularly good sensations and I'll use it only rarely, to create a contrast, or to help firm up his erection. Predominantly, I lick firmly and rapidly with the tip of my tongue. Holding the end of his cock in my mouth (and taking care to avoid getting my teeth on it), I concentrate on the underside of the ridge under the tip, flicking and rubbing with my tongue in much the same way as he might titillate my clitoris if he were sucking me.

This area, the frenum, reacts in a very similar way to the clitoris. It's essentially the male version of the same organ, situated at the top of the shaft, which is a close parallel of the female vulva. And as with the clitoris, the more stimulation the frenum gets, the more aroused the man becomes; though sometimes, for some men, direct stimulation can be unbearably intense, just as direct clitoral stimulation can become too intense for women.

Sometimes I knead his cock with the fingers of one hand

and titillate the tip with my tongue, giving little quick butterfly flicks to the most sensitive point. Then I take the whole thing in my mouth, bringing my head down as far as possible but keeping my chin up like a sword-swallower. I push down till I feel the tip at the back of my throat; if I relax enough I can usually – though not always – avoid gagging. I can't do much of it, but Colin gets very excited when his cock goes this deep.

I withdraw my head then, pulling back so that just the tip of his cock remains in my mouth, working round the sensitive edge of the head with my lips while my tongue explores the central eye from which delicious drops of juice emerge. With my hands I milk his cock, fondle and gently squeeze his balls, or hold the shaft tightly at the base so that it's maximally engorged and sensitive.

I get turned on by doing all this, turned on by his moans of delight, by his unique flavour, by the intimate contact. In fact, sucking and kissing his cock feels much more intimate, more personal, than fucking. Maybe because I don't lose myself in what's happening, I am hyper-aware of Colin as a whole person. I am demonstrating my love for him, not just getting very horny through what's happening to me. It's more of a mental turn-on.

As my excitement grows, I'll stroke my erect nipples against his thighs, fantasise about the sensations that he'll create in me, about the feel of this cock that's now so big, so hard, the embodiment of lust. I know that he'll fuck with tremendous enthusiasm when I've sucked his cock enough; he will be truly ready for it.

With young men and new lovers, it wasn't usually necessary to work on them so that they could give back all I wanted. They were enthusiastic anyway. But after decades with me, Colin needs foreplay as much as I do. It's a mutual delight, one that takes us higher than we ever realised we could get.

Sucking is the perfect way to arouse a man who feels a bit down, tired, or neglected. Colin loves to be woken by the sensation of my lips on his cock in the morning. It's a gift that tells him he's important and desirable. There's no demand, no pressure, just pure delight. If he's having difficulty getting it up, sucking will often gently solve the problem; if he's unsure about whether he has the energy for sex, sucking will usually give it to him. If Colin needs, for whatever reason, to receive love rather than to give it, or if I don't want to fuck, sucking him to orgasm is the greatest demonstration of love I can offer.

Usually Colin prefers not to come in my mouth, but if he does, I swallow it. Were I a man, I'd feel rejected if my lover spat out my come or dashed off to rinse her mouth out. Predictably, the majority of men want a woman to swallow if they come in her mouth.[13] Colin's spunk tastes lovely, but I have known other men whose come was bitter. The flavour seems less pleasant if the man hasn't had an orgasm for some time. The only problem for me is the sheer length of time it takes to suck Colin to orgasm – my tongue muscles tire and my cheeks begin to ache. Maybe the answer is more practice! I'm sure he would gladly co-operate.

Stimulating the prostate

There's one other trick that can enhance a man's excitement, a trick familiar to gay men but less well known among heterosexuals: stimulating his prostate. I do this by carefully inserting a well-lubricated finger (the nail short and smooth) into his anus and reaching in to stroke a small round organ which I can feel through the front of his rectum.

This is something I had heard of many times, but failed to do successfully. I can't really have been trying; like most people, I'm not too comfortable with exploring anyone's anus, even Colin's. Two things made me get serious: first, the fact that I write about sex, so I'm supposed to know about such things; second, the realisation that if this was a way to create wonderful sensations for Colin, I wanted to know about it.

I searched for Colin's prostate several times before I found it. It seemed unexpectedly deep, as deep as I could reach with the tip of my longest finger. But when I did finally locate it, I was able to produce sensations that Colin had never experienced before. 'I can feel it all the way to the tip of my cock,' he panted. 'It keeps me right on the edge . . . right on the edge . . .' I believe that most men come rapidly with prostate stimulation; Colin doesn't come easily whatever happens, however much he enjoys it. I can't complain: I'm just the same, I don't come easily either.

Sexy pictures

I am not the same, though, in the sort of things that turn me on. For Colin – like most men – visual stimulation is very potent. Watching sexy videos, or looking at anything sexy, turns him on far more than it does me. He likes to keep the lights on so that he can see me when we're making love; looking at my body, and especially my cunt, is exciting to him.

I used to feel silly, lying with my legs spread in front of him. I couldn't imagine how he could find my cunt beautiful or why he should want to take photographs of it. But now I understand that he really enjoys looking at me, looking closely at my sexual organs and watching the way they change with arousal, why should I refuse?

Male delight in looking at women – pictures of naked women, women masturbating, women with their legs wide apart, women having sex – is obvious. Men – both gay and straight – spend millions on sexy-picture magazines, many enjoy porno films and videos, strip-shows, peepshows and revealing underwear. Only 17 per cent of Shere Hite's sample denied that they looked at pornography.

Few women keep erotic picture-books under their beds – though they do enjoy reading romantic, sensual, and erotic writing. For men, it seems to me, sexual desire is more linked with the tangible, with things revealed, whereas for women, the erotic is more hidden. Blatant sexual symbols interest men far more than women.

Many women feel threatened by the male desire to look at sexual images. I don't worry about what Colin does or sees, but I am aware that I feel uncomfortable with some of these images of women. I tend to compare myself with the pneumatic models in the videos as they writhe in simulated excitement; they seem alien, unreal. Is this super-sexy behaviour? It makes me seem dull and plain. I can't easily empathise with these exaggeratedly female creatures; my body is less curvaceous, my responses are less dramatic.

Watching *The Lovers' Video* with a woman friend, I discovered that she felt precisely the same way as I did. Every woman in the video had breasts larger and rounder than ours, every one was half our age. Sex videos, like fashion magazines, promote images that ordinary people can't match; real women are nowhere in the fantasy sex-symbol stakes. It is unjust that the media can portray ugly men as sexy – just think of Jack Nicholson – while women must conform to the cultural stereotype. No wonder women get angry! The cardboard-cut-out men are strange too: unfeeling, cocks with people attached. Women prefer a story, complete with emotion and desire. Sexual action isn't attractive unless we're ready for it.

Stiff cocks and spread-eagled women mean different things for each sex. To men, stiff cocks are always associated with pleasure; if the pleasure isn't there, the erection won't be there either. But a woman can look sexy to a man when she feels no desire at all; she can be raped. To an unaroused woman, a stiff cock can be threatening. It suggests pain, not pleasure. When a woman who doesn't want sex lies with legs wide apart, she invites painful intrusion. Both images can be deeply disturbing to women.

I don't want to deprive Colin of pleasure, nor would I suggest that sexy pictures should not be available. If there were no sexual censorship, I believe that more sensuous, imaginative material would be produced as the art of creating erotica became more sophisticated. I wish film-makers would consider the woman's point of view more often – but women have to be open about what they want, and make their voices heard. Are any women's groups making erotic heterosexual videos?

There are erotic videos that we both enjoy. Slowly, we're building up our own collection. Some are films where the courtship sequences enhance our sexy mood: *The Witches of Eastwood* is one. (I *love* Jack Nicholson – ugly and flabby though he may be!) Others are videos with little story and a lot of sexual action. We pick something that suits our mood and cuddle up on the sofa to enjoy it together. I acknowledge his desire for the visual turn-on; he accepts my need for a slow build-up. Our tastes may differ but there's enough common ground to find things we both enjoy.

And that's the secret: to discover how male and female can match their desires to find complementary delights. This means acknowledging our differences, telling each other about ourselves and our feelings without embarrassment, adapting our behaviour so that we can go further together into new realms of closeness, sensuality and pleasure. Male and female, the two halves of the human race, can become whole together. But it takes a lot of understanding on both sides.

13

Loving and Fighting

I wasn't just naïve about sex when I first married, I was naïve about all aspects of relationship dynamics. The fact that Bob and I never fought was a source of pride to me; I believed this showed we were totally compatible, our relationship completely harmonious, our choice of each other absolutely correct. How far that was from the truth! It should have been taken as a serious warning. How we deluded ourselves!

With hindsight, experience, and a vast increase in self-knowledge, it all makes sense now. Afraid of losing the security of my relationship, feeling too weak in myself to cope unsupported, I didn't dare question life with Bob. Instead, I set about creating a relationship that seemed above question: our life of apparently perfect harmony.

We agreed on everything. We had the same taste in everything. This was good taste. (What an arrogant pair we were!) I made sure of this by expressing an opinion rarely, speaking *after* Bob when I spoke at all, and always, but always, seeing his point of view. Even when it was a negative view of me.

Poor grey thing that I was, I had shelved my individuality, sacrificing myself for a fragile illusion of security within this relationship. I had relegated myself to non-personhood; it seemed safer. No wonder I became depressed! No wonder

I was lonely – as a non-person, I had no friends. Nobody noticed me. I was Bob's woman, not me.

How things have changed in twenty years! Colin and I fight; we've been fighting for years. We have heated discussions, fierce arguments over more or less rational things; sometimes we're physically vicious with one another. Fortunately our style of fighting is predominantly verbal, but it can be very painful. Words can cut deep; bruises are usually superficial.

In a way, I wish we didn't fight; I catch myself longing for that mirage of perfect harmony. But I understand now that we must both retain our individuality and integrity, and sometimes we have to fight for them. It is essential that we remain distinct people within our relationship, or paradoxically we will lose the love that we nurture between us. Sometimes we infuriate each other and lash out irrationally at one another, but that doesn't prevent us from loving each other. It's part of the whole relationship. As the song says, 'Love hurts', and that pain is necessary. It's part of being fully alive. An intimate relationship is all or nothing.

But fights can be frightening, and not only because there may be an implicit threat of violence. Even if we are sufficiently socialised not to damage each other physically, we do hurt each other and we fear the yawning gulf that opens up between us. When you fight within a close relationship, you are alone.

Why people fight

Sometimes we fight about rational issues, because of disagreements in the way we see the world and how we should deal with particular matters. More often, we fight because of pent-up emotional tensions: usually because we feel trapped, frustrated or powerless. Through fighting, we vent our frustrations and seek a new power balance. By raising the emotional temperature, we try to impress the other person with the intensity of our feelings in such a way that they cannot be sidestepped or ignored.

Often, the real frustrations that underlie our anger are hidden behind apparently rational justifications. We may not know what we are really fighting about: the anger surges up from inside, producing inappropriate behaviour and actions that we later regret.

Anger is frequently misdirected. We may fight with those closest to us when the real cause lies outside the relationship. Among many species of animals, when one is forced to submit to a stronger member of the group, he or she will attack another who ranks lower in the group hierarchy. So it is among humans; the person who is humiliated at work is liable to turn on his partner in the relative safety of their home.

We may think we are fighting about one thing when in fact we feel angry about something entirely different, something we feel unable to acknowledge. We may be completely unaware of what is making us angry, especially if we repress our feelings because we are ashamed of them. For example, if I feel angry with Colin because he forgets things that are important to me, I might suppress that feeling because I see my own reaction as unreasonable. Emotions are often neither reasonable nor socially acceptable, but they are nevertheless powerful. So my anger would be displaced and I would attack him about something different. Far from solving the problem, denying feelings leads to conflict that is more difficult to resolve because its roots are not understood.

Lack of commitment to the relationship is one factor associated with aggression; depression and alcohol problems are others. All these act as disinhibitors, allowing irritation to flare into conflict by reducing the strength of the taboos that prevent us from fighting. Aggression, depression and alcoholism often have the same underlying causes, which are likely to contribute to the lack of commitment that leads one or both partners to feel the relationship is not sufficiently valuable to restrain the urge to attack.

For some people – particularly men – conflict is attractive

in itself. It produces excitement, exhilaration, a rush of adrenalin; and humans can become addicted to this. People who feel this way and also value their relationships have to learn to resist the temptation to feed their addiction by fighting with an unwilling participant; instead, they need to find a dangerous hobby like riding a fast bike, going bungy jumping, or joining Greenpeace or Earth First! in direct action to defend the environment.

Sex and aggression

Sex and aggression are intimately linked. I don't mean that aggression is inherent in sexual behaviour – that mixture is abhorrent to me, although I recognise that some people find it exciting – but that the physiological systems that drive our sexuality can also fuel aggression. The link goes right back to the design of our brains and hormone systems. When I was a psychopharmacologist, I saw the link clearly in my own research. I was working with a drug (para-chloro-phenylalanine or PCPA) that depletes the brain of one particular neurohormone, serotonin; this produces a simultaneous increase in sex drive and aggression. Rats who have been given PCPA get very irritable, very randy, and have difficulty sleeping. If they have access to females, male rats will copulate night and day; caged with other males, they fight.

The human brain is basically the same as a rat's. We have the same neurohormones, linked in similar ways, controlling the same types of behaviour. The same brain systems control sex, aggression, and sleep in humans.

These interconnected systems do not have interchangeable effects. Suppressed lust breeds conflict; suppressed anger kills love. To nurture lasting sexual desire within a relationship, we have to learn to express both lust and anger when we feel them, and deal with these strong emotional forces before they distort and become damaging.

When our sex life is satisfying, we sleep better and we're less aggressive. But when we're deprived of sleep or sex, we're liable to become irritable. And irritable people pick fights. The sixties cliché, make love not war, was based on biological reality.

When Colin and I fight too much, the solution often lies in reviving our sex life. However, there is a problem. The last thing I want is to fuck with someone with whom I've been having a row. I don't fancy him when he's being foul to me. I don't trust him enough to relax with him. I don't feel sexy when I feel battered.

I presume people who say 'You're so sexy when you're angry', and for whom fighting can blend into fucking, do exist; I hear about them often enough. Romantic fiction is full of such characters: women who melt into the hero's arms despite the insults he was flinging moments earlier, passionate rage that turns into equally passionate love. I've never experienced this, and I've yet to talk to someone who has. Play-fights are one thing; you can wrestle and tumble around the room and end up in a tight embrace. But real fights cause too much emotional bruising for an instant turnaround to be possible.

Nevertheless, a turnaround there must be. And when you are able to touch each other, to embrace and caress again, the pain of the fight will be soothed away. It's quite likely that the closeness achieved afterwards was what was needed all along.

But it's not a good idea to submit to sex because you want the fighting to stop. It doesn't work. I've done that, allowed Colin to make love to me when I felt washed out and feeble in the aftermath of a row. Still hurting emotionally, I wasn't able to respond and I ended up more miserable than ever. He was trying to be kind to me, to demonstrate that he loved me, but I felt victimised. I have to work at staying in touch with my own feelings and not passively seek to placate him by allowing him sexual release at my expense.

The answer is to take a slightly longer-term view. While lack of sexual contact might well have been one of the factors that precipitated the fight and it would be helpful if we could relate sexually, we have to wait till we're *both* ready. Part of the pattern that leads to conflict between us is that he wishes I would want sex as often as he does. He starts feeling resentful and rejected while I begin feeling pressured. This makes the problem worse because feeling pressured to have sex when I feel no desire turns me off even more. In fact, sex therapists recognise pressure from a partner as one of the most important factors contributing to loss of sexual desire.[1]

Sometimes we can build bridges through non-sexual physical contact. The healing power of touch is the subject of Chapter 15.

Reasons for rows: sex, money and children

Whatever the underlying emotional problem that makes us prone to initiate fights, the most common triggers are sex, money and children, not necessarily in that order. Lack of sex and lack of money make us feel undervalued. Desires build up, only to be frustrated. Often, features that seemed particularly attractive in the early stages of a relationship – like Colin's sexiness and generosity – can become sources of tension later. Colin can't be spontaneous with money when we don't have enough, and his high sex drive becomes a problem when mine doesn't match it.

Disagreements about children can lead to the most furious arguments because children are so precious. Parents will go to extraordinary lengths to defend their children. If they see each other as threats to the children's future happiness, they may stop at nothing. When each individual has a different view about bringing up children, the potential for conflict is enormous. Many conflicting attitudes may remain submerged for years, emerging only in the presence of children. This pattern is particularly common in cross-cultural marriages, where conflict over different ways of rearing children can become extreme, and very difficult to manage.

All you can do is discuss the issues, for reasons for disagreement are amenable to reasoned discussion. Listen to each other's views and negotiate. Probably, neither of you is completely right. Your attitudes were formed by the previous generation; children have to learn to cope with the future, whatever that may entail. The only thing that's certain is that it won't be the same as the past. In the end, the most important thing is that parents *care*: children usually survive their parents' mistakes, if there's enough love.

Children can also become the focus for problems within the relationship, like the feeling that your partner doesn't have enough time for you. The father, in particular, may feel left out when his partner seems obsessed by the children; many feel jealous, but can't readily admit it.[2] Both parents have to learn to give time to each other, time spent alone, nurturing their own relationship. When children are included in a warm, loving environment, they don't need access to their parents all the time. And they ultimately benefit when their parents give each other sufficient attention because their parents' relationship is the example that will teach them how to form good relationships when they grow up.

Pain, passion and change

There are those who seek perfect harmony in intimate relationships that are free from pain. I believe that's a dangerous illusion: pain always accompanies love and intimacy at some time during the life of a relationship. If it's a short-term relationship and it's wonderful, the pain comes when you part; if it goes on for years, the pain comes in dollops at irregular intervals. Sometimes it occurs frequently when you're going through periods of difficulty, change and adjustment, sometimes more rarely when you're sailing along. But passionate relationships always bring pain.

We learn from painful experiences. They force us to

develop. As we develop, we become stronger. I'm not advocating masochism, just realism: pain makes us grow up. Pain can also stimulate creativity; after the death of a much-loved cat (remarkably painless love, terribly painful grief), I began to write poetry. Pain can open up paths within our minds that might otherwise remain closed.

Most of the time, we're so busy avoiding painful experiences that we fail to recognise the benefits they can bring. The most effective therapeutic processes I've experienced have usually been painful. I've spent many sessions with Charleen exploring the pain of living with Colin. She encouraged me to relive the pain in all its depth, to feel it so totally that I could understand its full meaning and learn how to move forward and leave it behind.

I experience emotional pain as physical pain: a lump in the diaphragm, a blockage in the throat that makes it difficult to talk or swallow, a tightness round the head, migraine. Others experience it in the form of digestive problems, angina, skin disorders, persistent infections. If you don't admit you feel pain emotionally, your body is liable to make you feel it by producing symptoms of illness. Emotional pain can kill, but it has an important function: it forces us to change, to find better ways to live.

But change itself can be painful, scary, disturbing at the very least. Learning to be honest about things that bother me has been particularly difficult. I tend to be afraid of facing the consequences of admitting to some of my feelings. I'm afraid of rejection, of hurting Colin, of being hurt in return. Every time I confront this situation, I flounder, trying to think of ways to deal with it that won't hurt.

When I'm being sensible, I remember to apply the First Rule of Bicycle Riding. That's the best way I know to minimise the risk of unnecessary pain. Focus on what you want and go for that rather than getting angry or unhappy about what you don't want. Of course, if your emotions are driving you to fight because you're in pain, such knowledge tends to disappear into inaccessible recesses of the mind.

But things aren't always that desperate, especially if you attend to problems before they fester.

In theory, it's possible to head off confrontation every time and still be true to oneself. If I were totally perceptive, totally sure of myself, if I were never nasty or careless or demanding, I might be like one of those saintly people with whom it's almost impossible to be aggressive. But pacifists and saints do get slaughtered, and for most of us a life without quarrels is simply impossible.

At times, I really want to express my anger and aggression directly to Colin. Brought up in a household where anger was rarely expressed, where temper was taboo and I was punished for attacking my sister (they didn't know how much she deserved it!) I grew up afraid of anger. Recently, I've been able to tell Colin when I feel anger – and sometimes, I back up my words with action. One evening, I picked up a tin tea-tray and banged it on his head. What a noise it made! It was wonderful! I didn't really hurt him, but I was able to express my feelings as forcefully as I felt them, and I felt much better for it. After several loud bangs, we both ended up laughing.

Play-fights, where we don't bruise or damage each other, are a safe way of being honest without hurting one another. They help us to get anger out of our systems so that we can talk in a more relaxed way. We have soft balls to hurl at each other; we wrestle but we don't hit each other – or at least, Colin doesn't hit me! When we play badminton, we fairly smash the shuttlecock over the net, each intent on thrashing the other. The physical and symbolic action helps us feel better; we don't want to cause real pain, merely to express pent-up aggression unequivocally. By getting these feelings out of our systems harmlessly, we are able to avoid serious, damaging fights.

Anger is often a response to emotional pain. Sometimes when I bring up distressing issues, I don't feel angry at first; I just hurt inside without really knowing why. Anger comes later, when I begin to see how the pain originated. I've learnt to stay with emotional pain, not for the sake of suffering as a helpless victim, but to explore it in the hope of discovering its meaning.

One technique, through which Charleen guided me, is to tune into the precise location of the pain. It might be a lump in the throat, a sensation like a tight band around my head, or a sickness in the belly. Then I use my imagination to exaggerate it. As I sit there hurting and shaking, understanding seeps into my mind: I remember, perhaps, when I felt like this as a child; when I needed comfort and never got it; when I suffered and the emotional wound didn't heal completely. I realise how present events trigger off buried memories and I'll relive the past to heal the old cause and find ways to cope with current experiences more effectively.

This process sets off a whole chain of events and a lot of talking with Colin, when I'm able to explain how I feel and why I react the way I do. Then he understands too, and acts with more compassion. When we both know what's going on, the power of the situation to hurt gradually diminishes. For example, I react very badly when Colin behaves like a schoolmaster to me. With Charleen's help, I recalled my first schoolmaster, who used to slap my legs and rap me over the knuckles with a ruler when I had problems learning to read. Predictably, my problems persisted until I changed schools and had a teacher who didn't hit me. Then, suddenly, I became the best reader in the class. I realised that Colin reminded me of that bullying teacher, and I was reliving the fear and misery I'd felt in my first years at school.

Understanding this, I was able to find support for that hurt child in the more mature parts of my personality: the gentle, nurturing, maternal side of myself. I ceased to be impatient with the sense of panic that wells up from the depths; instead, I learnt to be kinder to myself and to explain to Colin, from my adult perspective, why he should think before he shouts if he believes I'm making mistakes.

As time goes on, I'm slowly becoming less delicate, better able to cope with tribulations, better able to react appropriately as the adult I now am, rather than the hurt child I used to be. Discovering the emotional basis of these reactions has made them less intense, easier to handle, and easier to explain.

There are no quick answers to emotional reactions that are tied to events in the past. Merely finding out that I feel the way I do because of something that happened when I was a child is not enough to change my feelings. No theoretical explanation can make sufficient emotional sense to change the way I feel without experiencing those journeys through past pain.

Colin is the same. Some events trigger off apparently excessive reactions because they cue painful memories from his past. Often, the memories aren't readily accessible; they filter through gradually, sometimes coming back in unexpected flashes. But when they do surface and he's able to relive them and share them with me, they lose their power to damage our relationship.

We both need emotional support when we're dealing with the strong feelings that linger in memories of rejection or oppression. Reason isn't enough: we need comfort, cherishing, the love we missed at the time. These aren't rational processes and there's little point in trying to work through them at a rational level. We have to allow ourselves to feel whatever we need to feel, and to feel it together. I need to cuddle close to Colin at such times to know that however unloved I felt then, I am loved now. Having him there to hold me helps me recover. And as we work through this process, the bonds between us grow stronger and our relationship becomes deeper, fuller, more constructive.

It is important to realise that we are not dealing with right or wrong. Believing a thing is wrong – especially something we feel – is unhelpful. There's a part of me, as there is in all of us, that does judge in those terms; but judging, and especially condemning, just drives real feelings underground where they cause more damage. We have to stay with what is, and, to a lesser degree, what was, not what we believe ought to be.

We can't expect to agree all the time, and neither one of us knows best. A couple is made up of two different individuals, and if our differences are not acknowledged, full acceptance of each other will not be possible. We have different priorities, different interests, we see things differently. He's a man, after all, and I'm a woman. So we may agree to disagree, knowing where the other person stands, but recognising that we don't both stand in the same place. Coming to terms with this means that we first accept ourselves. We may adapt our behaviour in order to live peacefully with a partner, but there have to be limits: we cannot afford to sacrifice personal integrity for the sake of a quiet life.

I'll consciously compromise in my actions when compromise is of little consequence to me. For example, I don't tend to wear jewellery at home, although I like it, because Colin has told me he hates it. When I go out on my own I'll indulge my delight in intricate shiny things by wearing whatever I wish. It's a small enough sacrifice to be insignificant, but it's one I make because we have talked about it and know our respective positions.

When we cannot accommodate differences, we face recurring conflict over the same issues. Most people are prepared to accept a certain amount of conflict if the relationship as a whole is valuable. It's when conflict recurs so often, or becomes so violent that damage spreads to the rest of the partnership, that change becomes essential.

Physical and emotional violence

Most couples fight with words; when one attacks, the other is likely to respond in kind. Verbal conflict tends to fall into habitual routines: the same accusations are rehearsed repeatedly, producing the same responses again and again. Conflict can also take the form of sulking, withdrawal and silence; this too is communication. These are emotional weapons which we use to express rejection of the other person. Physical violence, often seen as the worst manifestation of conflict, is just another form of expression of discontent within the relationship. Fights tend to become ritualised, with each partner taking a predictable role. These rituals are symptoms of persistent unresolved problems.

About a third of married and cohabiting women report experiencing physical aggression on at least one occasion during their relationship.[3] Verbal aggression is more common than physical violence; 16 per cent of American couples report this type of violence at least once a year. The more often women are exposed to verbal attacks, the less they are able to view the relationship in a positive light. One woman quoted in a study of marital violence[4] said, 'Bruises, cuts et cetera heal within a short time. When you listen to someone tell you how rotten you are and how nobody wants you day after day, you begin to believe it.' Emotional violence can be very painful, chipping away at your belief in yourself.

But backing down in an attempt to keep the peace and avoid conflict is equally likely to damage belief in yourself. When I feel something strongly, or when Colin does, neither of us may feel able to back down, compromise, or eliminate the source of the difficulty by pretending it doesn't exist. I have to say, 'That's how I am: that's how I feel, that's what I believe: take it or leave it'; and he'll just have to accept that and find a way to cope. If I deny my feelings, I risk turning myself into a shadow and losing my integrity, becoming depressed as unexpressed anger eats away at me. Inevitably, I lose interest in sex.

In my experience, conflict is always painful. The pain can be both physical and emotional. Very rarely – and not recently – our fights have led to bruises. I would refuse to live with any man if the relationship involved repeated physical violence, for men are stronger than women and that degree of suffering would be unacceptable to me. It's a pattern of interaction where women are almost always the losers.

However, male violence is, to some extent, controllable. I have been able to prevent men from injuring or raping me, although I don't imagine I'd always succeed. I stop them by confronting them with their behaviour, coolly and firmly telling them it's not going to help; I manage to keep my head when I'm really at risk because I know that fighting back, with emotional or other weapons, can increase the hazard, escalate the conflict. So I aim to reduce the emotional temperature.

This strategy does work. Colin's previous wives (there are two; I know and love them both) have scars from injuries inflicted by him; he too has scars. However, I will not take on an unequal fight and I would not risk smashing a heavy pot over his head or throw scalding spaghetti at him straight from the pan, as his other wives have done. Knowing he is much stronger than I, I do not provoke violence by behaving violently towards him. Through experience, I've learnt to recognise the limits of his self-control and I don't push him beyond them.

There have been times when I've been very aware of potential aggression in him, and that scares me. Fighting with Colin is always frightening, even though he doesn't hit me. I would prefer not to have to go through with it. There have been occasions when I've found our arguments exhilarating; some of our editorial discussions over books have been really stimulating, heated without being threatening; but that only happens when I feel very sure of my ground and I'm not personally under attack. Most of our serious arguments are ugly, nasty, brutal, though thankfully short affairs, with me or both of us ending up in tears.

What a crazy sequence it is! When we row, we usually lose the best part of a day and at least one night's sleep. We feel ill and miserable. I will be left with a dreadful headache that may take a couple of days to clear; we'll fall behind with our work. And at the end of it all, we will have discovered that our feelings *are* important and should have been communicated openly and clearly in the first place. Why don't we understand that, and so avoid these rows, after nineteen years together?

Fearful of the pain and rejection that accompanies rows, many people do their best to avoid them. If your partner seems insistent on some arrangement that doesn't suit you, you may say to yourself, it's not worth risking a row by bringing up this or that; better to try to live with it. We all have to make judgements about whether to confront or not, and there are times when it makes more sense to accept minor inconvenience or irritation than to fight it. It may be possible to find a way round disagreements and avoid head-on confrontation. This is often the best strategy for peaceful co-existence. But we have to be very careful about these judgements. When we feel we're putting up with too much, the fight happens, in one form or another, whether we like it or not.

Colin and I don't fight as much as we used to and we're able to make peace more easily and more quickly because we understand ourselves and the process better. But we can be terribly forgetful of the things that really matter in our relationship, even though we love each other, even though we hate to hurt each other. We may try to change, to avoid behaving in ways that annoy the other, but slip back into old habits when we're under stress. We both have blind spots and a sort of stubborn pride that makes us soldier on in the face of a degenerating situation. We'll cling to resentments when we should talk them through, pretend we can carry on without changing anything when it should be obvious that we need to find another way.

So we do still have rows. There was one just a short time ago. I'd been away for a long weekend with the Women's Environmental Network while Colin stayed at home, managing the farm single-handed. Usually, I am primarily responsible for the welfare of our flock. That weekend, he took over.

I was feeling marvellous when my train drew in at Carmarthen station. Colin was waiting with one of our dogs, but he didn't give me the expected hug and kiss. He turned away from me, distant. He was reticent about his weekend, noncommittal. There were no events to report. It was boring. Eventually, his resentment came to the surface. He was angry (irritated, he insisted – not angry: as though I didn't merit anything as strong as anger) because he had been unable to find what he needed to look after the sheep. I'd left them in the wrong places. I was a klutz. I made the place into a shit-heap. I just create chaos; it's one step forward and two back when I'm around. The house is squalid. He had been cleaning mould and crap out of the vegetable rack – when did I last do that? Why do I leave things around to get mouldy? So it went on. On and on and on.

I felt I was being battered. When you're emotionally battered, the bruises are of a different nature from those you get from a physical attack. It's difficult, sometimes, to know when you are being battered. It's difficult to discriminate between grievances which may justifiably be aired, and a wholesale attack that cannot be justified within a loving relationship. Shocked and astonished, I found it hard to know what to do, how to react, how to protect myself.

I couldn't deny most of his criticisms. I am chaotic. I am forgetful. And I had been worse than usual recently, because I had been overloaded with visitors, haymaking, business, and too many obligations. But all this Colin knows, and lives with me in the knowledge that I'm a klutz. There's no point railing at me about it; who gains from that?

I felt utterly miserable. My head ached. Eventually, I became furious. I wanted to hurt him back. But it was late at night, I was exhausted, and I would have to be up before seven next morning. I hissed my rage at him and considered sleeping in my own room, separately from him. Then I thought, why the hell should *he* push *me* out of my own bed? So I lay tensely, far out on my side of the mattress, facing the wall and gripping the duvet tightly lest he try to grab my share. I slept fitfully and woke unrefreshed.

I drove away before he was awake and considered my position. I pondered his behaviour: how he had failed to welcome me home, clearly saying that the place was the worse for my presence; how he had tried to redefine my reality, tell me how I felt, as if he knew better than me – and as if this made his attacks acceptable!

It all added up to a totally unacceptable picture. Either he would have to withdraw those accusations and apologise – unreservedly – or I would leave. I had no other alternative. It was not an easy decision but I knew I could not accept this sort of treatment. It was intolerable.

I returned that evening feeling strong. I knew where I stood. My weekend with ecofeminist friends had strengthened my resolve; I had to tackle this business with Colin.

But when I walked into the house, there was no confrontation. His first words were apologetic. He was unreservedly sorry for all he'd said, the sentiments he'd expressed. He had been feeling unhappy, negative. Now, after a twenty-mile bike ride – his first for more than a year – he was feeling positive again.

He was a completely different person. A person I can live with. The Colin I love. Yes, there is sometimes a monster there; but I know that. So long as the monster stays in his cave and emerges rarely, I can forgive its occasional appearance. After all, he puts up with my chaos, something I can no more control than he can control his monster within.

Aggressors and victims

In our relationship, rows nearly always start with Colin feeling neglected, lonely, and unloved. He's vulnerable to these feelings – who isn't? – especially when he's feeling unwell, unhappy or exhausted. I can be vulnerable too, especially when I'm premenstrual, when I'm tired, overworked and neglectful of my own needs. When I'm fed up with him or the world – feeling exploited, unappreciated, unloved – I stop cuddling him and lose interest in sex. This isn't deliberate policy: I'm not consciously trying to punish him: but it is a recurring pattern between us.

When this has been going on for a few days, Colin starts attacking me. He'll find fault with what I do or fail to do, or with things I say. And unless one of us realises what's going on and acts quickly and assertively to stop the process by doing something about the way we're both feeling, a hideous row will develop.

Because I'm not an aggressive person, I tend to become the victim, he the aggressor. For most heterosexual couples, it's that way round: many more men batter their wives than vice versa. Women submit, act as victims, feel inferior. It's the way we're reared, the role our culture creates for us.

All too often, women co-operate fully with dominant male/submissive female behaviour patterns. By acting weak, we attract men who need to prove they are strong. I'm sure I have done this myself, wanting a man who seems strong so that I can hide behind him. I did it because I was afraid of responsibility, afraid of having to be decisive; lacking confidence, I imagined – just as my mother used to – that others knew better, could cope far better than I. Being passive seems like an easy option, it allows you to avoid blame. But in the long term it is no good; the martyr role creates resentment on all sides.

Intellectually, I have rejected that role, even if I sometimes have difficulty acting as assertively as I would like. I know I must stand up, use the strength that is within me, take responsibility for my own decisions. Otherwise I could end up, like so many women, battered. We can avoid that fate by calmly insisting that our rights be respected, rather than begging for mercy. Cringing, begging and passive victim-behaviour tend to bring out male aggressiveness.

Taking an assertiveness course helped me to learn to stand up for myself without being aggressive or eliciting violence. It was based on Anne Dickson's book, *A Woman in Your Own Right*,[5] which I strongly recommend.

Sometimes, taking responsibility and recognising our own rights means acknowledging that a partner's attitudes are unacceptable. If negotiation is not possible, there is the ultimate sanction of withdrawing from the relationship. Although this book is about making relationships work, we have to accept that that is not always possible and it is important to remember that we don't have to take everything that's thrown at us. If we don't allow ourselves to accept the possibility of divorce, we can become very vulnerable indeed. The threat of leaving – made in all seriousness, as the end game that it is – can be enough to cause even the most stubborn of partners to reconsider.

This is not a threat to use casually: that would devalue it. We should never bluff about breaking up an important relationship. Nor is this a move to consider before other avenues have been thoroughly explored. It may be that your own attitudes need to be questioned at a deeper level; or it may be possible to renegotiate the relationship, to change your expectations of one another.

Learning to cope

When Colin and I are going through a bad patch, I remind myself that periods of conflict don't continue for ever. Our relationship goes up and down; sometimes it's loving and harmonious, at other times it's antagonistic. The crucial point is that we do love each other, so we must try to deal with antagonism, limit the damage it causes, and understand what underlying pressures make it develop. Then it's possible to do something about the real causes. A row, after all, is a symptom, not the disease.

The pain of the symptom can be reduced, allowing you to work on the underlying causes of recurring rows. I'm slowly learning how to cope and avoid getting crushed. I'm rarely sufficiently together to remember everything I should do when Colin gets angry (often because I am so *un*together)

– and I don't imagine he'll ever stop being irascible! These are my guidelines:

First, I must not assume that there is a rational reason for his anger, nor that I am to blame. I have to try to discover where he's hurting, and not necessarily expect to deal with it rationally. The problem is on an emotional level and it will have an emotional solution.

I have to make myself look straight at him, right in the eyes. When I'm afraid, I bow my head and avoid his eyes; by acting like a victim, I encourage continued attacks. I must hang on to my courage and not let my body language show fear of violence, for by anticipating violence I make it more probable.

I must tell him how his behaviour makes me feel, at the time, clearly and directly, so that he is aware of what he is doing.

I have to forgive myself for the crimes of which he accuses me even if I feel the accusation is valid. I cannot deny that I do things that annoy him but that's not my intention; I'd change for my own sake if knew how. Maybe one day I'll learn to be tidy, but it's not so terrible to be the way I am. I should not expect myself to be perfect and he should not punish me when I'm not.

Finally, I must remember that everything can be discussed, even if this seems impossible during the heat of the argument. If we keep our lines of communication open, we can resolve things. Constant negotiation (which I cover in the next chapter) is at the heart of lasting relationships. Problems must not be brushed under the carpet, avoided because they're too painful, or dismissed as too trivial for any effort to be worthwhile. Unresolved, problems and accusations fester, eating away at affection. That way lies divorce.

For all that we intend to be positive in our interaction, we don't always succeed and talking can degenerate into a shouting match. The best way I know of coping when this happens is to switch to physical activity – using the adrenalin that's flowing round my body by vacuuming the house, chopping wood, pedalling away furiously on my bike. By the time I'm physically tired, I'll be calm but alert, and able to return to talking without aggression interfering destructively with communication.

If, despite our good intentions, we still fight, we have to build in space to resolve the conflict afterwards – space for affection to return, space for apologies, for making up, for strokes and cuddles. We need to find ways to rebalance the relationship, to relax and return to each other's arms. Positive action is important. If you have the energy, you might enjoy a game like squash or badminton, where you can burn up any remaining aggression in a playful way. Or try dancing to music that reflects your mood: dance through your feelings, throwing your body around. Then change the music as your internal state changes.

Alternatively, you can change the context of your interaction by distracting yourselves with a good film that takes your imagination somewhere quite different. Laugh at your favourite comedy actors or go and listen to live music. One thing that doesn't tend to work well for us is passively watching TV at home. We have to find something that takes us further from the ordinary, further from the domestic focus of the row, something that has a direct influence on our minds and bodies. I don't relax properly in front of the telly; I twitch, get restless, start worrying about the million things I haven't done around the house and farm.

If I don't take positive action to deal with ragged emotions, they linger to damage me, nagging like an arthritic joint. The aftertaste of a bad row takes days to disappear by itself. We have to clear up the mess afterwards, just as we may have to tidy away the physical debris of smashed crockery and broken furniture. The clearing up process is part of the healing; it may cause feelings to surface that need talking through; it may make us realise the power of the tensions in our relationship, tensions that must be resolved. But unlike clearing up in the house, sorting out problems in our relationship doesn't mean putting everything back the way it was before.

Rows can clear the air, and if they're handled effectively things can be much better afterwards – especially if you are able to work out why they developed in the first place. A row is like a spot bursting. You have to look deeper than the immediate issue that sparked off the row, to understand the origin of the pent-up emotions that generated the explosion of fury. The specific reasons for the fight are often trivial, not the real problems at all; we've had the most awful fights over things that make little sense afterwards. Yet somewhere in the heart of the mess there are issues that have to be confronted, and these we must deal with when the rage has blown over.

Unless we let the anger go and forgive each other for the things we said in the heat of the fight, a row can make it harder to perceive and solve underlying problems. When we're fighting, we say horrible things, picking up weapons – any weapons – that we wouldn't normally dream of using. Try not to let words flung in the cruelty of the moment hang on between you, continuing to hurt like wasp stings. We all do things that we later regret; we all say things that should not be said. Let them go: let it be. Let forgetfulness do its healing work, but remember that the underlying issues will need attention.

Getting over the row

What we can't afford to do is get judgemental about the things our partners do when they're upset. I can't hang on to ideas like 'Colin's such a bloody adolescent, why do I put up with him?' unless I want to perpetuate the row. I have to resist any tendency to feel superior, because I wouldn't have done what he did. He reacted to his own unhappiness; he doesn't need me to be self-righteous now. Nor do I need it: it could create a chasm between us.

Blame has no place in effective communication. Blame is a cul-de-sac. Usually the important issue is not who is right or wrong: it's how we can best relate to one another. Our focus must be on the quality of our relationship.

So it's back to the First Rule of Bicycle Riding. What do I want? Love, peace and harmony at home. To share my life with the generous, funny, lovely Colin who shares a body with the cruel, selfish and destructive Colin I'd rather not have to deal with. I try to accept him as he is: a mixed blessing, but a whole person, and focus on those aspects that please me the most, to encourage them to flourish.

After all, he has the same problem with me. I drive him mad, sometimes. Sometimes he just can't bear my squalor any more. If he were alone, he wouldn't have this. He wouldn't be tidying up all the time because he wouldn't create a mess. Or so he imagines.

But he finds me too attractive to want to live apart from me, and so he's stuck in Melville chaos. I suggest he could do more housework. He says he would, but he can't stand dealing with the mess I've left – why don't I ever put things away? And on it goes, the perpetual domestic merry-go-round.

Still, I'd rather live with the differences between us, even if occasionally they blow up, than submerge or sacrifice my individuality to try to fit another person's desires. I'd rather have rows than no-go areas, things we can't talk about for fear of the consequences. I'd rather have fights than a dead, passionless relationship.

Maybe one day we'll achieve passion, integrity and honesty without rows. People do mellow with age. Maybe it's starting to happen . . .

We've got a long way to go yet – and it's unlikely this journey will ever end.

14

The Keys to Love

Communication is at the heart of every relationship; without communication, there is no relationship. While there are many ways and means of communication, I shall concentrate in this chapter on talking. Talking together is the most conscious mode of immediate communication and it's crucial to long-term trust, because it allows us to define and work through the most complicated issues, to bring them up into shared consciousness.

When a relationship is actively evolving, constant communication allows partners to renegotiate their partnership and grow together. It's particularly important to continue talking during periods of change. It may seem reassuring to believe you know what your partner thinks and feels about everything, but such assumptions don't allow for deeper exploration or for change. In one study of married couples in Scotland,[1] three-quarters made comments like, 'I can tell you what she's thinking before she says it,' and 'When you're married you know one another inside out, you know what they're going to say next.' Beliefs like this put partnerships at risk: they can become excuses for ceasing to bother to listen. When a partner seems that predictable, the relationship must be stultifyingly dull, limited by narrow assumptions.

To maintain a stimulating dialogue, we have to remain

open to new facets of the other person and give opportunities for unexpected views or feelings to be expressed and shared. We have to encourage each other to talk, never taking it for granted that we know what's going to be said. Both partners have to be aware of the importance of continued communication, especially about issues like sex which are crucial to their happiness together. These are not matters that most people are accustomed to discussing, and talking about them can seem risky or embarrassing. But the more we are able to share our deepest feelings, the closer, more resilient and more satisfying the relationship is likely to become.

Colin and I have to work at talking about intimate matters, things that are emotionally important and potentially painful. Neither of us finds it easy. I get tongue-tied and fearful about his reactions. When things are at their worst, I can't talk at all, it's as though my throat is blocked. But we've learnt ways of coping – principally, by talking before problems get too serious – so that I rarely end up in this state.

For his part, Colin finds it difficult to open up about issues that are potentially painful to him. Like most men, he isn't used to trusting anyone totally, especially when he feels I might trivialise or dismiss his feelings, or use them against him. It's especially hard for men to allow themselves to become vulnerable; our competitive society teaches them to keep protective barriers in place lest others take advantage of their weaknesses.

It's all very well knowing we must communicate: the problem is *doing* it. I used to hold back because I didn't want to provoke him; I didn't want to appear stupid, childish, demanding, unreasonable. I was afraid of angry reactions, aggressiveness, afraid to make myself vulnerable. But by holding back, we allowed problems to accumulate and bottled-up feelings came out in uncontrolled ways like loss of desire, irrational irritation and depression.

When I was growing up I didn't tell my parents much

about my feelings. Instead, I suppressed emotions like anger, which my mother had consistently denied, so firmly that I was hardly aware of them. 'I'm not angry, darling,' she'd say when I did something wrong, 'I'm just hurt.' From her, I learnt to feel hurt when anger was more appropriate, and I would cry instead of standing up for myself. Similarly, I was never able to talk to my ex-husband about the way I felt.

Every time one of my relationships hit rock bottom, there was a massive backlog of unspoken resentment. When I was alone after leaving Bob, I became aware of a great deal of suppressed anger. But I didn't use this awareness to mend our relationship because I was never able to work through these feelings with him; to be honest, I didn't care enough about the relationship to make the effort. It takes a long time and a lot of determination to go through all the unresolved issues that smother love as they build up over years of failing to talk through difficulties.

Colin and I knew we had to talk when we hit rock bottom but there was so much stored pain that every attempt at communication seemed to get bogged down in argument. Discussion would degenerate into blazing rows and mutual recrimination. He'd shout, I'd cry. We would both end up feeling wretched, feeling there was no point even trying. But eventually we succeeded in airing our grievances and listening to each other. We worked through problems as they surfaced, over a period of years. At last, we had found the keys to lasting love.

Now that we've dealt with the past, we can work in the present, dealing with conflicts and problems as they arise. The danger period is behind us. I don't believe there's anything we can't share now.

The first step is to recognise the vital importance both of talking freely and honestly, and of listening intently to the other person. We realised that the only hope of staying together lay in getting through to each other; even if we were to part, there was a lot of talking to do. At that time, neither he nor I was convinced that we wanted to continue to live together, but we couldn't know what sort of relationship we might have without better communication. Whatever the future held for us, we had to renegotiate our relationship because it was too horrible to continue as we were. We learnt to take talking seriously – we had to!

Misunderstanding between the sexes

Of all the problems women complain about in long-term relationships, lack of communication is the most widespread and the most dangerous. Ninety-eight per cent of women in Shere Hite's huge study of love[2] said they would like more verbal closeness with the men they love; they wanted the men in their lives to talk more about their own personal thoughts, feelings, plans and questions, and to ask them about theirs.

The most common complaint men make is that women don't want sex as often as they do, and that they don't initiate sex enough.[3] These two grievances are closely connected; women tend not to want sex with men who refuse to listen to them. Many men don't realise, when they fob off their wives' attempts at opening up communication channels, that they are putting their whole relationship in jeopardy. Few understand that by refusing to talk, or to listen when women want to air grievances, they turn us off sexually as well as emotionally; men who want a more exciting sex-life would be more likely to achieve it if they recognised the importance of better communication.

Women need to feel close on all levels, emotional and verbal, in order to respond sexually after the initial passion has faded. Closeness is essential to trust, to the sense of certainty that we are desired not just because we are anatomically female but for our whole selves. But the female need for communication for its own sake, to maintain contact, is not always shared by men. Many men believe talking should be used to transmit novel information, not just feelings.[4] Unfortunately, this can mean that women feel rejected.

Many women – including me until quite recently – give in to men's reluctance to discuss difficult emotional issues. They tend to suppress their frustration and turn instead to those who *are* willing to listen, usually their women friends and trusted female relatives. The importance of the man in her life shrinks as the woman shares less and less with him and is forced to look elsewhere for close companionship.

Intimate sharing means putting pride on one side, which is the hardest thing for most men to do. Men tend to bottle up their feelings. Many don't talk about intimate aspects of their lives to anyone – or, at least, not until they are in such misery that they cease to care about keeping up appearances. At that point, they feel they have nothing to lose.

I have learnt that I can only have a satisfying long-term relationship if I do talk about things that matter to me. I know I must not give up talking, though I have to choose the right time to do it, and perhaps work out how to put my point of view over in a way that allows Colin to accept it.

Putting out clear messages

Good communication has two facets. First, it means giving out clear messages, free from ambiguity and untested assumptions about what the other person understands by what you say. Before we can do this, we have to know what it is we want to say.

Talking clearly can be unexpectedly difficult. It's all too easy to retreat into clichés like 'you know' and fail to check whether he – or indeed you – really do know what you mean. We take short-cuts and end up missing crucial points. We imagine the other person can read our minds when the whole problem is that he can't. Men's minds are different from women's – they only have half a brain, after all – and each individual is unique. We have to risk being boring and follow the path we need to share for its full length.

Sometimes we put things ambiguously because we are too embarrassed to say them clearly. We try to minimise the difficult bits – even though these may be crucial: it takes courage to talk clearly about painful or embarrassing issues, but building a strong relationship demands that we hold on to that courage and persevere. I've often had to swallow my pride, struggle to say things; sometimes they come out in a tiny voice, but at least they do come out and get heard.

Making yourself heard

The second facet of good communication is putting the message over in a form that can be received. One of the reasons men don't seem to want to listen to women, and women feel they are not heard when they try to talk, is that the message often isn't transmitted in a form that men can readily receive.

I think of this situation as akin to using a dog whistle: the dog can hear it, humans can't. Men can't always interpret messages correctly when they're pitched at a level that other women would understand. Men can't be expected to fill in the gaps where things are left unspoken. And the same is true for women listening to men.

I believe there are some sorts of communications that men have particular difficulty in hearing. Typically, such communications are heavily loaded with emotions. Men find these emotions disturbing, so they block them out – and so block out the whole message. If I want to communicate something important to Colin, I have to put it in a non-threatening way and choose a time when he's receptive. This may not be when it's really important to me, but it's better to wait till he is willing to listen than try to make him understand when he isn't ready.

I have to be calm, to use straight statements and avoid the high-pitched tone that characterises nagging, whingeing, demanding, and all the other types of voice that are dismissed as women's specialities. What I say will have more impact if I can put it more coolly. Similarly, I know I block communications from Colin and tend to forget the substance of what he's said if he puts his points aggressively. He has to make an effort not to shout at me if he wants me to take in what he's saying. We have to find a common wavelength, to tune in to each other.

A problem that tends to arise between men and women is that men, because they are more concerned with talking as information transmission than as a means of sharing closeness, attach too much importance to the literal meaning of words. Metamessages – the underlying meaning of the communication in terms of personal relationships – are often more important to women. Deborah Tannen gives an example of the conflict that can arise from these different interpretations.[5]

A wife had told her husband that it would be impossible to find a painting of the particular size and shape he wanted. He had found one and wanted his wife to admit she had been wrong. She claimed that she had said it would be difficult, not impossible, and suggested that she hadn't meant her remark in the way he'd interpreted it. But he would not accept compromise; he wanted her to admit defeat. Their argument grew heated and could not be resolved because he never wavered from the message level – the literal accuracy of what she had said – while she had moved on to the metamessage that his position conveyed about their relationship: 'Why do you always want to prove me wrong and rank me out?'

The tone of voice we use carries just such metamessages. A forceful voice carries the metamessage that what the speaker has to say is important, and people should listen and take note. Women, who are more likely to speak in a higher tone of voice, more quietly, and who often phrase their ideas as questions, don't tend to be taken seriously. Their attempts to raise issues they feel are important may get ignored because the way they habitually speak does not carry the metamessage: Listen to me! This matters!

When I'm tense or upset, the pitch of my voice tends to rise. But this higher pitch sounds more like a child, who is more easily ignored, than a powerful adult. If I pause, breathe deeply, and try to relax before saying something important, my tone of voice will be lower and Colin is more likely to accept what I'm saying.

I can't pretend it's easy. Even now, when I want to share difficult feelings, I can't always put them over in the best way. Colin may feel alienated or distressed by the messages he perceives – although these may not be messages I intended to transmit. Equally, I can't always deal with what he has to say, especially if I feel I've contributed to the problem and I can't come up with a solution.

My desire to solve problems – a reaction more typical of men, according to Deborah Tannen – can actually be counterproductive, because it can prevent me from helping Colin to talk about the way he's feeling. It's not always possible to find a solution; simply being there, listening and caring, may be what's needed.

Recently, a whole weekend was taken up with a struggle for communication, with each of us blocking the other in different ways. On the Saturday, Colin was miserable and his hurt came out – as it so often does – heavily coloured with anger, larded with personal attacks and insults. At first I rejected his aggression, then I began to cower, afraid. He reacted with more anger: 'You're full of bullshit. You don't want to listen to me. You don't care how anyone feels but yourself.'

He desperately wanted me to hear him. But he was right: I didn't want to listen to him. I was more concerned with protecting myself. I wanted to block him out, to run away. He began to feel even more despondent and isolated.

For hours this continued, on and off, apparently getting nowhere. At first I heard only his anguish, blame and resentment against me; most of the day went by before other messages, messages on which we could act, began to come through. Finally there was a breakthrough. He expressed his sense of isolation; I heard, and was able to show him some of the things we share. I made a list of everything I could remember that we enjoy together and matters on which we agree; it ranged from political beliefs to tastes in food, from sexual delight to environmental concern, from writing to our mutual love for the sheep. Reading the list, Colin accepted that he was not alone and was comforted.

Then I volunteered to work with him on a small job to which we could both contribute: mending a doorway. I did the fiddly bits, because I'm patient enough to get the details right; he did the heavy engineering work that required strength and planning. Working together in this way reminded us that our skills and aptitudes are complementary, both valuable. As a couple, we have access to a wider range of abilities than either one of us has working alone.

Finally, acknowledging the backlog of loneliness and distress that had led to his outburst, I gave him a gift of loving, undemanding sex that night: sex that was primarily for his pleasure. Still hurting a little after the emotional battering of the day, I didn't come to orgasm; but we were coming closer again, and I was glad.

Next day, the emotional pressure was reduced and we had an agenda for action: to look together at the ways we could ensure that his needs were better met. We discussed strategy for the business venture about which he was worrying, then went out and created a new garden in the sunshine. By the afternoon, he was fine.

That night, he returned my gift of undemanding sex by making love to me tenderly, unselfishly, putting my desires before his own. At last I was able to relax totally and sleep off the emotional exhaustion of the previous two days. But I know I must remember the message of Colin's outburst, not just forget it now that particular crisis has passed. We have to do something together every day, however small it may be, so that our relationship doesn't degenerate into co-existence. I have to make a bit more effort to avoid sliding into my hermit ways, to propose that we do mutually desired things together rather than leaving him to get on with them alone while I work at something else.

You can't be there for your partner every time you're wanted, and indeed this may put unacceptable pressure on women, who tend to want more time away from their partners than men do.[6] But doing things together – even if it's just walking the dog or washing up – maintains that essential sense of active connection between you. It's sometimes easier to talk during shared activity, if you don't have to think about what you're doing, because physical activity can aid emotional relaxation. And that's especially important for men, who often find it difficult just to sit and talk spontaneously.

Communicating the message

It's often not *what* we say to each other that leads to tension, it's the *way* we say it. I would have been much more understanding and more ready to listen to Colin that weekend if his sense of loneliness had not been hidden behind aggression.

It helps to separate facts from feelings, to talk quietly about facts and discuss the links with emotional reactions separately. I have to think about how I'm going to say some things so that I don't go in with all guns blazing; the crucial thing is to get the message over in a form that allows it to be heard. If I feel like screaming at Colin, I'll take a walk or retire to my room and write down my thoughts until I've worked out what I really need to say. It's okay to say I felt like screaming at him, it may not be helpful to do it.

I do end up shrieking at Colin when I feel he's refusing to hear me. But that's like shouting at foreigners when they don't understand your language. It doesn't make communication any clearer, it just raises the emotional temperature. I have to insist, quietly and calmly, that what I want to say to him really matters to me, and perhaps remind him that we can't expect to have a close relationship (and the rewarding sex-life that goes with it) if either one of us chooses to ignore attempts at communication.

Abuse, like screaming, blocks communication and widens the distance between us. We do abuse each other occasionally, of course, though not nearly as often as we used to. We're learning less damaging ways of expressing ourselves. I retort quite sharply now to insults, especially general-purpose put-downs like 'stupid woman'; I simply won't tolerate them. Time was when I just felt hurt and kept quiet; now, I'm more likely to ask why he feels he wants to hurt me, what it is that's hurting him. That way, we can make progress.

Having acknowledged the importance of talking, we make time for it. If something's bugging me, I'll tell him I need to talk before the pressure builds up too much. We'll agree a time to do it when there are no distractions. We'll make sure we're relaxed, turn the TV off, ignore the telephone, shut out intrusions. We accept that we must concentrate totally on each other.

I have had to ask him to co-operate, to have patience when I get tongue-tied. He understands that spoken words come slowly to me and I hesitate and repeat myself when I'm hurting inside or when I'm talking about subjects that I've never talked about before. He's learnt not to interrupt – I speak sharply to him when he does! – and not to anticipate what I have to say. It's for me to say it, not him. I can't handle distraction and I get led off-course easily, so he has to wait, and listen. We've learnt to allow for each other's strengths and weaknesses.

Learning to listen

Studies of group discussions involving both sexes reveal that men interrupt women far more often than women interrupt men. I believe this is an in-built difference between us. Women have to be constantly alert to the needs of dependent children, to drop whatever they're doing and respond instantly. So women are more easily distracted, they find it more difficult to fix their exclusive attention on what they want to say, and they tolerate interruption better than men do. Caring people have to learn to listen without interrupting.

Listening is not always easy, especially when you're listening to someone expressing their hurt. The listener has to stay fully attentive, help the talker by making that attention obvious, and reassure the talker that there's no time-limit. The listener's turn will come later, when the talker has finished. This is difficult for Colin; patience is not his strong point and I can be very slow to get out what I have to say. But when I'm talking, I hold on to the knowledge that my feelings are important, and insist that Colin respects that.

It helps the process of communication if we are aware of non-verbal messages. We pick up cues from expressions, body language, even smell, without necessarily being aware of them, and usually communicate them without conscious intent. Part of effective communication is working at putting over helpful body messages: good listeners may give reassuring touches and hugs, avoid showing boredom or rejection by drumming fingers and staring at the ceiling or indeed looking anywhere but at the speaker.

Sometimes, especially early in the process of working through relationship problems, talking can be too difficult and listening too painful for couples to continue for long enough to sort out their conflicts. The help of a counsellor can be very valuable at this point. When I was doing relationship counselling, the most crucial part of my role was to facilitate communication, preventing the listener from ignoring or cutting off the message that the talker was struggling to put over and encouraging the talker to go on, even when progress was painful. The only exception is when the listener doesn't understand what's said; he or she must feel free to ask for clarification.

When relationships are in trouble, talking about what's going wrong is always painful. Counsellors keep boxes of tissues handy. If I'm going to try to talk about something difficult, I try to remember to equip myself with a handkerchief even if I feel calm at the beginning. I don't try to avoid crying, nor did I try to stop my clients crying: it is a natural cathartic process which helps to get the pain out of your system.

Using 'I' statements

We try to talk primarily about our own feelings. I'll say 'This is how *I feel* when you do/say that,' rather than '*You make me feel* this way.' My feelings are my own, created within myself; I cannot put the responsibility for them on to Colin. Talking in the first person like this helps to prevent us from getting into pointless accusations and attacks. It allows us to get to the bottom of the issue without fighting.

Using 'I' statements prevents communication from degenerating into blame. Colin has a tendency to seek a villain in any situation, and he's all too ready to allocate blame when he gets angry. When he expresses his feelings in this damaging way, it pushes me into a victim role. It's a very negative process. Both of us end up miserable and the underlying problems remain unsolved. Somehow, one of us has to shift the focus away from blame towards a more positive way of viewing the situation. Once again, we return to the First Rule of Bicycle Riding.

I try to tell him what I would like him to do in a similar situation in the future, not what he should or shouldn't have done. Oughts and shoulds create anxiety without solving anything. I try, too, not to get hung up on what I imagine I ought to do: we're dealing with wants and needs, not oughts; desires and feelings, not obligations and duties.

Raising difficult subjects

Some desires seem embarrassing. I have often felt ashamed of myself, wishing I didn't feel the way I did. But shame has no place in the crucial business of opening up to each other so I know I must fight it. Colin understands that; he realises that I was brought up as a dutiful girl who was taught to put others first, and that a passive attitude can lead me to ignore my own feelings. It's been a recurring part of the problem between us. I have to express those feelings and look for ways to deal with them.

Ultimately, there can be no taboo subjects, but it takes a lot of time and trust to get around to sharing everything. In a lasting relationship, we have that time: time to learn to accept ourselves and each other, to grow into new dimensions with each other's encouragement. There are no limits.

Recently, I wanted to tell Colin how I felt about masturbation. I found this surprisingly difficult. Masturbation isn't something women normally discuss – if it were, we'd have a shorter, more expressive word for it.

When emotional reactions make communication difficult, if there's antagonism between us or I'm too embarrassed, uncertain or tongue-tied to talk sensibly, I'll often work through my feelings on my own, writing down the points I want to share with Colin. Then I'll use my notes to help me talk through the issues and make sure no essential points are missed.

On this occasion, I raised the subject when we were relaxing one quiet evening. I didn't need my notes; the fact that I had them was enough to allow me to proceed. Haltingly, I explained the problem as I saw it.

I had been going through a period when orgasms with Colin were unreliable. I wanted this pleasure, this closeness, this deep-down relaxation, but I'd grown nervous because of a fear of failure, a fear that we'd get worked up and I'd be left unsatisfied. These anxieties were causing me to lose interest in sex. Sometimes I turned off partway through, and things got worse; my cunt dried up and I got sore. At the same time, I acknowledged that Colin wanted sex and he is prone to get bad-tempered if he doesn't get it.

I'd thought about the issue on my own for some time

before I remembered to apply the First Rule of Bicycle Riding. What did I want? Orgasm with Colin. I knew I could achieve orgasm through masturbation, so instead of precipitating all sorts of distress with negative comments about his ability to give me orgasms, I told him that I was having difficulty coming (it didn't matter why), and that I wanted our sexual interaction to incorporate clitoral stimulation with my vibrator.

I explained that I understood that he was having problems too: he was under stress at work and he had health problems. I didn't want to put pressure on him, just to do what I could to ensure my orgasm when we had sex together. He agreed wholeheartedly; like most men, he wants me to have orgasms, he doesn't like to come alone.

Talking about it proved wonderfully liberating. There was no confrontation, no rejection, and in the end, no problem. Later, he watched me masturbating, joined in when I asked him to, and did what I suggested. He found it very exciting, very stimulating. To our mutual delight, we both had intense and satisfying orgasms.

Another evening, we talked through my feelings about masturbating on my own. Sometimes I preferred to masturbate rather than have sex with him, but I felt guilty because I imagined I should share every feeling of desire with him. He says he wants sex more often than he gets it, and it seemed unfair for me to satisfy myself on my own. But talking cleared the air; he quite understood that I sometimes wanted reliable, effortless orgasms, and he didn't resent that. I realised that I had completely misjudged his reaction and become needlessly anxious.

I would never have anticipated that I would hit such blocks around discussing masturbation. I suppose it's yet another leftover from my childhood, my mother's disapproval preserved deep in the recesses of my mind. I felt very relieved when I finally succeeded in talking about it. Now another block has been knocked away; I wonder how many more there are lurking beneath my consciousness, making me anxious about acting in ways that are consistent with my beliefs.

When we're discussing difficult issues or areas of potential conflict, it's always helpful to make positive suggestions. I find it easier to talk if I can suggest improvements to the way we interact, and there's a much better chance of a positive outcome. For example, rather than say 'Your love-making doesn't satisfy me,' I might say 'I'd like more kissing and cuddling when we make love, so that I feel more turned on.' But when I can't see how a problem can be solved or I'm not sure of the precise nature of the problem, I'll still talk about it so that we can work towards a solution together.

Sometimes, Colin can't cope with what I want to say; sometimes, I can't deal with the issues he wants to raise. We've learnt to say, 'Let's not talk about that right now, I'm feeling too vulnerable,' but we don't leave anything hanging in the air for more than a day or so. We'll choose a time when we're feeling stronger or calmer and return to the discussion. The crucial thing for us both is not to run away from the issue. If you try to avoid it, pretend it doesn't matter or sweep it under the carpet, sooner or later you trip over it again. All our feelings matter, especially our feelings in relation to each other.

We try to share the positive as well as the negative, to balance potentially hurtful things with loving comments. That way, talking becomes a pleasure not an ordeal. It's always helpful to say, 'I really like the way you do that, I'd love it if you did it more often'; and I now try to bring those good things up into my awareness and share them with Colin, so that he feels good too.

The other side of this is accepting compliments. When I'm feeling down, I have a tendency to shrug them off and not to hear them, especially if they don't fit in with my poor self-image. This is sad, because they would help me to feel better about myself. Gradually, I'm learning to internalise compliments as readily as put-downs; the more I do this, the more Colin compliments me and the less he puts me down. Part of being loving is encouraging each other to express loving feelings by accepting them with grace when they're offered.

The struggle for clear and continuing communication is an ongoing process, an essential part of a loving relationship. The quality of our relationship is crucial to our well-being and our ability to withstand the pressures of the outside world. And we know – not just in theory, but from experience – that communication is vital to maintain closeness.

This relationship matters to both of us, so we make conscious efforts to ensure that it works for both of us. The key is to discuss everything before major problems build up. While we continue to talk, we shall continue to love each other; for communication is an expression of our love.

15

The Power of Touch

When I'm with people from almost any other culture, I notice how readily they show warmth to one another. The British touch and hug each other less than other national groups, and I'm convinced that this makes it harder for us to establish and maintain loving relationships. Did our grey island weather, I wonder, create the chilly British temperament? As I write, rain drums remorselessly on my window; the sky is overcast, bright summer butterflies all flown from the garden. These conditions aren't conducive to warm, expansive feelings!

I am typically inhibited about touch. I envy those who can unselfconsciously throw their arms round each other, for whom touching is the most natural and easy form of communication. For touch enhances trust, creates connection between people.

My problem stems from childhood, from a cultural pattern of limited touch that I both experienced directly and observed around me. I cannot recall being touched or hugged at all when I was small. It must have happened, but clearly not enough, for I developed strong barriers around myself, a protective shell that's difficult to break down. This, I know, is part of the pattern of inhibition and fear that has made it hard for me to nurture close relationships.

Colin often feels the presence of these barriers. They

show in my body language when I wrap my arms protectively round myself, shutting others out. I've seen the same self-protection in films of monkeys separated from their mothers at birth, reared without the constant reassurance of touch that all young animals need to grow up emotionally whole. I don't mean to shut him out, at least not consciously; but I do it all too readily, and he is aware of it. It's inevitable that he should feel rejected and unloved when he wants to be close and I shrink away. I feel the same way when he shuts me out.

Touch has the power to heal the spirit and the body. Untouched children wither, sicken and die. Untouched adults are sad and lonely, isolated at a deep level even if they relate in other ways to their community. However much we may talk, we must also touch.

When we can't talk, touch allows us to rebuild closeness, to communicate tenderness, reassurance, comfort. If I'm feeling hurt, I need a cuddle more than anything else. When I'm anxious, I need Colin to hold me close to him; when I'm miserable, I need someone to stroke me. See me, feel me, touch me, heal me,' sang the Who in their rock opera *Tommy*. In the seventies, this idea became the basis of encounter groups, which were designed to overcome anxieties about touching each other.

Even when we can talk, we share delight, transmit warmth and maintain trust through touch. Touching makes it easier to discuss difficult subjects or approach potentially threatening ones. It tells your partner that you want to remain close even though you're saying things that might be interpreted as unkind. These things do sometimes have to be said, and when you don't want to hurt the other, it's essential to maintain closeness.

So I tell myself to touch more readily, more often; to overcome the barriers that have held me back, isolated me from other people. I'm learning to translate inner feeling of warmth into overt demonstrations of affection and amplify the pleasure that is created. It becomes easier with practice.

I found myself spontaneously hugging my neighbour after the shared labour of haymaking – that surprised her! It is good to get closer, to break through those British inhibitions. There is no doubt that I'm much happier for it. And when I'm happier, I feel stronger, and those around me tend to be happier too.

Colin and I touch in more ways, more freely, than we used to. At first, of course, we touched a lot. When I'm madly in love, I'm impetuous, I don't hold back; but over the years I withdrew, especially when our sex-life wasn't working. For us, increased touching is a reflection, and an integral part of, the progress we've been making in building a richer relationship. It's been necessary for us both to understand that touching needn't be a sexual invitation – although sometimes it is. I used to hold back when I didn't want sex, fearing that he would misinterpret my behaviour. But by withholding touch, I was also holding back my own sexual feelings, burying sensuality deep within myself. It was part of the process that smothered my sexual fire.

When we're tense and antagonistic, going through one of those horrible phases when we are far apart, seeming to mishear, misunderstand or misinterpret everything the other says, or when we're locked into a destructive power struggle, determined to score points from one another, win arguments and prove the other wrong, words deepen the gulf between us. At such times, touch allows us to bridge it. I've found that sort of destructive cycle can be broken by saying to Colin, 'Please stop talking, it makes me anxious,' and insisting that we change over to touch.

Massage

Soothing the tension through massage allows us to stop fighting and get in touch with our underlying affection for each other. We massage those parts of the other where we know from experience that tension builds.

The best situation, even if we are still prone to the

occasional snarl, is to be naked in a warm bedroom. It is more difficult to maintain a negative façade without clothes. Our mattress is on the floor (I am in the process of building a huge bed, but it's not yet finished) so we have a firm base on which to work. If we had a yielding bed, we'd massage each other on a duvet or thick bathtowel on the floor.

I usually start with his feet. He lies on his back with his lower calves on my thighs, his feet placed conveniently within easy reach. Using warm perfumed oil, I stroke the sole of one foot firmly and manipulate his toes, pulling on each toe in turn, oiling it all over, moving it without forcing it through its full range of motion. Then I work carefully and steadily over the whole of the foot with my fingers working in a circular motion, pressing quite hard on the sole. I imagine that I'm pulling energy through the foot, stimulating forgotten centres. Foot massage is used in therapy in many cultures. Mine is a relatively unsophisticated sort of therapy, but one on which I concentrate my whole awareness as I try to feel where reactive pressure points lie. When I've finished, his foot will move freely, without resistance, and his leg muscles are loose. Then I go on to the other foot.

It has been a source of wonder to both of us that I can do this. Colin used to have incredibly ticklish feet and would not let anyone touch them. Gradually I broke through this barrier – it was, after all, merely a manifestation of the chronic tension in the lower half of his body – by getting him to relax as much as he could, while I held his feet firmly. I wouldn't use light fingertip strokes here: they would make him tense again. Now I have learnt, with practice, how to induce relaxation, I can do it at will when I have sufficient energy.

Foot massage affects Colin's whole being. He lies back when I've finished in a state of total relaxation, enjoying the sensation and the warmth my energy has created. Then, after a couple of minutes, he's ready to work on me.

I hold tension in my back, neck and face. If my back's aching, as it often does after farm work, I'll ask for a back massage. If the tension is greater in my face, I'll ask for a face massage. I have to tune into myself and tell him what I need.

Colin readily took to back massage. He particularly enjoys working on my back because he finds it beautiful, appreciating the muscles that gym workouts and agricultural labour have created. He uses a variety of strokes; some quite hard, pushing up each side of my spine with his whole hand; some softer, stroking down my ribs. I like deep finger pressure around the vertebrae of my lower back; he works with a circular motion sometimes, other times with straighter strokes that follow the lines of the muscles under the skin. I sometimes ask him to massage my hairline around the base of my skull, where headaches build up; that makes him nervous but he's slowly growing accustomed to it.

Finally he massages my buttocks with a kneading motion, and that often turns him on. Before he started, I would probably have been too tense to respond in any positive way to his erection; but by the time he's finished, I usually appreciate it. I'm delighted that my body excites him still!

We've both had to learn and develop our technique over time. We help each other by giving feedback about the sort of touches that feel best, sometimes firm, sometimes gentle. It's part of the continuing process of learning about each other.

For a face massage, I lie with my head on his thighs, my eyes closed while he works from above. Sometimes we use light massage oil, sometimes face cream; free samples of anti-wrinkle cream always get used this way in our household! He uses light strokes, gentle fingertip pressure, all over my face, following the features, pulling gently at the tense areas around my mouth and forehead. Finally he works carefully around the eye-sockets, stroking the eyelids, massaging the area between my eyes and nose.

Face massage feels wonderful! I suspect that anti-wrinkle creams work as much through the massage used to apply them as through any particular properties they may have. My face always ends up smoother than when Colin started. And when my face looks smoother, I feel more relaxed, rested but not yet sleepy; and of course I'm grateful to him for making me feel so much better.

By the time this is finished, all the petty antagonisms of the day are behind us, forgotten. We are close again, content with each other, aware of the delights that mutual touch can bring. From that point, we can move on to making love, if we fancy it, or to loving embraces and rest.

It's important to me that sex should not follow inevitably after massage, for then I might feel pressured to respond sexually when I'm not ready for it. But in practice, we often do end up making love. We feel so good together that the sexual turn-on is natural and easy. Massage enhances loving feelings between us, feelings that shift readily into sexual desire.

Without mutual massage, I think it would have been very difficult for us to rebuild our sex-lives after our years in the doldrums. It was something I'd thought about but felt nervous about doing: I hadn't been trained, I imagined I'd get it wrong, I thought I didn't know how to do it. I got through my fears of massaging Colin by reminding myself that it wasn't a performance, on which I would be judged; it was something I was doing to make him feel good, to communicate warmth. Once again, I had to tell myself to focus on the positive and put my fears aside. When I tried working on his face, hands and feet, I didn't have any preconceptions, any beliefs about what I should be doing, to inhibit me. My methods evolved gradually, through experience.

It probably would have been easier to start if we – or I – had done a massage course. Maybe I'll find one yet, to develop my skills; it would be beneficial for both of us. Books on massage can be useful; the discussion of massage in Anne Hooper's *The Body Electric*[1] is the best I've ever read. I recommend it.

We are building up a collection of massage oils with different perfumes to suit our moods and the effects we want to create. The perfumes we use undoubtedly affect the way we respond. Aromatherapists are the experts in this field and books about aromatherapy can be helpful, but shops that sell essential oils often offer information about their properties. We're still experimenting, and this is an area about which I am determined to learn a lot more.

Casual touching

Deliberate, conscious uses of touch are only part of the story. Casual, even accidental touches are very important because they contribute to closeness on a day-to-day level. Like massage, they help to establish trust and enable us to relax with one another. But ignore touches, or brush them away, and you risk creating resentment.

I know this all too well. Distracted by farm worries, I took no notice when Colin touched me one recent morning when we woke. Instead of reciprocating, I got up, dressed, and started trying to work out how best to use our fields. When he turned up for breakfast he was irritable and thoroughly nasty to me. I had rejected him and he reacted by punishing me.

Being brushed away like a fly is even more hurtful than being ignored. When that happened to me, it made me feel deeply unwanted. Indeed, I was unwanted: I'd got the intended message. I left the man who did this to me repeatedly; *that* wasn't his intention, but he shouldn't have been surprised. This is not the sort of message we can afford to give to those we love, not if we want them to stick around.

Of course, I am human and given to unconsidered and careless acts. I don't always want to take notice of Colin's desires. But if I ignore or reject him without thinking and without offering any kind of explanation, he is bound to feel hurt, and his hurt affects both of us. It's important that

I remember to tell him if I just want to put his needs on hold since I'm too preoccupied with something else to concentrate on him, because unless communication is maintained, conflict is all too probable; and it can be so hard to make peace.

When we do make peace after a quarrel, it's usually through touch: through embraces, through stroking each other, through holding hands. I used to think grown-ups didn't – shouldn't – hold hands; now I know better. It is part of a repertoire of touch which maintains the connection between us, a connection that should not be allowed to lapse.

Sex therapy and sensate focus

There are sex therapists, and sex therapies, that rely almost entirely on touch.[2] The first well-known exponents of this approach were Masters and Johnson,[3] whose sensate focus exercises are prescribed by marriage counsellors around the world. Masters and Johnson report great success in treating loss of desire and other sexual problems using sensate focus. Problems as apparently different as premature ejaculation, impotence and vaginismus are in fact closely related; all are caused by anxiety, all tend to be associated with loss of interest in sex, and effective help is available for all of them.

The idea of sensate focus is to enhance awareness of physical pleasure through touch. It is a systematic technique for teaching couples to give and receive different types of touch which helps them to tune into their sensual natures and builds closeness and trust between them.

I cannot tell you what these exercises feel like in practice, nor the nature of the feelings they might arouse, because I have no experience of them. The main reason for this is that Colin has consistently refused to accept the first directive given to couples about to enter this type of therapy: that sexual intercourse is not permitted until the end of the therapeutic sequence.

The reason for the ban on sex is to reduce anxiety. If I were using sensate focus in the hope of restoring interest in sex, I believe I would not want to feel pressured to have intercourse because the exercises aroused my partner. He might not think he was putting pressure on me, but if he had an erection and his desire was obvious, I would tend to feel anxious. If sex was not ruled out, I'd be put in the position of refusing him again. But if both of us understood that we were not going to have any 'direct sexual interaction involving genital contact' (as Masters and Johnson put it),[4] then I could relax. I would not be making the choice so I would not be rejecting him. I could enjoy sensual pleasure without fear.

Another advantage of a temporary ban on sex is that it frees the participants from the desperate search of their emotions for signs of sexual arousal. When I've experienced what Masters and Johnson call 'inhibited sexual desire', or ISD (loss of desire for sexual contact), I fall all too easily into the trap of searching within myself for desire. I want to grab it, magnify it, so that I can feel and behave in a sexy way. What happens then is that whatever embryonic desire might be there gets killed because I become a spectator and judge of my own reactions rather than a participant. I get trapped by the desperation of the search. I'm only capable of experiencing desire when I don't feel I have to.

However . . . I cannot dismiss Colin's point of view, for I'm quite sure that many men would feel just the same way as he does. 'How can I spend all that time stroking a naked woman without blowing up,' he argues, 'when my balls ache with frustration and I'm denied sex for an indefinite period? This might be okay for a tiny selected minority who go for a fortnight's intensive therapy, but if you try to do it yourself at home you could precipitate very ugly situations.'

Dagmar O'Connor, director of the Sex Therapy Program of a major New York hospital, gives protests from sexually frustrated men short shrift. She refers scathingly to 'the famous "blue balls" defense'[5] and points out that men can always masturbate once the touching session is over. So they can – if they're willing to co-operate. Men who enrol in a sex therapy programme are more likely to commit themselves to following the therapist's advice than those who hear about the method from a woman who's read her book.

Using sensate focus demands patience, a mutual willingness to accept the situation, and, perhaps, a greater degree of tolerance of sexual arousal coupled with deprivation than Colin could contemplate. Both partners have to be happy with whatever strategy you use to improve your sex-life. It is no good for one partner to insist that the other must co-operate, if he is liable to erupt into rage or rape.

That doesn't stop me from feeling a bit resentful sometimes. I'd like to explore this method, to discover what it could do for us. Colin knows how I feel; I hope that one day he'll come round to it . . .

There are a variety of books on sex therapy for those who want to learn more about it. *Masters and Johnson on Sex and Human Loving* is pretty comprehensive. In their discussion of sensate focus, they describe the method as including two sessions in which each partner takes turns touching the other's naked body, but with breasts and genitals 'off limits'. The person touching (the toucher) does whatever he or she wishes, without trying to guess at what the one being touched (the touchee) wants or enjoys. It is not a massage session, nor is it intended to produce sexual arousal, although this might happen. The couple should only talk during the session if the touching feels uncomfortable. Over the next few days, the toucher may explore first the breasts then the genital area, but the session always begins with general body touching. The point is to develop awareness of physical sensations without anticipating or seeking to elicit any particular response.

In later sessions, the toucher should be guided by the touchee. Masters and Johnson recommend 'hand-riding', which means the touchee's hand is laid lightly on the toucher's hand to give feedback, indicating whether the touchee would prefer more pressure or less.

After this come sessions of mutual touching, but intercourse is still not allowed. Finally, the woman gets on top of the man, and if she wishes to insert his penis into her vagina, she may do so. From this point on, intercourse may follow.

If you want to know more, read Masters and Johnson or Dagmar O'Connor, or consult a suitably trained counsellor. A good way to find a counsellor is by making an appointment with Relate; the number will be in your local telephone directory. There are also increasing numbers of sex therapists in private practice, and details of how to contact them are given in the notes for this chapter at the end of the book.[6] Alternatively, your doctor may be able to recommend or refer you to a suitable person.

As with every form of therapy, it's worth searching for someone with whom you feel you have a good rapport; you will benefit most from a counsellor whom you feel really understands you, and that may not be the first person you consult. You have to trust your therapist when you're talking about intimate problems; otherwise, you can't open up and be completely honest. Intuition is important. When I was working as a relationship counsellor I didn't feel equally comfortable with all my clients, and it was the people with whom I had the warmest relationship that I was able to help the most – because they trusted me.

Sex therapy is most likely to be effective if it is used in a counselling context, where the other issues that affect sexual feeling are addressed. Interestingly, Masters and Johnson point out that the majority of time in sex therapy sessions is actually spent on non-sexual issues such as dealing with anger, self-esteem and power struggles. Helen Singer Kaplan[7] warns that partner rejection, which can underlie many sexual problems, cannot be bypassed through sensate focus; the couple must make up before they can make love. Anger and resentment have to be resolved, at least in part, before erotic feelings can emerge. If this is impossible, sex therapy will fail.

My experience is that if you can work through issues of this sort together, you can often resolve sexual problems without any specific therapeutic input. After all, we have overcome my lack of desire without using sensate focus! But we do use the power of touch – non-sexual touch – to create the mutual trust that is essential to a harmonious and mutually enjoyable sex-life.

Discovering your partner – and yourself

Although Colin and I haven't worked through any sex therapy exercises together, we have spent a lot of time exploring each other's bodies to discover what sort of touches we most enjoy. Our tastes differ: I like light butterfly touches on the front and sides of my body: they make me quiver with delight. He finds such delicate fingertip touch unpleasantly ticklish. I enjoy being scratched quite hard on my back, or scrubbed with the bath brush till my skin turns rosy pink; he's more sensitive, preferring whole-hand contact to fingernails, rubbing to scrubbing. We both react with pleasure to strokes along the inner thighs, over the buttocks, deep kneading on muscle; we both enjoy having our nipples stroked and licked, though he has to be careful if my breasts are tender before my period.

This exploration hardly started in earnest until we began to work consciously towards building a better sex-life. For years we hadn't taken the time and trouble to find out exactly what we both enjoyed. We worked on assumptions, many of which we discovered were unjustified. In retrospect, it seems that for years we hardly knew each other: we just did what we thought appropriate without checking that it had the desired effect. Inevitably, it didn't; I turned into a sack of potatoes (his phrase) while he seemed like an insensitive clod. No wonder our love almost died!

Touching myself has helped me to learn more about my

own responses. It has been important for me to learn to enjoy and accept myself more easily. I had to learn to appreciate myself before I could relate fully to sexual partners

Smoothing perfumed body oil on myself after a bath can get me into a sensual, relaxed mood. Others feel the same way; Anne Hooper likes to use suntan oil because the smell reminds her of holidays and the indolent pleasures of warm beaches. I've realised that time spent smelling different oils and moisturisers in shops is time well used when I find something that gives us pleasure at home.

Smell can be such a subtle sense. It can take us away from the mundane to another country, another life. It can also take us right back to somewhere we'd rather not be, with immediate effectiveness. That's why I have to wash the smell of sheep off myself so thoroughly before close encounters with Colin – he doesn't want to be reminded of the farm when we're in the bedroom!

Learning the importance of touch, and touching each other in new ways, has played a crucial part in reviving sexual delight in each other. We no longer go straight for the genitals: our whole bodies are sources of sensual pleasure. We don't concern ourselves with concepts like 'erogenous zones'; we don't look for overt sexual response; but the end result is a much greater whole-body involvement in sex.

Sensuous fabrics are part of this, although for me, there is a risk that if I'm wearing too much I'll lose out on the skin contact that I like and need. But I will put on hold-up stockings so that Colin can enjoy running his hands over silky legs, and I love wearing a short black slip with the satin feel of pure silk. I remember getting quite turned on by wearing close-fitting satin trousers and smoothing my hands over my thighs and buttocks – especially when I knew there was a sexy man watching!

It's time we had more of these fabrics in the bedroom . . . a velvet-covered stool, perhaps, satin sheets and cushions . . . there are always more sensations to explore, more sensuous delights to imagine and create! Touch brings a whole world of pleasure.

If it feels good, do it! Follow your desires, let them flower to bring delight that you can share.

16

Time for Sex

Colin knows a thousand and one ways to refuse sex when I want it.

'Not now, I'm busy!'

'Later, I want to do this first.'

'After *Newsnight*, when I've fed the dogs.' He then puts off feeding the dogs for two hours.

'Why don't *you* go to bed?'

Sometimes I feel Colin only wants sex when I don't.

Finally we're both together, TV off, the business of the day finished. I'm three-quarters asleep, twitchy because I wanted sex four hours ago and didn't get it, resentful because I no longer have any energy to put into it. Irritably, Colin pushes me aside. I'm not giving out the signals that make him want to make the effort to make love to me. I'm showing no conviction, he complains.

I roll away to my side of the bed feeling rejected, unloved, fed up. Next day I don't bother him. If I'm still in the mood, I may masturbate on my own but I probably won't mention it. When I'm sure he's interested, it may be worthwhile putting my ego on the line again. In the meantime, I'm not issuing invitations. Stuff that.

Colin's point of view is the same, but different. Another sequence of events unfolds . . .

I'm sitting at my word processor in the morning when he

comes into the room naked, sporting a fine erection. I start talking about my book. I've noticed his cock – how could I not? – but I'm preoccupied, so I ignore it. Or he embraces me in the kitchen, pulls up my T-shirt, fondles my breasts. I get on with the housework, taking no notice.

Or he is consistently charming and hints at his desire for sex. But I'm caught up in a seemingly endless round of obligations which continue till late in the evening. By the time I finish I'm exhausted. Yes, I find him attractive, but I'm just too tired for sex . . . In due course, we start rowing.

The same foolish pattern gets repeated in various forms, time and again, until we're forced to acknowledge that we can't continue to put sex last on our personal priority-lists. We can't behave as though it's the least important aspect of our lives, something that can be squeezed into the odd half-hour when everything else is over. Yet this pattern of behaviour, one of the many repetitive destructive patterns in our relationship, emerges again and again to undermine our happiness together.

When passion is overwhelming, finding the time and energy for sex is easy. But after years of living together, making time may require conscious adaptation, assertive action. As with cleaning the bedroom or taking exercise, Colin and I find it difficult to allow enough time for sex, even though we know it's essential to the quality of our relationship.

The pressure of time

We are living in a period of history when everything seems to be happening faster and faster. There's a pervasive sense of time running out. Inevitably, this feeling of having to rush damages our ability to enjoy sexual pleasure.

Good sex demands unrestricted time, and not just for the physical act that is so often the subject that we focus on. We need time to wind down from the pressures of our daily life, to slow down and open up to one another. We need time to adjust our mindset, to talk and remember affection, time to get in touch with our feelings, time to relax. When I analyse a night of wonderful sex in Chapter 17, I point this out: the preparations – both mental and physical – began many hours before we reached the bedroom.

Time-pressure, and the lack of energy for sex that goes with feeling there's too little time, is a problem for both Colin and me. We run many lives in parallel: writing, farming, environmental campaigning, business, running the household. I found it equally difficult when I had a nine-to-five job and Colin's children to look after. Like most people, we lead demanding lives.

Sex therapist Dagmar O'Connor writes of 'the one-minute marriage', the increasingly common situation where couples feel they have too little time for intimate talk and leisured physical contact. 'When intimacy is put under a time restriction,' she observes, 'something has to give and often it's our bodies that give up first . . . *Our most intimate emotions and sensual feelings refuse to be rushed*.' The productive, independent couples she sees in her New York clinic are so intent on not wasting a minute that 'sex tapers off to nothing or he comes too soon or she doesn't come at all'.[1]

Making sex a priority

Sometimes, we just have to put everything else on hold. Business can wait. Writing can wait. Housework can wait. The sheep can wait. Cleaning the barn, cutting the nettles, mending the tractor – all these time-consuming tasks can wait. Maintaining our closeness is more important: we'll return to work soon enough.

For people who work away from home, there are fewer choices, but even then there is almost always some leisure time when you can make conscious decisions about what to do. Most people have evenings and weekends when they are in control of their own timetables. There are jobs to do, commitments that cannot be ignored; but we can still decide to take time off for ourselves and our primary relationship, time to enjoy sex together. The crucial thing is to make that decision, to acknowledge that sexual closeness, and the intimacy that goes with it, is sufficiently important to us that we choose to give sufficient time to it.

For all that so many people complain that they don't have enough time to enjoy themselves, there are often many hours that could be used differently. The busiest group of people, according to British government surveys, are mothers in full-time employment – yet even they have an average of thirty-three hours' leisure each week, while the average man has forty hours a week for relaxation.[2] He has more time, of course, because he still doesn't share housework equally. I hope the boys who are growing up now will behave differently from their fathers!

What do we do with our time? Where does it all go, that there's too little left for sensual and sexual pleasure? Watching TV is a major time-drain, and social research reveals that removing the TV leads to a surge in frequency of lovemaking. Do we really want to spend so long watching trivia on TV when we can find much more rewarding ways to pass our time?

Time to nurture our relationship can become the most expendable item on our schedule. Even when Colin and I know we must spend more time together, we often don't. Sometimes, the demands on us are unavoidable: urgent appointments that can't be changed, ewes who can't be ignored, lambs who must have attention lest they die. But if we discuss the problem and make a conscious mutual decision to give ourselves more time for sex, at least we can return to it and remind each other of it whenever we feel our sex-life is getting neglected.

Colin and I are fortunate that we can control our time to the degree that we can – or maybe we've been very determined that this should be so. We don't have to clock in at an office, shop or factory each morning; we don't have to work till five o'clock, five days a week. We can choose to write when we feel able, to do farm work when we decide or when Nature demands, and in theory we can retire to make love pretty much when we want to. But this is a mixed blessing; it means that our work is pressing even when most people have time off; we can lose weekends, evenings, holidays, because we can't ignore the needs of our animals, or take time off in sunny haymaking weather.

City life is totally different, yet the end-result can be the same. I have friends who have so many commitments – evening classes, pressure groups, sports clubs and jobs – that they hardly ever seem to see their partners, let alone spend a whole day together. Others work such long hours, and commute such outrageous distances, that they only meet to sleep. But this situation is one that we bring upon ourselves: almost always, there is some choice, commitments can be refused and meetings may not really be necessary.

The arrival of children often coincides with the time of life when the desire to make rapid progress at work is greatest. Children require time, space and money – and the increased need for space and money adds to the pressure on their parents' time and energy. Predictably, both opportunity and desire for sex tend to decline during the child-rearing years. Arranging weekends without the children, hiring babysitters one or two evenings a week, and fitting a lock to the bedroom door, can help couples to maintain their closeness despite the pressures of parenthood.

During the honeymoon period of relationships, couples live *for* each other and can almost always find time for sex; but after a few years, Colin and I were just living *with* each other. Suddenly we realised this misguided focus was one of the forces that had brought us to the painful edge of parting. To get back to where we started, we had to look at our priorities and make time to meet our needs. When we ignore these, we cease to function effectively in all other aspects of our lives.

One of the most difficult features of feeling there isn't

enough time is that you cease to see the wood for the trees. Every job seems equally important, every need equally pressing. Sometimes it seems like there's a cacophony of demands in my mind, each of which requires immediate attention. And then I get nothing done effectively, I can't function, I panic. The answer is to slow down – however difficult that feels – to stand back and assess priorities. I find that writing lists and making judgements about what really matters to me, and what can wait, is helpful.

It's all too easy to allow priorities to get distorted, to imagine that housework is more important than emotional well-being, or that commitments to other people are more important than your commitment to each other. If your relationship is to remain strong for the rest of your life, you have to give it the attention it needs. It's a question of finding the right balance between time for yourselves, working-time, and time for others. If you get that balance right, you'll find you use your time more effectively because a well-balanced life generates creative energy. It's something all of us who work under time-pressure have to think hard about.

Time-pressure: an excuse to evade difficult issues

Sometimes it feels more comfortable to work than to spend time together. Reared in a culture where the work-ethic is dominant, we are not free from its pressures. We feel nagging anxiety about making sex a priority even though we know we sometimes need to do so for the sake of our relationship and our sanity. Or we may use time-pressure as an excuse to avoid confronting the reasons for an unsatisfactory sex-life. The real issue may be hidden behind the socially acceptable problem of time-pressure: it could be anxiety about sex, or anger with your partner. Inability to find time for each other can be yet another symptom of failing communication or loss of trust.

We have to tune in to our feelings, work out what is

going wrong for us, before we're likely to find effective answers.

Guilt about taking time for personal pleasure may be part of the problem. Some women believe they cannot please themselves until the house is spotless, the ironing done, the children asleep in bed. Never mind that this takes all their time and energy, leaving none for themselves and their partner: at least it feels safe and virtuous.

I find it difficult to cut myself off from what I see as obligations. Colin is not as guilt-ridden about duty, but he has problems putting aside his need for constant outside input. So much of his time is spent watching television, I sometimes wonder if I matter at all. Eventually I get angry about his choice of priorities. Gradually, the effects of mutual neglect set in; tension grows, irritability flares, time is squandered in self-protective habits and, eventually, protracted rows.

Almost always, our rows focus on outside pressures and our failure to cope with them. Colin gets angry because I don't find enough time for the finer points of farm maintenance. I get resentful because I'm too busy to do the things I most care about, and he's trying to push me into giving even more time to the mundane necessities of life. But the underlying issue is that we're not taking enough time to care for our personal needs, and for each other.

Internal clocks

It's not just sheer shortage of time that causes difficulties. We also have to co-ordinate the times when we're able to put energy into nurturing our relationship. One of the problems Colin and I face is that our internal clocks run differently. He comes alive at night; he likes to stay awake late and enjoys making love after midnight. For him, sex is often difficult in the morning, impossible in the early evening. Diabetes rules his time-schedules with unrelenting force: he must have his insulin and eat at the same time every day, and because of the physiological disruption sex is not an option for him for a couple of hours around mealtimes.

I wake earlier than he does in the morning and my sex-drive peaks in the afternoon, when we're both working. By midnight, I'm drooping; if I'm awake at all in the small hours, I'm half-dead. He often wants to talk far into the night, when I can't think straight; at other times, he wants sex when I'm far too tired to put any energy into it. Even without the pressures of work, there are only limited time-windows when we can get together and enjoy sex.

We have had to compromise. Colin has had to come to terms with what I am, understand that I can no more control my internal clock than he can control his. Even after almost two decades together, we find it difficult to adapt to each other's needs. But accept and adapt we must.

We cope by setting a time when we will get together, usually the middle of the evening. He promises to turn the TV off, or stop writing, earlier than he otherwise would; I try to keep my energy-level up with physical activity or half an hour's meditation if I start to feel dozy. We both modify our behaviour so that we can meet halfway. But this has to be a conscious choice; when we fail to schedule intimacy in this way, it tends to get neglected.

So arrangements and agreements are made. We plan, at least to a minimal degree. We prepare. We refuse to answer the telephone when it's time for us to get together, set the video to record if there's something crucial on TV, put all work and the very thought of work aside till the morrow.

Spontaneous sex has become rare. If we wait for passion to take over of its own accord, we find ourselves waiting too long. But frankly, I don't think that matters; scheduled sex is no less exciting, no less delightful, because it has been planned in advance. There's just one point we have to remember: if one of us doesn't actually want to make love at the time we have agreed, we don't go ahead regardless. There's no obligation. You can't schedule feelings, but we've learnt that we must never ignore them. So that time-slot is for potential sex: it doesn't necessarily happen. Sometimes we just cuddle and talk and enjoy each other's company.

Couples with more structured lives than ours often benefit by scheduling a couple of evenings a week as time for themselves, when they will refuse all other invitations and commitments. You might decide that you won't go out with anyone else on Tuesdays or Fridays; instead, you'll spend these evenings together. You might choose to have a romantic candlelit supper, followed by a sensuous perfumed bath and an early night in each other's arms; you might simply want to talk together about things that are important to you alone. The important feature of such times is that they're *your* times, when you concern yourselves with your own feelings and desires.

Time for intimacy

It's not just the physical expression of sexual desire that takes time. Even more crucial is finding the time to look after each other emotionally, to nurture each other. In our materialist world, we tend to forget that it's important to take time just to be together, to create our own private world. Too readily, we allow everything, anything to intrude: the telephone, visitors, worries, routine, work.

Giving ourselves unpressured time simply to be close to one another allows sexual feelings to develop within us. We can't rush into sex: our minds and emotions need time too.

Time for arousal

When we do go to bed, we usually need plenty of time for sexual satisfaction. Twenty years ago, we were both able to respond faster; now we're middle-aged, we need longer to adjust in mind and body. I don't know whether I've really changed, or whether I've come to understand my own needs better. It's probably a bit of both. But I do know I need lots of time for sex.

When I was young and wild, carried along on a tide of lust and novelty, arousal came quickly. Now we have to create that tidal flow between us and it takes longer. The rush still comes; I still get carried away; but it doesn't happen automatically. We have to allow sufficient time for the build-up.

For couples who have spent years together, sex is more relaxed, less desperate, than it was at the beginning. Long-term partnerships aren't like weekend affairs when pent-up lust is released in a great flood. They're long, flowing rivers of love with their origins way back in memory: deeper, more subtle, gentle yet powerful.

We cannot hurry if we are to savour the experience, to meet each other's needs fully. We must linger together, talking, touching, kissing, tasting, awakening the full range of sensual response. There's no rapid build-up, no quick release. We must remember that and go to bed early so that we have all the time we could possibly need before we're too tired to experience the feelings that we hope to awaken.

Time to enjoy sex

Sex itself cannot be rushed. According to Sheila Kitzinger,[3] women may take two hours from the beginning of lovemaking to reach orgasm. Different writers give different figures, but many make the same point: that women, in particular, cannot go from cold to orgasm in a matter of minutes. Women often feel guilty about this; they think they're taking too long and that they have a problem. The truth is, in many cases, that it is not the woman who has a problem; the *couple* has a problem acknowledging that sex doesn't satisfy if it's hurried.

Not only is rushed sex a problem for women, it teaches men unsatisfying habits. Premature ejaculation is one; dashing for penetration is another. Both men and women enjoy sex more if they take longer over it. Mature sex is a leisurely activity which only works for both partners if they feel they can take just as long as they want.

Colin and I never watch the clock – so I have no idea how long we may spend caressing each other, how long we lick and kiss and savour each other, how long fucking lasts. But I do know that each stage must last long enough for us both to get as much pleasure from it as we possibly can.

Communication is, as so often, the key. We have to communicate clearly with one another, and each be open to communication from the other. I've known this for years, but even so I've found it difficult to put into practice. I still discover strange and unexpected blocks within me, fears that Colin might not want to hear what I have to say, and often I have failed to tell him clearly how I feel.

To get over some of these problems, Colin proposed a simple but effective method to ensure clear communication when we're making love without having to get into a long conversation or risk disputes.

We use just four words: 'Wait', 'Next', 'More', and 'Stop'. 'Wait' means stop whatever you're doing for a moment; it provides a pause, an opportunity to make some minor adjustment. I use it when I want to rearrange my position, get a vibrator, or simply build in a little time. 'Next' means let's do something different – adopt another position, change to another activity; it may mean I'm getting a little bored, or uncomfortable, or I simply want to move on to the next step in a lovemaking sequence. 'More' means more of the same, please – carry on doing that, it's wonderful! More, more, more! I may ask for more, or he may ask me: 'More?' 'Stop' tells the other that there's a problem: something's hurting, my cunt's getting sore or he's suddenly got cramp.

Apart from 'Stop', these words aren't commands or instructions that must be obeyed: they are aids to mutual understanding. If I say 'Next' or 'More' he might reply with 'Wait'; or if he says 'Next?' I might reply with 'More!' and he'll carry on, if he feels okay about it. 'Stop' is a little different; it calls for a complete halt and it needs to be treated with care and respect. When either of us tells the other to stop, some explanation is required. If we need to use 'Stop' often, there's an underlying problem that must be discussed and resolved.

So now I don't feel rushed when we're making love. I tell him with one simple, non-threatening word – 'More!' – if I want to stay with what's happening rather than move on. If he's really enjoying something I'm doing, he can ask me to continue in the same way. And when either of us wants a break or a change, we can propose it to the other without any risk of misunderstanding.

These four words provide a communication structure within which we can try anything. They make communication safe between us at times when we are both very vulnerable. We both know about them, so they don't worry either of us; using these words won't throw Colin off his stroke, or make me feel anxious. But most important, it allows us to control the timing of our lovemaking so that we both get as much out of it as we can. It allows us to experiment without fear.

How astonishing that we took eighteen years to work out such a simple device! Who knows what we might come up with in another eighteen years: time to reinvent the wheel, perhaps?

Time for yourself

The energy for sexual feeling comes from reserves deep inside each of us that don't get entirely replenished when we're with another person. We all have a need for private time, when we can be introspective, time to get in touch with our innermost feelings. This may be active time: for me, it can mean a long bike ride alone, or solitary dancing to the music of my choice; or it can be relaxation, just lying on the bed with my eyes closed. It doesn't matter what I'm doing, so long as I'm alone and concentrating on myself, nothing else. Maybe I'll just drift, my mind unfocused.

Time alone feels like a luxury when you're surrounded by other people every day. But partners can demonstrate their love by giving each other time for solitude. One might take the children out so that the other can enjoy quiet time. In the past, I've asked Colin to go out for the afternoon so that I can have the house to myself.

Women generally seem to need more time to *be* than men do. Most men are more concerned with *doing*. Many of my women friends find, as I do, that their partners are constantly wanting to drop in on them, disrupting their solitude when they're quite happily alone. We have to explain to the men in our lives that we have this need for solitude, which they may find incomprehensible, firmly asserting our right to be alone sometimes. I call it recharging my batteries; I fall apart if I don't do it. And one symptom of falling apart is loss of interest in sex.

Time to dream – and think

We may want to dream alone, or together. Whichever it is, it takes time. Shared dreams, as I explained in an earlier chapter, bind us together; mutual fantasies shape our future. We need to connect as dreamers and thinkers, not only as people who do things together. And once again, we lose out if we don't allow ourselves enough time.

A long-term relationship certainly gives you time to think! What's essential is that we actually take time to do so.

17

Sexual Fireworks

Despite our occasional problems, I have to say that sex with Colin has been more satisfying, more enjoyable, and more exciting in the past year or so than ever before. When I'm in the mood, I invite him to come to bed early so that we can enjoy extended sex-play together. But it's not so long since I was never really in the mood; I accepted his desire passively and did very little to contribute. I put all the responsibility for sexual excitement on to him and we both missed a lot of pleasure.

I began to change when I accepted unreservedly that we were jointly responsible for sexual excitement. I ceased to see my lack of enjoyment as Colin's fault, and recognising that I played an equal part in creating the situation we were in, naturally led to changes in my own behaviour. As I changed, Colin began to change too. We became better lovers.

It might seem surprising that all our years of sexual exploration and promiscuity had failed to teach us how to make love to each other in the most exciting ways possible. Looking back, I think we had merely been enjoying the stimulation of novelty, of other people's approaches to us, without developing a sexual style of our own as fully as we might. We hadn't learnt to get the most out of sex because fun came easily. We were having lots of sex and sheer quantity made up for any lack of quality; with plenty of casual fucking, we didn't bother to explore the wider reaches of our sexual natures. But as time went by, our unsophisticated routine became boring, unstimulating. Passion and desire faded away.

Learning to make love to each other in more exciting and varied ways has brought us closer together, deepened our relationship. By creating a more vital sex-life, we learnt to appreciate each other more. It's not that we need or expect sexual fireworks every time we make love: far from it. If we demanded that, I'm sure we would soon feel such pressure to perform that making love would seem like hard work and we'd probably give up doing it. Indolent sex, sleepy sex and quickie sex have their place too.

But wonderful sex has to happen sometimes, to remind us that, together, we can scale the peaks of excitement; we don't need to look elsewhere. I know now that Colin is the only lover I need because he can give me the greatest pleasure I can imagine. In return, I aim to pleasure him to the limit of his endurance.

The relative poverty of our previous sexual routine was not due to lack of knowledge. Colin and I have had plenty of opportunities to learn about sexual techniques; we've read extensively, watched films, videos, enjoyed group sex with other couples. We've both had more lovers than we can count. But somehow, we weren't applying this knowledge. Our expectations were too low and we were to discover that we didn't know as much about each other as we thought we did. It's something that tends to happen to couples who take each other for granted. Now, we're exploring our sexual selves as never before, just for the sheer pleasure of doing it. And the more we find, the more there seems to be to find.

Perhaps it seems strange that we didn't bother to put sufficient effort or imagination into sex. We had grown complacent, set in our ways. For my part, I saw sex with others as really exciting; stimulated by the upsurge of immediate lust that overwhelms me early in an affair, I'd throw myself totally into it, worshipping my lover's body in every way I could. When I gave up sex with others, I gave up expecting excitement. Poor Colin just got the barest routine.

Poor me, too. Not for me the sexual marathons that other women enjoyed with Colin. I was the bread-and-butter bonk; sex between us was barely enough to keep frustration at bay, and that only when I was willing. As I grew increasingly fed up, I was less often willing. My behaviour and appearance became progressively less inviting, more smelly farmhand than delectable mistress.

Learning to be lovers again after our sex-life had been deteriorating for a decade and a half required a conscious decision. First, we had to face the facts. We weren't giving of our best, and we would both have to put more into sex if we were to get more out of it. We had to recognise that we both needed and enjoyed extended sex-play, and that we didn't, and shouldn't expect to, come primed and raring to go. Reaching the peaks of experience means getting it right from the start, and it demands commitment.

For the first year or so that we were together, we didn't feel we needed to make any effort to get the most out of sex. We were in love. The fires of lust were burning high. I was ready for Colin at any time, I didn't need preparation and we didn't tend to bother with more than minimal foreplay. Colin would get a hard-on just looking at me; I'd get wet just being close to him.

But over more than a decade of living together, our reactions changed. As the years went on, we increasingly came to see each other as irritating, nasty, predictable and dull. The sheer weight of time, familiarity and negativity undermined that early simplicity of delight in one another. If Colin were suddenly to fling up my skirt and attempt to fuck me as he could in our honeymoon years, he'd meet shocked resistance. The act, if completed, would be rape.

We now realise we need an extended warm-up period to

orientate our minds and bodies and prepare ourselves for sex. It doesn't just happen by itself, except on those rare occasions when I wake from an erotic dream to find that Colin has a convenient morning hard-on. You have to blow over the ashes of an old fire, no matter how fiercely it once burned, before putting more fuel on.

For some time, I fought against that knowledge. One of my reactions was a perverse disinterest: why should I bother to get myself worked up for his sake? I could leave him for someone who inspired spontaneous sexual excitement. My ambivalence about Colin and anger at the pressure of his sexual demands made me resent the idea that I should make more effort.

It was a risky time for our relationship. It's at times like this that we are open to flings with people who do stimulate instant, effortless lust. It's easy to fall into the trap of thinking that the marriage is dead and a new affair is true love. But I knew, when I was being honest with myself, that sexual boredom would set in very fast, as it had with man after man in my promiscuous years.

Colin was unaware of how little satisfaction I was getting out of our sex-life. I had been afraid to admit to the way I really felt. When I decided I wanted to make our relationship work, I had to do my best to make sex good for both of us. The first step was to have the courage to be honest about my feelings.

I believe in honesty. I have always believed that honesty is crucial to healthy, loving relationships. Yet when it was important to speak about my feelings, I was afraid to do so. I feared that if I said anything he might take as criticism – especially criticism of him as a lover – he would feel hurt and might react by hurting me in return. I lived in fear of his scathing tongue and suppressed violence. I felt anxious, guilty, and uncertain about my own feelings. For a long time, it was easier to pretend I didn't feel the way I did. But once I admitted to myself that I was being dishonest, I had to do something about it.

Finally, one calm evening, I decided to speak up. I started to tell Colin about my own reactions, explained what was happening – or failing to happen – to me, and what I thought I needed to start enjoying sex again.

I told him how dry I was, and how uncomfortable and miserable sex was without enough vaginal lubrication. He hadn't realised how bad the problem had become; but when he understood, he was willing to take more trouble to ensure that I was thoroughly wet before he tried to insert his cock. The best method, we discovered, was cunnilingus, extended tongue-work on my cunt. His saliva overcomes the initial dryness while his tongue and lips quickly cause my juices to flow.

For some reason, I had never asked him for this – nor, in fact, had I worked out that I needed it. I had felt he would offer it if he wished, I had no right to expect it. Silly me! For so long, what he'd really wanted was that I should enjoy sex; whatever I needed, he was happy to give – so long as it wasn't actually objectionable to him. And mouth-to-cunt contact definitely didn't fall into that category.

We had talked about it, but not enough. I knew he preferred mutual sucking (69 position), so I hadn't insisted on getting what I liked – solo licking and kissing, with him concentrating on pleasing me so that I could focus totally on the sensations he was creating.

He hadn't known how good it was for me, but once he knew, he did it. He encouraged me to ask for more, if I wanted more – as much as I wanted. I read in one of Alex Comfort's books that women might need half an hour's sucking to truly turn them on, so we began to joke about half-hours and now take just as long as we want, give each other as much as we can take. When I reach melt-down, I let him stop!

Sucking is good for both of us. Pleasuring me this way turns him on; my juices have marked aphrodisiac effects. It's so simple, so natural, so utterly delightful. Of course, the taste has to be good. Once, at an orgy, Colin got a horrible shock when he started licking a woman who had used a vaginal deodorant. The flavour totally turned him off. 'What's wrong?' she asked him as he pulled away from her. 'Tongue-tied by twinkle twat,' Colin eventually replied. He likes me to wash thoroughly an hour or so beforehand; I never use soap, just warm water.

Now, I feel I can ask for sexual delight and allow myself to relax and accept it. I need not worry about offering Colin some reward at the same time; that can come sooner or later. In most circumstances, Colin isn't reluctant to ask for whatever he wants. Sex was the exception. He didn't ask for particular sexual delights because spontaneity is part of the turn-on for him. He hoped I would know intuitively what he wanted and resented the fact that I didn't. And when pleasure wasn't mutual, I resented being expected to give – especially when I wasn't confident that he wanted what I was offering. So he lost out too. He is slowly accepting the fact that I can't read his mind.

While I understand his desire for me to know what he would most enjoy and do it spontaneously, this can become the mirror image of my belief that if he were the perfect lover, he'd know precisely what I wanted without being told. It can become a way of avoiding taking personal responsibility for mutual pleasure or coming to terms with reality, an excuse for blaming the other. Making desires and preferences clear can encourage the other person to act with more confidence, and that confidence inspires spontaneity. We have to achieve a balance between the two.

For all that, we both love it when the other person does something we never thought of. Reciting a menu to the other makes sex predictable. The most exciting sex is part familiar delight, part surprise.

Although we've been learning to ask for special pleasures, we have to be careful not to *demand* them. Neither one of us can afford to put pressure on the other: that's a certain turn-off. Both of us have to feel we can stop whatever we're doing if we're losing interest. What I do is try to *encourage*

Colin to give me what I want, perhaps by telling him how much I enjoyed it last time he sucked me, or maybe that I've been fantasising about his fingers massaging my G-spot.

I sometimes pair a request with an offer: I'll suck yours if you suck mine; I'll massage you if you massage me; I'll stroke you if you stroke me. When we feel especially loving towards each other, we can ask for sexual and other favours even when we don't have the energy to offer anything in return, because pleasing someone you love is inherently rewarding. But the truth is that nobody really feels like giving all the time; there has to be mutuality, a balance.

Colin and I have come to appreciate sex-play in all its variety more and more as time goes on. We rarely fall into bed without preparation and casually fuck before sleep, or wake up feeling horny and start the day with sex. That used to happen years ago, but now we're more likely to plan, prepare, and take our time. And we've been reaping the rewards of a more considered approach to sex.

We have been making conscious efforts to find new ways to delight each other. I've been working on turning him on more completely, exciting him more, getting in touch with the deepest levels of his sexual nature, seeking 'new perfumes, larger blossoms, pleasures still untasted . . .'[1] Concentrating on him, I forget myself and tune into his presence, his maleness, his desirability. And he concentrates on me, pleasuring me till I quiver and melt.

Ecstasy refound

Most emphatically, there can be lust after sexual boredom. After loss of desire comes the rebound resurgence, if you're determined to make it happen. I was determined, I was dedicated. I knew I loved sex, I had just forgotten how to gain access to the feelings . . .

To me, sexual fireworks means feelings so intense, they take me somewhere I can't normally go. It can be days before I recover. Let me tell you, as best I can, about a peak that followed one particular trough. A whole range of peaks await us, each individual, shrouded in the mists of the future. This is what we've been aiming for: this is bliss.

I quiver as I write, wriggling on my chair. My cunt is still hot and wet from last night. I can feel a pulse beating there, demanding attention. It's had so much fucking, it can't take any more – not just yet – but the longing's still there, still strong after uncounted orgasms. The higher I get, the higher I can get and the more I want. Love and lust create a positive spiral that takes me to heaven.

Colin and I made love till we couldn't do it any more. Then, sleeping, I dreamt of sex, more and more and more sex, a strange orgy organised in the back of a shop; Colin was there, and our friend Bill Levy, but I don't remember exactly what I did with them, just that it was incredibly exciting . . . I woke up thinking about sex, wanting to feel a man beside me, inside me, but Colin was still exhausted from the night before and anyway I was sore. So I kissed him and stroked him and pushed my buttocks against his stomach so I could feel him warm against me and he played with my nipples, pulling and tweaking just enough to delight me and make me want more . . .

This is how it happened. Colin had bought some sex videos[2] because he enjoys them. I never had, particularly. Usually, as I've said, they make me uncomfortable. But one video he found especially charming, and he wanted me to watch it with him, if I was willing. This one, he assured me, was not crude but beautiful.

I prepared myself consciously for an evening of sexual pleasure. I had a dance-workout in the afternoon so my body felt good, strong, supple. We ate a light supper of fish and fresh salad, enough to refresh without feeling full, and took a walk for togetherness as the sun was setting. Then I had a soak in a hot bath, lying back and reading Bill Levy's book *Is There Sex After Forty?*[3] which strikes many chords in my mind.

I dried my hair so that it fell in a perfumed red-gold cloud around my face when I stood up, put on a short tight-fitting dress, sheer black hold-up stockings and high-heeled dancing shoes. No underwear, no jewellery, no ornaments, no make-up: just me, my body shape emphasised without being constricted by clothes.

Colin had lit the log fire in the sitting room; I lit the candles. Incense perfumed the warm air. With a glass of wine each, we settled back to watch the video.

The scene he'd thought I would like was of two young Californian girls masturbating outdoors in the sunshine. It was indeed charming; it was obvious that they enjoyed what they were doing, the camera did not intrude and the music was good. But it was the next episode of the video that got me going: a scene of two lovers, the girl not unlike a younger version of myself, the man young but sexually sophisticated.

The sequence was simple: kisses followed by sucking and fucking. But each phase was so real, so natural and unselfconscious, that I couldn't help but be drawn into it. I identified with the girl in the film, watched both their faces, imagining the sensations, reliving memories of favourite lovers whose mouths and cocks have driven me wild.

When they had finished I was ready to go upstairs with Colin, eager to experience these delights in reality. He found my cunt hot and wet, rosy pink and swollen in anticipation. I put a pillow under my bottom to give him better access so he could lick my cunt all around, take the little knob of my clitoris between his lips and suck it, roll it and flick it with his tongue till I didn't know whether I was coming or going off into orbit, quivering and trembling . . . He paused. More? Yes, more! More, I can't bear it, more! With his fingers he parted the inner lips, felt for the sensitive spot inside and drove me frantic.

At this point I just had to have his cock. I had to feel its hardness, its power deep inside me, each blow against my cervix throwing stars through my body, right up to the top of my head. I wanted him to come against me then, when I was coming, to come deep into my cervix, so ready, so tight against him. I came and he was still there. I found him again when I returned to earth.

I came down enough to seek his cock with my mouth, to show him how I felt, to transmit those wonderful feelings to him; so I licked and nibbled and teased and swallowed his cock till it was so sensitive he was groaning and then I gave him some more until I couldn't resist the temptation any longer and I lowered myself on to him to fuck again, choosing my position so the most reactive parts of me were in contact with him, moving as the centres of sensation moved in me.

We were clasped together, one creature, driven by lust, wildly fucking, the core of life in our genitals, dominated by cock and cunt and the desperate delight of total contact.

He turned me over, working at me doggy-fashion as we like to do when we are close to the climax. He drove his cock so far into me it almost hurt, but it wasn't pain, it was perfect, it was what I wanted, this was what I wanted . . . I could feel the head, like a red round pecan nut, moving inside me. I knew it would be there, where I needed it, as we came . . . We cried out in unison, high voice and low together. Rings of colour appeared in my mind, each one expanding and flying outwards, fading as the next one arrived. My cunt was contracting on his pulsing cock. I couldn't let him go, not yet, not till I'd settled down . . . I shook with aftershocks, tremors that ran through me like echoes of my orgasm. I needed his arms round me. Holding me. Letting me down gently.

I strove to calm my quaking cunt by pressing it against his thigh. It refused to be quiet, it would not rest. I felt insatiable. I brought him croissants and apple juice, refreshment to aid his recovery. We continued to kiss and caress each other, rolling around on the mattress, enjoying each other's naked warmth. I was still turned on, wanting more, insatiable.

He sat and watched as I began to masturbate, stroking me gently while I held the vibrator to my clitoris. My orgasm turned him on again. Finally we both reached another overwhelming climax and fell back on the pillows, both well fucked, floppy all over, tingling from the soles of our feet to our heads.

We had turned each other on so much, he had enjoyed two tremendous orgasms within an hour; as for me, I don't know how many times I came. I found it amazing that this could happen still, after eighteen years.

Waking after sexy dreams I felt hot and eager again, though I knew my cunt wouldn't take any more till it had had time to recover from the battering of the night before. I can wait. He'll be here later, when we're both ready. Just don't let it be too long!

That afternoon, the women in Colin's office told me he looked worn out. 'What have you been doing to him?' they wanted to know. What's he been doing to me, they should ask. It'd been a long time since I last felt so insatiable.

I look back, analyse, isolate the components that were brought together to create this night of passion. It began with positive anticipation and preparation. Devotion to pleasure starts early. Feeling good in ourselves, we built up our energy through activity, and talked about what we wanted. On this occasion, Colin had said he wanted me to watch a sexy video with him; other times, we might talk about exploring some other aspect of our sexual selves, dressing up or trying out a new toy. How can you know whether you'll like it until you try it?

We didn't feel pressured in any way. There was plenty of time and freedom from everyday worries. We were in agreement; neither pushed the other; there was an easy warmth between us.

We bathed to ensure that we smelt and tasted good, and to relax us. I like to read erotica and fantasise in my bath, focusing my mind on sexual delight. If I'm going back to the sitting room, I dress with care to create an image that's attractive and consistent with the way I feel. Some of my clothes are chosen purely with sex in mind: I never wear them outside the house.

We watched the video in warmth and comfort. It need not have been a video, we could have listened to music and danced in soft candlelight; but whatever we did, our mental focus would have to be on sex. Distractions would reduce the intensity of the excitement later.

A glass of wine added to our pleasure. Not too much: we don't want to get stoned insensible, and all intoxicants, including alcohol and marijuana can, in excess, interfere with sexual sensitivity and pleasure. We select our aphrodisiacs with care; a taste of top-quality dark chocolate, a handful of roasted almonds, a luscious peach . . .

When we first begin to kiss, to touch, to feel each other's warmth, it is a gentle exploratory process, confirming feelings. We retire to the comfort and privacy of our bedroom to take touch further, to stroke and massage each other, to oil each other's body with subtle perfumes, to arouse each other, first with fingers and then with tongues and lips.

In a small covered dish by the head of the bed, I keep a cache of crystallised ginger. When we fancy intensifying the erotic impact of sucking cock or cunt, we chew a chunk each to make our saliva hot. Long known for its aphrodisiac qualities, ginger is especially exciting when we use it on each other's genitalia. Ginger can be wild stuff!

Sometimes we enjoy sex-toys. I have tried many, but keep only a small collection: a handsome brass-ringed black vibrator with a sponge tip (sold as the Non-Doctor, it has a selection of tips but I prefer the soft one on my clitoris); a slender vibrator for stimulating Colin's prostate; a dildo; KY jelly. We have various oils; rose-scented cock and cunt oil; massage oil perfumed with jasmine and patchouli; ylang-ylang body oil; foot oil with relaxing lavender.

We're quite conservative really. We don't go in for bondage, or spanking, or even toe-sucking. But if we enjoyed these things, or any of the many other variants on everyday sex, we'd make sure we were equipped to take advantage of our proclivities.

Mail-order services can be very useful if you live, as we do, in deepest countryside, or if you're unhappy about entering sex-shops. There are advertisements for all tastes in sex magazines. I've found Anne Summers (081–660 8958) efficient and their prices are reasonable.

But it's the attitude of mind, not the toys and accessories, that really matters. Knowing we wanted to enjoy all we're capable of feeling, we went for it with every level of our beings in harmony. We had prepared ourselves mentally and physically; we were ready for pleasure. And pleasure – the most intense pleasure – was what we achieved.

18

The Wellsprings of Desire

The expression of sexual desire is a natural function of a healthy body. So far, I've emphasised the psychological aspects of sexuality, but mind and body are inseparable. To concentrate on psychology and ignore physiology is to deny reality; peak sexual function requires a balanced approach to all aspects of ourselves.

Sexual activity is very physical. The fitter we are, the better our performance, and the more we enjoy it. Fit, healthy people are more desirable and usually experience desire more intensely than those who are out of condition. They certainly enjoy sex more often.

Physical competence creates the sort of well-proportioned body that looks sexy. Active people enjoy the benefits of more effective hormone systems, they have more energy, and they move with a supple grace that reflects contentment with their bodies.

I won't pretend that regular activity will make you into something you were never designed to be. It can't give me the body of a willowy dancer or a leggy fashion model because that simply isn't my body-type, but it does enhance physical attractiveness. And for all that I'm aware of the pernicious pressures on women, in particular, to be skinny, it's an undeniable fact that flabby, over-fat people neither look nor feel as sexy as those whose bodies are a healthy shape.

Physical inactivity is self-neglect

Keeping fit is a central part of a wider strategy for meeting the body's needs that brings a multiplicity of benefits, not just in improved appearance but in an inner glow that affects every aspect of our lives. When we neglect our physical needs, it reveals that we do not value important aspects of ourselves. A neglected body is a clear sign of a person who is out of tune with his or her physical self. Such people are more susceptible to illness, much of which is rooted in self-rejection. Rejecting and neglecting our physical selves damages both sexual feeling and the ability to fully share and experience sexual pleasure.

Becoming as physically attractive as we can be is a very positive, enjoyable process. Strategies based on suppressing natural desires, like calorie control and other forms of dieting, are ultimately doomed to failure because they involve self-rejection. When our aim is to function and feel better by ensuring that our personal needs are met, we naturally begin to look more attractive.

Perhaps it's because I've been aware of this that I've always fancied athletic men. I like men whose legs and arms and buttocks are well-proportioned with muscle, not wasted or flabby with disuse; men who move with the confidence that regular physical activity confers. I know from my promiscuous days that (all other things being equal) physically fit men make the best lovers. I used to love fucking with dedicated sportsmen, not just because their muscular bodies felt wonderful, but because they could sustain sexual enjoyment for so much longer.

It doesn't matter if a man no longer has the slender outline of youth, nor that his skin is wrinkled with age: my father, nearing eighty, is still handsome. He walks his dog each day with the energy of a young person, scarcely noticing the many miles they cover together. The point, for both men and women, is that it's good for us, and especially for our continued sexual enjoyment, to ensure that we feel and look as desirable as possible at every stage of life. I'm not concerned with superficial things like using moisturisers or colouring our hair, but about the way we function deep inside. We can't stop time going by, but we don't have to allow ourselves to degenerate unnecessarily. Bodies are wonderful but we have to treat them with respect – and that means meeting our needs for regular activity.

Not that Colin and I are paragons; we have phases when we neglect ourselves. When there are too many demands on my time, I walk and cycle too little. Fat begins to accumulate on my body, hormone and period problems start to creep back. When Colin's fed up, he'll spend hours slumped in front of the TV; when he's feeling stressed, he'll drink too much coffee, eat too many chips, use his muscles too little. His face turns grey, his gut expands, his temper flares. For both of us, the unwanted effects of inactivity are predictable and obvious.

Sooner or later, we acknowledge that we've got into a harmful negative cycle. We pick ourselves up, help each other to make fresh resolutions, and act to incorporate more pleasurable exercise into everyday life. We return to playing badminton, taking walks, we get our bikes on the road. We don't criticise and we try hard not to nag; instead we encourage each other with gentle reminders that we need physical activity and we cannot afford to ignore that need.

Soon the benefits become obvious: not just in body-shape, but in a more positive outlook and an upsurge of sexual energy. In fact, energy for life in all its aspects increases, so long as we stay within the limits of our physical capacity. We gain more energy from activity done purely for ourselves than we put into it.

Activity and pleasure

Colin and I both prefer each other without large rolls of surplus fat (though certainly not bony), skin healthy with the glow of an active life, legs and arms passably shapely.

We don't expect perfection, faces free from the marks of passing years, or eternal youth. Experience has taught me that I gain from keeping myself fit, not only in the pleasure his appreciation brings, but from the direct benefits of physical activity: continuing health, enhanced emotional stability and resilience, and the sheer pleasure of using my body.

When I was younger, I neglected both my emotional and my physical needs, concentrating excessively on my rational self. I was suffering the disastrous effects of a passive upbringing combined with a general tendency to do everything very slowly. I'd been something of a slob as a girl; hopeless at games, I knew nothing of the delights of physical competence. It wasn't till I reached my thirties that I discovered that using my body could be fun.

My attitude started to change when I learnt to ski. I was no worse at it than any other member of my beginners' class, and the combination of snow, mountains and speed was unbelievably exhilarating. Having discovered one activity I really enjoyed, I then – with Colin's constant encouragement – found others.

I started to explore and develop my physical competence when we were very poor. Working on our first book, we had to find ways to balance long hours spent sitting in front of typewriters. That was when I learnt to run, ride a bike, discovered delight in gardening, sawing logs, and even shifting piles of earth and stone. I became strong and proud of my strength.

The real breakthrough was the realisation that physical activity could be *fun*, that muscular effort could bring pure, unadulterated pleasure. I know it can bring discomfort too; unaccustomed physical work leads to aches and muscular soreness, but that's no more than a temporary phase which can largely be avoided with careful pacing. Once I'm over that barrier, pushing myself harder brings excitement and exhilaration. I find new energy reserves and a sense of physical power that I'd never anticipated. In addition, I find I'm more in tune with my body, I appreciate myself more, and I enjoy life more. I had suddenly discovered a whole dimension of myself that had lain unrecognised for years. Physical passivity had meant I'd been missing a great deal of pleasure in life.

My reactions are not unusual. Hilary, who wrote to *New Woman* magazine in response to their survey on women, sex and body image, expressed feelings very much like mine:

> From the age of 15 onwards, I developed a loathing for my body. I was obsessed by dieting, obsessed by my imperfect shape. I believed that if only I could be a better shape, then the door to success would somehow magically open.
>
> It wasn't until I was 28 that the door *did* open – but not in the way I expected. A girlfriend had started running and I agreed to join her. As my performance improved, for the first time I felt physically capable – not something that, as women, we are encouraged to be. This fitness gave me a confidence that came from within, and was not dependent on whether I'd lost or gained weight that week, or eaten 'good' or 'bad' food.
>
> My figure has certainly firmed up in the year since, and although it may not be model-perfect, I like it and have learnt to enjoy my own unique shape rather than hanker after someone else's.
>
> If women really want to be 'liberated', I think the importance of feeling physically fit and confident is paramount. Otherwise we will be locked forever in this constant dissatisfaction with our bodies, the endless craving for perfection. The good news is that the answer is in your hands, and the moment you recognise it you're halfway there already.[1]

Colin was the friend who encouraged me to develop my physical power, and I shall always be grateful. As a teenager, he had been a cross-country runner, he swam for miles in the sea, cycled great distances for pleasure. He went in for serious weight-training to rebuild his body after the wasting effects of undiagnosed diabetes had reduced him to little more than a skeleton. When I met him, he too had been neglecting his physical needs, but the collapse of his business led to a total change in his way of life. Through sustained physical labour he changed his body-shape to that of a much younger, more desirable man. His blood pressure fell, his paunch disappeared, and his circulation improved. Because of this, he has retained a capacity for sexual pleasure that would probably have been lost through physical deterioration. He's much more handsome now than he was when I first met him!

Activity for older people

In the longer term, we both know that we're likely to have, and enjoy, each other for many more active years if we continue to ensure that our physical needs are met. I don't want Colin to degenerate to such a degree that he's incapable of enjoying sex or pleasing me; we're mature enough to know that that can happen surprisingly quickly if he neglects himself. When he gets out of condition, his diabetes becomes less controllable and his sexual potency could fail. And I fancy him less.

When we look after ourselves, we can look forward to a more enjoyable future. For women, one advantage is that menopause is easier to cope with. Physically active women sleep better and suffer less from hot flushes because their temperature control systems are more effective.[2] In addition, using their bodies – and in particular, their legs – protects women from post-menopausal osteoporosis. Just twenty minutes' brisk walking, three times a week, is enough to keep the bones strong well into old age, as well as enhancing resistance to many other forms of illness. Women who have been through the menopause should not overdo strenuous exercise, however; walking and cycling are beneficial but anaerobic activities like weight-training are not.[3]

So Colin and I keep fit. Running a small farm undoubtedly contributes to this: I have only to look at my neighbours, the farmers around me, to see how regular physical work keeps them looking well and vital. Many are older than we are, but they move with an energy that belies their years. However, we don't have to be farmers to use our bodies. I recall the elderly members of the nudist club to which we used to belong. Those who used the sports facilities regularly were as fit and attractive as anyone could wish to be. Nudists cannot disguise the state of their bodies; the benefits of sport were obvious for all to see.

A positive attitude

Physical activity must be regarded in a positive light. If you're not accustomed to it, you may be convinced that exerting yourself will be uncomfortable, even painful. If you're a habitual dieter, you may not have the energy you need for activity. The answer is to build activity gently into a totally changed lifestyle: eat enough good food (see below for more on this) to boost metabolism and get energy flowing, and don't try to do too much too fast. Your body will gradually grow accustomed to the change. As you become used to a higher level of energy output, your capacity for pleasure in activity – all physical activity – will increase.

I had to throw out my belief that I was hopeless at sports and that I didn't enjoy exercise and learn to think about it in a positive way. Now, I appreciate myself far more than when negative ideas like 'I can't ride a bike', 'I don't run', 'I can't hit balls', 'I mustn't eat' and 'I'm fat' controlled my leisure hours.

How to get moving

There are five key principles for effective physical training regimes. Ignore any of these, and good resolutions fall by the wayside. Disillusionment sets in, blocking the will to continue. Torture is no fun. Forget 'pain means gain': the point is to care for yourself, not punish yourself.

The pleasure principle comes first because it's the most important. Pleasure is your body's way of telling you you're doing the right thing. You must find forms of activity that you enjoy. There's no point in taking up jogging to get into shape if you hate jogging: you won't carry on doing it. If you believe physical activity is unpleasant, it may be because you haven't discovered the form that best suits you; or, perhaps, that you're hanging on to the conviction that you're not going to enjoy it. Try something different! Try something you've never done before!

I was amazed to discover how much I enjoyed riding a bicycle. I made the effort to learn to do it without realising how good it would feel. I hadn't anticipated the thrilling way the momentum would carry me along, giving me a sense of freedom and delight in the countryside. I proved myself wrong. It happens all the time. Until you have the confidence to explore unfamiliar possibilities with an open mind, you don't give yourself a chance to discover new pleasures.

When you find an activity you enjoy, it's easy to keep it going. Physical activity is something no one can afford to give up at any age. If you like doing things with other people, enhance the pleasure component of your chosen activities by doing them with your partner or in a group.

Make sure you're comfortable by equipping yourself with shoes and clothing intended to withstand the stresses of the form of activity you choose. It's important to wear clothes that absorb sweat and don't restrict movement. Well-fitting shoes with cushioned soles are essential for sports that involve running and leaping about. Buy them from a specialised sports shop where tough, serviceable shoes intended for active people are usually cheaper and more durable than fashionable look-alikes.

When Colin and I lived in London, we used to work out in a local gym. Now, we've invested in some basic equipment at home: an exercise cycle that allows us to keep fit while talking or watching TV and a mini-trampoline on which I bounce to energy-enhancing music. I like to dance or work out to music; it boosts the spirit and adds excitement to activity. So make sure you enjoy whatever you choose to do!

Second, you must work within your capacity. That means not doing too much at first when you're not accustomed to your chosen activity. Start again gradually after taking a break, recognising that you won't be capable of achieving as much as you could last time you were fit. A good rule is to do half of what you think you're capable of doing. That way, you don't end up stiff and sore. Slow, steady progress is much better than a fast crash.

Third, exercise for *yourself*. Don't seek to prove anything to anybody. Do what feels right, not what might impress others. Get used to impressing yourself, it's much more satisfying.

Fourth, exercise frequently. There's little point in obsessive exercise on Sundays, followed by inactivity for the rest of the week. We benefit most when we do something – however limited – every day: it might be a brisk half-hour walk, a session on the bouncer, a dance/workout in the sitting room, a swim or a cycle ride. Little but often is far better than too much or nothing at all.

Fifth, aim for balance: a programme of varied activities that use a whole range of muscle groups and are wide enough in scope to develop stamina, strength and suppleness.

Exercise should be part of a balanced lifestyle, with plenty of good food to fuel activity and sufficient rest to permit recovery and development. Each one of us needs to learn the balance that feels best. Try to concentrate on improving weak points without allowing strong ones to deteriorate.

We wrote in detail about exercise and its effects on the body in our book *Eat Yourself Thin*.[4] One of the things that our research revealed was that burning up fat requires prolonged steady exercise. Find time for activities that continue at a moderately demanding pace for an hour or more if possible. A fifteen-minute workout can keep you supple and help maintain muscle definition, but it'll do little to get rid of excess fat. An hour's brisk walk a day is what you need for that.

Activity requirements change with age but they never disappear. Physical power and speed are characteristics of youth; as we grow older, we need to shift towards gentler, lighter activities which can continue for longer. At mid-life, we slow down somewhat but we still have great stamina; later in life, joints become more vulnerable and recovery is slower. Allow for these changes, recognise that your needs and abilities will not remain constant.

Ten years ago, I used to keep in shape by running. Now I'm in my mid-forties, I prefer less demanding activities that are easier on my joints. So I cycle, dance and walk, and leave the running to younger women. What you cannot afford to do is imagine that physical pleasure is only for the young. Sexual pleasure can be enhanced at any age by building up endurance in other types of physical activity.

Fitness has made me a better lover because I'm more in tune with my body, more appreciative of its abilities. Becoming physically competent has enhanced my sense of self-esteem. Exercise is the most effective way of improving body-image; I flex my muscles proudly in front of the mirror, admiring their rippling contours – they make me feel good! Confidence grows along with physical competence.

Eat well

Attention to diet is the second major aspect of looking after yourself. Always go for food of the highest nutritional quality. Colin and I choose wholefoods, organic whenever possible, because they provide the nutrients we need for high energy and optimum function in every area of our lives. Organic food is high in essential nutrients. At the other end of the spectrum, highly-processed junk food is not only nutritionally poor, it doesn't contain the right balance of fats, complex carbohydrates and protein for optimum health, and it's contaminated by chemicals which disrupt body function.

We eat plenty of fresh fruit and vegetables, nuts, fish and wholemeal bread, and try to avoid sugar and other refined and processed foods as much as possible. Admittedly, we do have a weakness for high-quality chocolate: we're convinced it has aphrodisiac properties! But we can't allow chocolate to become part of our everyday diet: it has to remain special.

A balanced organic wholefood diet is naturally high in all the vitamins and minerals necessary to sustain good health and sexual function. The micro-nutrients that are known to be particularly important are the B-group vitamins, vitamins C and E, the minerals magnesium, iron, zinc and boron, and essential fatty acids.

B-group vitamins are necessary for energy and stable mood. I take extra vitamin B – especially B6 – when I'm feeling miserable and lethargic. Rich sources of vitamin B6 include oily fish, egg yolks, grains, nuts and seeds, bananas and avocados.

Vitamin C is essential for the production of sex hormones. It is concentrated in the adrenal glands, which produce testosterone, the hormone that makes both men and women feel sexy. People with higher testosterone levels tend to have higher sex-drives, they are more assertive and less prone to depression. Smoking, infection and exposure to pollution increase vitamin C requirements. The best sources of vitamin C are fresh fruit and vegetables, especially citrus fruit, berries, and most tropical fruits. New potatoes, water-cress and broccoli are also rich in vitamin C. Storage and cooking reduce the vitamin C content of food, so make sure it's as fresh as possible.

Vitamin E has been called the sex vitamin because deficiency causes impotence. It is essential for female fertility and can reduce menopausal symptoms, including hot flushes. Sunflower seeds, almonds, hazelnuts and peanuts, avocados and wild blackberries are all good sources of vitamin E.

Magnesium and iron are necessary to maintain energy and hormone balance. The first symptom of deficiency of either of these elements is lack of energy and loss of stamina. Magnesium deficiency is very common because conventional farming methods, which depend on chemicals, produce food that's especially short of it. The best sources of magnesium are nuts, especially almonds, brazils, cashews and hazelnuts, organic wholegrains, and tofu.

Iron is particularly important for women who have heavy periods. Dark green vegetables and red meat both get their pigment from their iron content. The foods richest in iron are kelp, yeast, molasses, sunflower seeds, wheatgerm and liver.[5] Nuts and raisins are also good sources. Iron absorption is enhanced by vitamin C, and reduced by drinking tea and soft drinks.

Zinc is a crucial mineral for the development and function of male sex organs. Boys who grow up on a zinc-deficient diet have tiny genitals; they don't develop into sexually mature men unless they get adequate zinc. Serious zinc deficiency causes impotence, while less severe deficiency reduces fertility. Semen is very rich in zinc.

Zinc is essential for women, too. Deficiency reduces sex-drive, causes anxiety, depression and anorexia, and reduces resistance to infection. Intense physical activity and infection increase zinc requirements.

The richest source of zinc, by far, is oysters – believed by many to be the most potent aphrodisiac food. Other zinc-rich foods include red meat, nuts and organic whole grains.

Boron is required in very small quantities, but it's especially important for middle-aged and elderly women because it raises the level of oestrogen in their bodies. Oestrogen keeps our sexual organs young, lubricated and elastic. Fresh fruit and vegetables are rich sources of boron.

Essential fatty acids keep our sex hormones in a healthy balance and protect our cardiovascular systems from ageing. There are two major sources: oily fish, and seeds such as sunflower and pumpkin. Evening primrose and blackcurrant oils are readily absorbed sources of essential fatty acids. If your diet is high in animal fats or processed fats, you will need more essential fatty acids to maintain a healthy balance. If you suffer from PMT or period pain, reduce the quantity of animal fat and processed fat in your diet at the same time as increasing your intake of essential fatty acids. People on low-calorie diets are especially susceptible to essential fatty acid deficiency; indiscriminately avoiding fats can cause a wide variety of problems, ranging from PMT to arthritis.

Nuts, avocados and whole, unrefined grains crop up repeatedly as the most valuable sources of nutrients for good sexual function. Some people avoid them because they see them as fattening. Don't worry about that! Forget calories! Foods like these will enhance your metabolic processes so that you burn food more effectively, producing energy rather than fat. Dieting makes you fat; look after yourself properly, stay active and eat well, and you will never consider returning to the misery of food deprivation.

When I was anxious about enjoying food, I was unable to enjoy my sexuality. Before I could function as a whole person, I had to learn to appreciate the importance of maintaining a balance within myself without rejecting either my capacities or my desires. Learning to eat well and to look after my body was crucial to my development.

Sometimes, however well we try to eat, we still don't get enough crucial micro-nutrients. Colin and I both use nutritional supplements: he takes a variety of supplements including chromium, magnesium and B vitamins every day; I take the same group of micro-nutrients during the second part of my menstrual cycle. But while supplements can be valuable, they are no substitute for a healthy diet.

Rest and relaxation

Along with exercise and a balanced diet, adequate rest and relaxation are essential to health. For me, like many women, this is sometimes difficult to achieve; I tend to be anxious, to feel I must dash about caring for others – especially my sheep – to the detriment of my own well-being and my relationship with Colin. I have to be constantly aware of this pitfall, to remind myself that activity must be balanced with rest, stress with periods of peace. When I neglect this need, I lose interest in sex. My mind must be stilled before I can focus fully on my sexual self.

Drugs and poisons

Finally, we cannot expect to be optimally healthy – and therefore sexy – if we poison ourselves with drugs, including medicinal drugs, alcohol and nicotine. In the long term, these substances cause physical damage which reduces sexual function.

In the short term, some drugs can help us feel sexy: nicotine has both tranquillising and energising effects, while alcohol, cocaine and marijuana help to free us from inhibitions. Marijuana can also intensify sensation and sexual pleasure. But we have to be careful with such substances, not only because some of them are illegal in Britain. If we use them too frequently, or in excessive quantities, they diminish sexual competence.

Making the best of ourselves

Why are these things – fitness, good nutrition, relaxation, looking after ourselves physically – important to long-term relationships? The answer is that they are important to our selves, to the creation and maintenance of our whole being. We cannot expect to fulfil our individual potential if we do not, literally, make the best of ourselves. And if we want to get the best out of a relationship, we have to put the best in that we can.

Improving your relationship starts with looking after yourself. Even if the relationship seems perfect, that perfection will only be maintained if we do what we can to maintain ourselves and each other in a state of maximum well-being.

Keeping the wellsprings of desire flowing is something we can, indeed should, do together. Encourage your partner to join you in your quest for greater physical competence. Teach by example: you won't need to nag or bully when the benefits of a self-respecting lifestyle start to show. This may take a few weeks, but you can afford to be patient if the lifespan of your relationship can be measured in years or decades. Unless your partner is very unusual, he won't want to be left behind.

Stable relationships are about balance. Being fit and whole will help to sustain that balance. Be the best you can – but don't expect to be the same as anyone else. Use your strengths to complement the balance of your relationship as a whole and trust your partner to do the same. Sharing the best will make it even better.

19

Can Sex Improve With Time?

'Sex gets better and better,' my mother told me when she was seventy-five. 'My greatest problem is removing your father from his workshop and all his preoccupations. He will carry on working so late. You know what he's like.' After nearly fifty years, she enjoyed her marriage tremendously; her only complaint was that she didn't get as much time with my father as she wanted.

There had been difficult periods. She used to tell me, when I was newly separated from Bob, how she longed for a younger man. That was a passing phase which my father recognised but accepted with impeccable tolerance, knowing her to be a colourful, emotional and sometimes capricious woman. His love for her never faltered. In due course, he reaped the rewards of his steadfastness.

My father adored my mother. She used to worry about growing fat and wrinkled but he never noticed; he saw her as utterly beautiful till the day she died. Old age brought its problems, but my parents had achieved a wonderful sense of peace together. I was delighted to realise that this really could happen; it gave me hope in a culture where many people seem to find it difficult even to think about sex between the older members of society.

How culture affects sexual interest

Who can really be surprised that sex and old age make a taboo combination? When young means desirable and old means ugly, sexy equals young; when sex is portrayed only between the young, sex between the old becomes unacceptable. The fact that the phrase 'old man' or 'old woman' is so often prefixed by 'dirty' reflects a view of sex in old age as something disgusting: good, wholesome sex is strictly for the young. Our culture – reflected in, and dominated by, the popular media – values youth and rejects age.

Faithfully repeating the dominant scenarios of our culture, many people give up sex when they pass middle age. For some women the menopause is seen as an opportunity to give up bothering with sex for ever; only a minority of people continue to have penetrative sex after the age of seventy, although non-penetrative sex and masturbation are more common.[1] Nevertheless, in one survey of sexual activity among a group of healthy people over the age of seventy living in California retirement homes, over 60 per cent of men and 30 per cent of women reported intercourse at least occasionally, while 28 per cent of men and 17 per cent of women enjoyed some form of sex-play every day. Another survey found that 46 per cent of men and 16 per cent of women over seventy were still having intercourse.[2] Not surprisingly, the sexually active group had more positive ideas about sexuality and age.

The difference in the rates of sexual involvement between the sexes is largely due to the much greater numbers of women who survive to this age; because women live an average of eight years longer than men, many are widows and their chances of having a sexual partner are lower. In addition, women are usually younger than their partners and the decline in their sexual activity is bound to reflect, at least in part, the health problems of older men.

There is, unquestionably, a reduction in sexual activity with progressing age, but this reduction is more cultural than biological in origin. What other reason could explain the fact that loss of sexual interest among women around the time of menopause is twice as common in less affluent, lower-class groups than in the highest social classes?[3]

How sad that for some, the delights of sex are so diminished that they are happy to give them up! This is the end-result of life in a culture which devalues sex, where negative attitudes to sex are so predominant. It's a long-term effect of regarding sex as dirty, of ignorance and guilt which limit sexual experimentation even for married couples, of the idea that sex as fun is indecent. When acceptable sex is still linked with procreation, it becomes unacceptable when the fertile years are past.

Ceasing to have a sexual relationship may also reflect an accumulation of problems within the relationship generally. The bonds between older couples may remain strong – after all, most have been through a great deal together, rearing a family and maintaining a home – but it's often true that a whole range of issues have been ignored for many years because they seemed too difficult to resolve. For many couples, there are areas of life and feeling that are never discussed by unspoken agreement; they reach a compromise which allows them to coexist without broaching these awkward topics. But the cost of such gaps in communication can be a stunted relationship where sexual pleasure is an early casualty.

Age and sexual potency

We can remain sexually active until we die. Even if our physical functioning is not what it was and the driving force of desire has diminished, sexual pleasure is still available in most of its many forms. Old age is a time of freedom from obligations to work and look after children, a time when we can be truly our mature selves and focus on the things we personally believe to be important. We miss so much if we see ageing only in negative terms. We can adapt without difficulty to increasing age so long as we don't accept limiting assumptions about what we should or should not be doing.

At forty-four and fifty-three, Colin and I are noticing some effects of age, but for me, the drawbacks are more than balanced by the benefits of increased understanding and trust as our relationship matures. It's obvious to both of us that arousal takes longer and orgasm usually comes more slowly than it did a couple of decades ago. But this is no disadvantage, it poses no real problem; it encourages extended delights, lovemaking drawn out to pleasurable length.

Colin can't achieve the repeated orgasms and near-permanent erection that he had when he was younger. But neither could I cope if he did; my vagina and vulva get sore more easily than they used to, even if there seems to be plenty of lubrication. I could not fuck for hours on end even if I wanted to. But we *can* make love for hours together, when the energy and the desire are there.

There are physiological changes to which older couples have to adapt. Men need more direct stimulation of the penis before it becomes fully erect, more rubbing and caressing with hands and tongue. In women, vaginal lubrication generally begins more slowly, and it's likely to be less profuse. Both of these are due to reduced blood-flow to the sexual organs. Changes in muscles and nerves mean that orgasm usually becomes less intense, and many men feel less physical need for ejaculation.[4]

It's difficult, of course, to distinguish the effects of ageing from the effects of familiarity, living and loving with the same person for many years. There isn't the novelty to keep the adrenalin pumping, just love and pleasure: softer delights, not so demanding that they keep us awake once our sexual appetites are sated. As we get older, Colin and I aim to enlarge our sexual repertoire, grow ever more sophisticated in mutual understanding and practice, and to extend the range of our pleasures. In this way we hope to compensate for the loss of the driving power of hormones, unfamiliar pheromones and fierce lust.

Using age as an excuse

It's all too easy to use encroaching age as a safe and convenient explanation for loss of sexual interest. It seems less threatening to tell ourselves that we don't want sex or that we have sexual problems because we're getting on in years, than to admit that we've allowed our sex-lives to become unimaginative or boring, or that we have to resolve difficulties in our general relationship.

Using your age as an excuse lets you off the hook – any hook. Age is a handy reason for refusing all sorts of things you don't enjoy, and as I've explained earlier in this book, there are a great many possible reasons for ceasing to enjoy sex. But these may be painful to confront; solving them demands that you look closely at yourself and the way you interact with your partner. The path to reawakening sexual pleasure can be a rocky one. It may seem a lot simpler to avoid the issues by putting loss of sexual desire down to increasing age.

Nobody can be blamed for getting older. You can't do anything about it. Attributing problems to old age permits passivity and complacency, even if in the long term the cost is terrible because there's no going back. If you stop doing something because you're too old, you're not likely to take it up again next year, when you'll be even older.

Six years ago, Colin attributed my lack of lust to my age. I never seemed interested in sex; I didn't approach him for it; my cunt stayed obstinately dry. Blaming my age made the situation more acceptable to him. It certainly meant he was in no way responsible. It also meant that neither of us had to look too closely at what might actually be going on: we didn't need to confront the potential pain of change.

Then – like many another middle-aged holiday-maker – I had that affair with a much younger man. I was very aware of the contrast between us: Johann's smooth limbs against mine, blue-veined and flabby; his playful, irresponsible manner breaking through my seriousness; his lack of commitment to anything while I had a home and career to return to. At times, when my mind wasn't preoccupied with the sheer delight of our sexual games, I felt ninety years old.

But my body responded as it had when I'd been his age. We made love all night and felt no need for sleep. The difficulties I'd been experiencing with Colin disappeared: I was high on lust, my juices flowing as profusely as they ever had before. I was insatiable. A glance at Johann's face would turn me on, my cunt burning with longing. I just wanted more and more. It was like a dream. That brief affair forced me to recognise reality. My loss of desire for Colin was nothing to do with my age, it was bound up with problems in our relationship.

Despite that experience, I found myself, quite recently, falling into the same trap again, imagining that Colin's erection and orgasm difficulties were purely caused by his diabetes and his age. It was threatening to me to face the possibility that his potency problems were actually symptoms of sexual dissatisfaction. Although he wasn't fully aware of it, he felt unsure that I wanted him, and this inhibited him.

I hope that these difficulties are part of the past: we acknowledged them and started to work on them, and we continue to make progress. The improvements we have achieved in our relationship endure. As we grow older together, we grow closer, more understanding. The chances are, we'll relapse; but we won't give up so easily in the future, not now we know we can recover our mutual pleasure in sex.

Ours is a maturing relationship, mellow, rich, full of depth. I look back over the progress of the last four years with satisfaction; I look forward with some trepidation (it's still not always easy) and optimism. Growing older together feels good to me. Wisdom can't be bad.

In my view, this is what maturity is all about. Growing in wisdom, learning how to be more fully ourselves without limiting each other's development. Shedding the unwanted baggage of imperfect upbringing while finding new dimensions of consciousness and self-expression.

The sexual problems of older people

Impotence is the most common sexual problem among older men. While erection difficulties may be due to unresolved problems in the wider relationship, physical causes become more common with increasing age. Many older men suffer from circulatory and other health problems which directly affect their ability to achieve and maintain erections. High blood pressure and heart disease, and the drugs used to control them, are ofter associated with impotence. There's a lot we can do to reduce the severity of such problems so that we can minimise our need for drugs, although we cannot always prevent them completely.

Drugs for cardiovascular disease have been promoted widely by the pharmaceutical industry over the past couple of decades, and they are frequently prescribed inappropriately, and in unnecessarily high doses.[5] Forty per cent of people over the age of eighty in Britain are prescribed diuretics for high blood pressure, and these are known to cause erectile failure in a large proportion of men.[6] If you or your partner are using medication, it's worth going to some trouble to check that it's really necessary; often it is not. A good herbalist or homoeopath will be able to offer less dangerous remedies.

Colin has succeeded, through a combination of physical activity, good diet, rest, and mineral supplementation, in reducing his blood pressure to a healthy level without medication. He is now totally free from the symptoms of circulatory disease from which he used to suffer. Growing older need not necessarily imply worsening health if we take good care of ourselves.

Older people are also more likely to suffer from mature-onset diabetes, which affects an increasingly large proportion of people as a lifetime of over-processed food and insufficient exercise takes its toll. Diabetes is a common cause of impotence; among men, failing sexual potency is often the first symptom, and for this reason men who become impotent in later life should ask their doctors to check their blood sugar levels.

Fortunately, diabetes can be controlled by appropriate lifestyle changes and medical treatment. Colin has been diabetic for over forty years; his cock only works properly when his blood sugar is stable, neither too high nor too low. Quite often, we have to pause in the middle of making love so that he can eat.

Major surgery is another common cause of loss of sexual interest in later life. Prostate surgery, colostomy, mastectomy and other operations that lead to disfigurement, embarrassment, or damage to the nerve and blood-vessel structures around the sexual organs are especially likely to cause both physiological and psychological damage. People who have been through traumatic experiences like this often feel they are no longer desirable afterwards; and the change in the partner's role from lover to nurse can make renewed sexual closeness difficult. We should do all we can to help those we love through the misery of serious illness by making them feel desirable and rebuilding sexual contact when it becomes possible again.

If you or your partner are diabetic, or hypertensive, or suffering from any other disease that reduces sexual potency, don't give up hope! Use multiple strategies to regain full physical function. But also question your attitudes, your assumptions about illness and disfigurement, your relationship, and the way you interact sexually; it's a terrible waste to give up sex because you imagine you can't possibly be desirable or you're incapable of doing it any more.

Adapting to the changes in our bodies

While we can take steps to improve matters, physical ageing can't be avoided completely. Older couples have to learn to adapt, to change their patterns of lovemaking to allow for changes in their bodies.

The secret, I have come to believe, is to enlarge our sexual repertoire so that we have plenty of ways to enjoy ourselves together even if some options cease to be available to us. If Colin becomes impotent, we shall concentrate on making love without fucking. If I should start to lose my fight against arthritis, we shall find positions that don't hurt my joints. We can compensate for decreased vaginal lubrication with a combination of saliva and other lubricants, from KY jelly to our favourite sex oil. As with so many aspects of sex, the answer lies in an amalgam of imagination, playful experimentation and continued communication.

Even if a man can't achieve an erection or can't make it to orgasm, sexual stimulation remains extremely enjoyable and you can continue to make love. Colin assures me that his cock is highly sensitive if he's mentally aroused, even when the physiological signs aren't there. He loves me to play with his cock and balls whether he has a hard-on or not. If a time comes when vaginal penetration is no longer possible, he will still be able to enjoy sex, and if I want penetration, his fingers will be available for mutual pleasure.

Many older men find that they don't achieve orgasm every time they make love. Talking about it makes it easier to come to terms with this change in sexual response. Intermittent loss of orgasmic capacity need not affect pleasure if you don't worry about it. As men grow older, sex ceases to be the driven, goal-directed activity it once was; it has a different, more subtle quality.

Obviously, I can't write from personal experience of the problems of old age, but here's what one seventy-eight-year-old man told Masters and Johnson:[7] 'In my mid-sixties, I had a real problem getting it up. Sexual intercourse became impossible and I got very upset over it at first. But my wife found other ways to excite me, and after a while – when I relaxed more, I guess – my problem disappeared.

Now, even though she doesn't always want to have intercourse when I do, we still use our mouths and tongues on each other, and we plan to keep doing it, too.'

Sex and the menopause

For my part, I know that menopause is not far ahead, and that knowledge used to make me nervous. Quite apart from anxiety about the potentially unpleasant symptoms of menopause itself, I wondered what implications it might have for my sex-life.

Researching these questions for my book *Natural Hormone Health,*[8] I discovered that there was no need for anxiety. In my view, the reality of what happens at this time of change does not justify the apprehension with which many people approach it. Popular beliefs about menopause and women's experience of it are closely tied in with more general attitudes to sex, the role of women, and ageing. Our cultural beliefs about menopause are very negative because Western cultural attitudes to all these issues are negative, and menopause triggers anxieties about them.

Just consider what we're dealing with.

First, as I've already said, our culture devalues age, particularly in women. Older women, in general, are at the bottom of the social heap. Not only are they women, and as such less valued than men, but they no longer have the gloss of youth. Menopause is the passage through which we move into old age. When you see it in this context, is it any wonder that women dread the menopause?

Second, our culture continues to regard sex beyond a certain age as dirty, especially for women. The fact that a young woman is potentially capable of becoming pregnant legitimises sex, but the idea of sexual pleasure with, or for, an older woman disgusts many people. In addition, these women grew up before the changes in attitudes that have made sexual pleasure more socially acceptable. So older women are even more likely than younger ones to feel guilt and shame about sexual desire.

Add to these attitudes the medical view of post-menopausal women as creatures in a state of hormone deficiency, lumbered with useless reproductive organs which are nothing more than potential centres of disease, and you get a deeply depressing picture. The medical literature about sex among older women is dominated by reports of the problems they suffer. Older women are reported to experience lack of lubrication and vaginal atrophy. It's very difficult for women to feel good about themselves as sexual beings in the face of such pressures.

Sure enough, surveys of sexual behaviour reflect these combined pressures. The average age at menopause is fifty-two; 40 per cent of women report that they lose interest in sex between the ages of fifty and sixty. The precise timing of such widespread loss of desire can be no coincidence.

But what is the real problem here? Does female biology, the failure of Nature to equip us for lifelong reproductive activity, actually condemn us to a sexless old age? I don't believe that. And the fact that some women *do* continue to enjoy sex for the whole of their adult lives convinces me that we are not looking at a failure of biology, but a failing in our culture.

I see menopause in a different way. It's actually one of Nature's triumphs. The value of an older woman to the social group in which she lives is in the wisdom she has accumulated. Nature, in her wisdom, removes the increasingly dangerous hazard of child-bearing in order to enhance the older woman's chances of survival. I can see no other reason why women should be designed to go through such a complex hormonal readjustment as the menopause. Menopause heralds a period of life when women are important for their *minds*, for *themselves*, not as breeding stock.

For many women, menopause is a time for taking stock of their lives. Free at last from the responsibility of looking after children and the rollercoaster cycle of reproductive hormones, they come into their own, to enjoy an Indian summer of uncluttered energy and productivity.

One area of later life that is bound to come under scrutiny is sex. After menopause, sex is purely about pleasure, bonding and love. But if sex is not a source of pleasure, not an expression of love, there's no point in it. And when the biological imperative of reproduction no longer exists, the physical structures that support it may cease to function.

Research has revealed that the most important single determinant of continued sexual pleasure in post-menopausal women is the presence of an interested and desirable partner.[9] If both want to continue with an active sex-life, the woman's sexual function and desire remain effectively unimpaired. The physiological changes are under psychological control.

The situation is quite simple. If a woman wants sex, she can continue to enjoy it for as long as she likes. If she doesn't, her body will make it painful, if not impossible.

Post-menopausal women have to decide what *they* want. Duty is no longer relevant: Nature has seen to that. At this time of life, it is perhaps more important than ever before that women act to ensure that they get what they want. This may be a change towards a more loving, harmonious relationship where sexual closeness reflects closeness on every level; or it may be an honest admission that sex is not – and perhaps has never been – a source of pleasure for them.

I don't believe that older women should feel any obligation to continue in sexual partnership. Some will be quite content without this. It is an individual choice. But it is a choice that must be made on the basis of desire, nothing else.

Women are offered a mirage of eternal youth, and, by implication, eternal sexual receptivity, through Hormone Replacement Therapy (HRT). Clever marketing plays on our fears of ageing and sexlessness, our fear that we will not be valued as people if we allow ourselves, through uncorrected hormone deficiency, to turn into crones. But the benefits of HRT are oversold, its shortcomings underestimated.

HRT will not help to resolve underlying tensions in a relationship where sex has ceased to bring pleasure to the woman. It will not revive desire when the reasons for its death lie in the sort of problems that I've been describing in this book. The real answers are on another level: in creating greater communication and sensitivity, in honesty and the rebirth of closeness. These answers are in our own hands, no doctor can prescribe them.

While hormone treatment may help some women to cope with the stresses of menopause, there is much we can do to help ourselves. I described a variety of strategies in *Natural Hormone Health*. In addition, women who suffer from post-menopausal vaginal dryness may find oestrogen creams, available on prescription, useful. But just as dryness before the menopause is almost always due to lack of desire, the same problem after menopause often has a similar cause. Women have to *want* penetration before it becomes enjoyable. They may need more love-play before intercourse. If sex has become a stunted, perfunctory act, many women will refuse to co-operate. Menopause allows them to opt out of a sex-life that they have come to regard as a chore.

When sex is a source of mutual delight, it can continue indefinitely. One thing that really stands out in surveys of ageng couples who do continue to have an active sex-life is that the older they are and the longer they've been together, the greater the pleasure they experience. With every decade that passes, the consensus is that sex is better than ever before, just as my mother told me.

What a delightful future we can anticipate! But it doesn't just happen. We have to build understanding, continue to learn how to please ourselves and each other. Growing older can challenge our ingenuity, but rising to challenges extends and teaches us.

Just don't give up. Don't give in to the cultural pressures that deny the pleasures of sex to older people. Make sure you get all the joy you can: it keeps you alive! I don't intend to let any part of me die prematurely, certainly not my sexual self. Why should I? Colin loves me for myself, not for firm breasts or unwrinkled skin. I love him for his total self; he's not a golden youth but I don't care, he understands me better than any boy could.

20

Sexual Fire in the Social Forest

This book has proved to be the most demanding I have ever written. Looking as closely as I did at myself and my relationship with Colin, I had to confront issues that I might otherwise have left unexamined, and to relive experiences that affected me very deeply. In our years together, we've lived through some of the most intense emotions of our lives: the greatest joy, the most profound despair. Often these emotions were inspired by events outside our relationship, but they always affect the way we feel about each other. Our partnership reverberates and resonates with all our feelings.

This is the nature of marriage and close long-term partnerships. Sometimes the strains are too great for the integrity of the relationship to hold; but when partners weather crises together, they build a resilient raft of shared experience that becomes ever stronger.

Sex is the part of the bond where stresses are quickly revealed. After many years together, the sensitivity of our sex-life to problems of all sorts has become acute. It's like an early-warning beacon – even if we don't always know what the warning is about.

There's tremendous media fascination with sex in the nineties. Yet this attention tends to miss the crucial point: focusing on sex during courtship, sex among the young, and variations on sexual acts, it ignores the complexity, the multidimensional nature of sexual bonding over the long term. The potential for both joy and pain associated with sex becomes, if anything, greater with time.

Sex may be a pressing biological urge for the young, but when we're older it's so tied up with psychological needs and social pressures, with memories and dreams, that its influence goes much deeper. But these deeper currents that affect our sexuality are largely ignored. Paradoxically, the longer we've been in a relationship, the more confused we are likely to feel when things go wrong, wondering why we feel the way we do, worrying in isolation.

I went through years of distress, not understanding why I had turned off sexually. Now I realise that millions of other people go through the same process, the same misery. I hope my voyage of introspection will help some of them to find the courage, take the risks and reap the rewards of a similar exploration of their own lives and feelings.

The process of getting to know oneself affects every relationship. As we grow to understand our own motivations more clearly, we learn to accept ourselves. Then we can stop pretending, playing prescribed roles, acting out mother's guilt, father's fear. We have to have the courage to become fully ourselves, to go through whatever is necessary, to learn what we need to know.

As we mature, we change profoundly. The process may not be as dramatic as the caterpillar's metamorphosis into a butterfly, but it produces similar upheavals at every level of our being. The potential form of my present self was always within me, but it was overlaid and hidden by assumptions about what I should be, the roles I'd learnt to play that did not truly fit me. Crucial aspects of myself remained undeveloped, unrecognised, unappreciated.

As I went through my recent metamorphosis, my relationship with Colin underwent profound changes. He is, in many ways, a new man: he looks at his behaviour in new ways, he challenges himself as well as me. Superficially, he may seem less secure, less dogmatic; underneath, he is stronger. And our relationship has a greater feeling of durability and commitment than ever before.

Now, when I need to talk, I do so – and he listens. When he needs to share his feelings, he can do so without reservation; and I listen. The depth of communication between us has developed as our understanding, both of ourselves and each other, has grown. And with it, we have found a new level of trust.

We weren't aware of keeping secrets from one another; we thought we were totally honest, indeed we prided ourselves on our honesty and integrity. But we weren't able to be truly honest until we knew ourselves well enough to express our feelings and desires. We didn't even realise when we were hiding from one another, because we didn't know what we were hiding.

We've come to understand that sometimes we had misunderstood each other because of the differences between us: that the same words, the same gestures, could mean something different to the other person. We've learnt to watch for misunderstandings that develop because Colin's male and I'm female, or because of the social class differences of our backgrounds, and the differing attitudes we learnt in our formative years. Getting to know another person continues for decades.

We've learnt to look for assumptions, to question and check on them. We're still finding out what the other means when we talk: we know nothing is as obvious as it seems.

When our relationship was going downhill, we looked for simple reasons for our problems, easy ways to blame the other and validate ourselves. Colin called me boring. I called him a bully. We nurtured bitterness between us: not deliberately, but because we didn't know how to resolve our differences or cope with the pain of mutual rejection.

Looking back, I can see that it was inevitable that desire should die between us. I'm just amazed he didn't switch off to a greater degree, that I alone showed that symptom of the breakdown of our relationship. It's another difference between men and women: women tend to turn off more readily in response to relationship problems. Perhaps I shouldn't be surprised; males of all the species I've ever observed are more consistently randy than females.

Love is a constantly evolving dance whose steps and nature we are never likely to understand totally. Inevitably, we sometimes trample on each other. But if we're determined to keep love alive, we can and will learn, adapt, discover ways to step around problems or overcome them.

Rekindling desire meant thinking about our whole relationship. It's been a slow process, with stops and starts and many frustrations. Sometimes we relapse into our bad old habits and we have to pick ourselves up again. At least we know we can do that. We have learnt about the critical areas that we have to examine: the adequacy of our communication, the acknowledgement of our feelings, recognition of stresses that might be grinding us down. We know the sorts of actions we'll have to take: giving ourselves time to stand back and tune into ourselves, discovering neglected needs, looking after ourselves.

I'd like to quote the end of the postscript from Sheila Kitzinger's book on women's sexuality; I believe it's true for men as much as for women. She wrote: 'Question all received knowledge, however authoritative it may appear. Trust your feelings. They are valid. And share what you discover about yourself with other women. Gradually we shall be able, as if piecing together fragments of a mosaic, to learn more and more about who we are as women.'[1]

I hope that women will share their growing understanding of themselves with men, too, for most of us live with these strange but sometimes desperately lovable creatures. And then, with luck, men will begin to find it easier to share their hidden feelings and perceptions with us. As we get to know each other better, relating becomes easier.

In our mutual struggle for self-knowledge and closeness, we come up, again and again, against barriers of our culture which are internalised in our minds. We hit distrust and suspicion, anxiety and shame. When we try to relate, we confront hypocrisy and cultural distortion. When sexuality is belittled, we encounter rejection of our very humanity. It's hard to fight against the pressures of a culture that treats sex as superficially as ours does.

Powerful Western cultures are dominated by institutional values. To the institutions of our culture – whether State, Church, medical or business, – individual human beings are but cogs in machines, numbers in computers. As individuals we are interchangeable, expendable. Who can put a cash value on human expression, human interaction in close personal relationships? Who profits? When nobody expects to profit, the power centres of our culture aren't interested.

People need intimate relationships. We have to care about our real selves and the future we create for our children. Even those who seem to be the winners in institutional life often end up losing in their personal lives. Think of the overstressed businessperson, whose job demands constant effort to act a part in an organisation rather than responding to human feelings. The stress of such work shatters people, they become incapable of unwinding and relating to their partners at home. Individuals self-destruct, break down, have heart attacks.

For most of those outside the protective – if demanding – walls of institutions, life can be much worse. For the poor, the unemployed, for mothers trapped at home with babies, self-respect is eroded by lack of social contact, lack of purpose and opportunity, lack, even, of the basic necessities of life: nourishing food, clean air, pure water. The very fabric of society is falling apart around them – and they know it. In situations devoid of hope, caring is an early casualty.

This is what we have to stand up against. We are fighting for the preservation of the self and human relationships in a world we have created beyond human scale, in a world-culture that cares nothing for the values of individual humans and human relationships. We are facing a global crisis, not only of the environment, but of human society.

As society fragments around us, we depend more than ever on the strength of our closest personal relationships. Living as a whole being in a whole relationship is part of living in a harmonious relationship with everything around us. We are not separate from one another, nor from the planet that sustains us. We are each unique, multifaceted life-forms who need to relate to others for the sake of present sanity and future survival. As we come to understand the full richness of our selves, we become more able to create enduring relationships of great richness and depth.

That way, I believe, lies ecstasy.

Notes and References

FOREWORD

1 Riley, Alan, 'HSD: A Disease of the 90s', *Journal of Sexual Health*, Vol. 3, No. 1, January 1993, pp. 5–6.
2 Reinisch, June and Beasley, Ruth, *The Kinsey Institute New Report on Sex*, London: Penguin, 1991.
3 *Ibid*, p. 173.

CHAPTER 1: SEX IN THE NINETIES

1 ACSF Investigators, 'Aids and sexual behaviour in France', *Nature, 360*, 3 December 1992.
2 Haskey, John, 'Patterns of marriage, divorce and cohabitation in the different countries of Europe', *Population Trends, 69*, 1992, pp. 27–36.
3 OPCS, 1992.
4 OPCS, *General Household Survey*, 1989.
5 *Divorce Statistics for England and Wales*, London: HMSO, gave the recorded cause for 60,011 divorces granted to women in 1990 as unreasonable behaviour by the husband. Adultery by the husband came second, with 25,893, and adultery by the wife third at 18,145.
6 Friday, Nancy, *Women on Top*, London: Hutchinson, 1991; *My Secret Garden*, London: Quartet, 1979.
7 Friday, 1991, *op. cit.*, p. 3.
8 Kitzinger, Sheila, *Woman's Experience of Sex*, London: Penguin, 1985, p. 29.
9 Friedan, Betty, *The Feminine Mystique*, Harmondsworth: Penguin, 1963.
10 Greer, Germaine, *The Female Eunuch*, London: Paladin, 1971.
11 *Social Trends, 23*, 1993, London: OPCS.

CHAPTER 2: YOUNG BEGINNERS

1 Freeman, Dorothy, *Couples in Conflict: Inside the Counselling Room*, Milton Keynes: Open University Press, 1990, p. 98.
2 Assagioli, Roberto, *Psychosynthesis*, Wellingborough: Turnstone Press, 1975.

3 *Arena/New Woman*: Survey of Sex in the 90s, *Arena*, March 1993.

CHAPTER 3: FLYING BLIND

1 Freeman, Dorothy, *Couples in Conflict: Inside the Counselling Room*, Milton Keynes: Open University Press, 1990, p. 150.
2 Wolf, Naomi, *The Beauty Myth*, London: Vintage, 1991, pp. 142–3
3 Pre-trial interview with Arabella Melville and Colin Johnson, held at New Scotland Yard in the presence of our solicitor, David Offenbach, in 1976.

CHAPTER 4: FROM FREEDOM TO FIDELITY

1 Zelda West-Meads of Relate, in telephone conversation with Arabella Melville.

CHAPTER 6: LEARNING ALL THE TIME

1 Botwin, Carol, *Is There Sex After Marriage*? London: Bantam Books, 1990.

CHAPTER 7: VALUE YOURSELF!

1. Many wives still feel like their husband's property, despite cultural changes over the past two decades, according to Zelda West-Meads of Relate in telephone conversation with Arabella Melville. Older women, and those who are dependent on their partner's income, are particularly vulnerable.
2. Kitzinger, Sheila, *Woman's Experience of Sex*, London: Penguin, 1985.
3. *New Woman*, Survey on Love, Sex and the Dieting Woman, June 1991.
4. *New Woman*, June 1991, p. 15.
5. Dickson, Anne, *The Mirror Within*, London: Quartet, 1985.

CHAPTER 8: TRUST

1. Hite, Shere, *The Hite Report on Male Sexuality*, London: Optima, 1981.
2. Hite, Shere, *The Hite Report on Love, Passion and Emotional Violence*, London: Optima, 1991.
3. Russell, Bertrand, *A History of Western Philosophy*, London: Allen & Unwin, 1946, p. 35.

CHAPTER 9: DESIRE

1 See Anne Dickson, *A Woman in Your Own Right*, London: Quartet, 1982. Women have told me that learning to be assertive, through courses like Ms Dickson's, has been crucial to their ability to re-experience desire for their partners. See also Kaplan, Helen, *Disorders of Sexual Desire*, London: Ballière, Tindall, 1979. Sex therapist Dr Kaplan believes that the primary causes of loss of desire are fear and anger.
2 Freeman, Dorothy, *Couples in Conflict: Inside the Counselling Room*, Milton Keynes: Open University Press, 1990.

3 Hooper, Anne, *The Body Electric*, London: Pandora, 1991.
4 Weideger, Paula, *Female Cycles*, London: The Women's Press, 1978.
5 Melville, Arabella, *Natural Hormone Health*, London: Thorsons, 1990.
6 Hooper, *op. cit.*, p. 91.
7 Hite, Shere, *The Hite Report on Female Sexuality*, London: Collier Macmillan, 1976.
8 Ladas, Alice, Whipple, Beverly and Perry, John, *The G-Spot*, London: Corgi, 1983.
9 Masters, William, Johnson, Virginia, and Kolodny, Robert, *Masters and Johnson on Sex and Human Loving*, London: Macmillan, 1986, pp. 36–7.
10 *Ibid.*, pp. 35 and 37.
11 Jong, Erica, *Parachutes and Kisses*, London: Panther, 1985, p. 327.

CHAPTER 10: DREAMING

1 Melville, Arabella, *The Good Sex Diet*, London: Thorsons, 1991.
2 Stanway, Andrew, *The Joy of Sexual Fantasy*, London: Headline, 1991.
3 Friday, Nancy, *Women on Top*, London: Hutchinson, 1991.
4 Dickson, Anne, *The Mirror Within*, London: Quartet, 1985.

CHAPTER 11: CONTRACEPTION AND SEXUAL FEELING

1 Clark, David (ed.) *Marriage, Domestic Life and Social Change*, London: Routledge, 1991.
2 Kitzinger, Sheila, *Woman's Experience of Sex*, London: Penguin, 1985, p. 185.
3 *Social Trends, 23*, 1993, London: OPCS.
4 Kitzinger, *op. cit.*, p. 187.
5 Grant, Ellen, *The Bitter Pill*, London: Elm Tree Books, 1985.
6 Kitzinger, *op. cit.*

CHAPTER 12: THE OTHER HALF

1 Tannen, Deborah, *You Just Don't Understand: Women and Men in Conversation*, London: Virago, 1991.
2 See, for example, Doreen Kimura, 'Sex Differences in the Brain', *Scientific American*, September 1992, pp. 80–87.
3 Tannen, *op. cit.*
4 Finch, Janet and Morgan, David, 'Marriage in the 1980s' in Clark, David (d.), *Marriage, Domestic Life and Social Change*, London: Routledge, 1991.
5 De Angelis, Barbara, *Secrets About Men Every Woman Should Know*, London: Thorsons, 1990.
6 Tannen, *op. cit.*
7 Hite, Shere, *The Hite Report on Male Sexuality*, London: Optima, 1990.
8 Comfort, Alex, *More Joy of Sex*, London: Quartet, 1988, p. 117.
9 Hite, *op. cit.*
10 *Ibid.*
11 Stanway, Andrew, *A Woman's Guide to Men and Sex*, London: Century, 1988.
12 Hite, *op. cit.*

13 *Arena/New Woman*, Survey of Sex in the 90s, *Arena*, March 1993.

CHAPTER 13: LOVING AND FIGHTING

1 Kaplan, H.S., *Disorders of Sexual Desire*, London: Ballière, Tindall, 1979.
2 Litvinoff, Sarah, *The Relate Guide to Better Relationships*, London: Vermilion, 1992.
3 Stets, J.E., 'Cohabiting and Marital Aggression', *Journal of Marriage and the Family 53*, 1991, 669–80.
4 Herbert, T.B., Silver, R.C. and Ellard, J.H., 'Coping with an abusive relationship: why do women stay?' *Journal of Marriage and the Family*, *53*, 1991, 311–25.
5 Dickson, Anne, *A Woman in Your Own Right*, London: Quartet, 1982.

CHAPTER 14: THE KEYS TO LOVE

1 Askam, Janet, *Identity and Stability in Marriage*, Cambridge: Cambridge University Press, 1984.
2 Hite, Shere, *The Hite Report on Love, Passion and Emotional Violence*, London: Optima, 1991, p. 5.
3 Hite, Shere, *The Hite Report on Male Sexuality*, London: Optima, 1990.
4 Tannen, Deborah, *You Just Don't Understand: Women and Men in Conversation*, London: Virago 1991.
5 *Ibid*., p. 176.
6 Blumstein, Philip and Schwartz, Pepper, *American Couples: Money, Work, Sex*, New York: William Morrow, 1984.

CHAPTER 15: THE POWER OF TOUCH

1 Hooper, Anne, *The Body Electric*, London: Pandora, 1991.
2 O'Connor, Dagmar, *How to put the Love back into Making Love*, London: Columbus Books, 1989.
3 Masters, William and Johnson, Virginia, *Human Sexual Inadequacy*, Boston: Little, Brown, 1970.
4 Masters, William, Johnson, Virginia and Kolodny, Robert, *Masters and Johnson on Sex and Human Loving*, London: Macmillan, 1986.
5 O'Connor, *op. cit*., p. 168.
6 Registers of therapists, both NHS and private, are kept by The Insitute of Psychosexual Medicine, 11 Chandos Street, London W1M 9DE (071–580 0631) and by The British Association for Sexual and Marital Therapy, PO Box 62, Sheffield S10 3IS.
7 Kaplan, Helen, *Disorders of Sexual Desire*, London: Ballière, Tindall, 1979.

CHAPTER 16: TIME FOR SEX

1 O'Connor, Dagmar, *How to put the Love back into Making Love*, London: Columbus Books, 1989, p. 13.
2 *Social Trends, 23*, 1992, London: OPCS.
3 Kitzinger, Sheila, *Woman's Experience of Sex*, London: Penguin, 1985.

CHAPTER 17: SEXUAL FIREWORKS

1 Levy, William, *Natural Jewboy*, Amsterdam: Ins and Outs Press, 1981.
2 Available from Hand Picked Films, NZ Voorburgwal 66, Suite 95, Amsterdam 1012SC, Netherlands.
3 Published by, and available from, Invisible Language Society, Fokke Simonsz Straat 28 I, 1017 TH Amsterdam, Netherlands.

CHAPTER 18: THE WELLSPRINGS OF DESIRE

1 *New Woman*, June 1991, p. 16.
2 Reitz, Rosetta, *Menopause: A Positive Approach*, London: Unwin Paperbacks, 1981.
3 Notelovitz, M., 'Non-hormonal management of the menopause,' In Studd, J. W. & Whitehead, M. L. (eds.), *The Menopause*, Oxford: Blackwell Scientific, 1988.
4 Melville, Arabella and Johnson, Colin, *Eat Yourself Thin*, London: Michael Joseph, 1990.
5 Although liver is very high in nutrients, it concentrates chemical contaminants and cumulative nutrients such as vitamin A, which can be dangerous in excessive doses. These hazards can be avoided if you eat liver from organically reared animals.

CHAPTER 19: CAN SEX IMPROVE WITH TIME?

1 Kellett, J M., 'Sexuality of the Elderly,' *Sexual and Marital Therapy*, vol. 6, no. 2, 1991, pp. 147–55.
2 Persson, G., 'Sexuality in a 70-year-old urban population,' *Journal of Psychosomatic Research*, *24*, 1990, pp. 335–42.
3 Hallstrom, T., 'Sexuality in the Climacteric', quoted in Kellett, *op. cit*.
4 Masters, William, Johnson, Virginia and Kolodny, Robert, *Masters and Johnson on Sex and Human Loving* London: Macmillan, 1986.
5 Melville, Arabella and Johnson, Colin, *Cured to Death: the Effects of Prescription Drugs*, London: Secker & Warburg, 1981.
6 Editorial, 'Need We Poison the Elderly So Often?', *The Lancet*, 2 July 1988, pp. 20–22.
7 Masters, William, Johnson, Virginia and Kolodny, Robert., *op. cit*., p. 184.
8 Melville, Arabella, *Natural Hormone Health*, London: Thorsons, 1991.
9 Fordney, Diane, 'Female Sexuality and the Menopause', in Studd, J. D. and Whitehead, M. L. (eds.), *The Menopause*, Oxford: Blackwell Scientific, 1988.

CHAPTER 20: SEXUAL FIRE IN THE SOCIAL FOREST

1 Kitzinger, Sheila, *Woman's Experience of Sex*, London: Penguin, 1985, p. 311.

Index